BASICS OF THE FAITH:
A CATHOLIC CATECHISM

Basics of the Faith: A Catholic Catechism

Alan Schreck

SERVANT BOOKS
Ann Arbor, Michigan

Published by Servant Books
P.O. Box 8617
Ann Arbor, Michigan 48107

Cover design by Michael P. Andaloro
Cover mosaic from Art Resource

Printed in the United States of America
ISBN 0-89283-618-0

88 89 90 91 10 9 8 7 6 5 4 3 2

Nihil obstat: Monsignor Joseph P. Malara
Censor Librorum
Imprimatur: † Most Reverend Albert H. Ottenweller
Bishop of Steubenville
June 25, 1987
The *nihil obstat* and *imprimatur* are official declarations that a book or pamphlet is free from doctrinal or moral error. No implication is contained therein that those *who grant* the *nihil obstat* or *imprimatur* agree with the contents, opinions, or statements expressed.

In this Marian year, 1987-1988,
this book is dedicated to
Mary
Mother of God
Mother of the Church and all Christians
My mother.

Our Lady, Queen of Peace, pray for us!

Contents

Abbreviations in Text of Documents of Vatican II

AA—*Apostolicam Actuositatem,* Decree on the Apostolate of the Laity of the Second Vatican Council

DV—*Dei Verbum,* Dogmatic Constitution on Divine Revelation of the Second Vatican Council

GS—*Gaudium et Spes,* The Pastoral Constitution on the Church in the Modern World of the Second Vatican Council

LG—*Lumen Gentium,* The Dogmatic Constitution on the Church of the Second Vatican Council

SC—*Sacrosanctum Concilium,* The Constitution on the Sacred Liturgy of the Second Vatican Council

UR—*Unitatis Redintegratio,* The Decree on Ecumenism of the Second Vatican Council

Abbreviations of Other Documents

DS—*Henry Denzinger's Enchiridion Symbolorum, definitionum et declarationum de rebus fide et morum* (A collection of Roman Catholic papal and conciliar definitions and declarations on matters of faith and morals)

FC—*Familiaris Consortio,* Pope John Paul II's Apostolic Exhortation on the Role of the Christian Family in the Modern World (1981)

Foreword

GEORGE WILLIAM RUTLER REMINDS US quite sensibly, in his introduction to the collected works of G.K. Chesterton, that: "Love must know its object or it is sentimentalism." His reminder is particularly apt because he is talking about Chesterton's conversion to Catholicism. Chesterton already had Catholicism's "vast pattern," but he required its particulars, which he proceeded to study "page by page from the Penny Catechism."

Perhaps one can still buy a catechism for a penny. Whatever inflation has done, however, or sophistication, neither misfortune has eliminated the need for the catechetical approach, at least for those wise enough to recognize with Chesterton that we really can *not* truly love what we don't truly know. Alan Schreck's *Basics of the Faith: A Catholic Catechism* might be well described as dedicated to this premise.

I am happy to see Dr. Schreck's work published. It meets the need he intended it to meet, the need for an in-between size work, more comprehensive than the Penny Catechism, less voluminous than a major work in apologetics. More importantly, the author gives us a straightforward, highly readable catechetical presentation of the basic teachings of our faith. I like particularly his interweaving appropriate passages of key documents of the Second Vatican Council throughout the text, applying and interpreting such documents as the Council Fathers intended.

I fear neither the extreme right nor the extreme left in theology, neither the ultra conservative nor the ultra liberal. I do fear ignorance, for ignorance leaves us vulnerable to both extremes. Dr. Schreck has rightly seen the need for a work that makes ignorance unnecessary, even for those with limited backgrounds. In responding to that need he has given us a highly useful book.

John Cardinal O'Connor
Archbishop of New York

Acknowledgments

I gratefully acknowledge the generous support of all who assisted me in writing this catechism. My colleagues in the Theology Department of Franciscan University of Steubenville read the chapters related to their specialization and provided valuable advice; thanks to Fr. Daniel Sinisi, T.O.R., Fr. Giles Dimock, O.P., Andy Minto, Michael Brees, and Dr. Mark Miravalle.

Special thanks are due to Norma Donohue, who typed most of the manuscript of the book with its endless revisions and additions, to Jim Fritz Huspen, my graduate assistant, and to Dawn Recznik who also assisted with the typing.

Finally, I acknowledge the prayers and support of the vibrant Catholic community to which I belong, the Servants of Christ the King, and of my loving family, Nancy, Paul, Jeanne, and Mark.

Introduction

"WHY DO WE NEED ANOTHER CATHOLIC CATECHISM?" some may ask. In reviewing the Catholic catechisms available for adults and informed older teenagers, it appeared that some of them are short, presenting the faith of Catholics without much explanation, while others are lengthy, suitable for use mainly as reference books. Few catechisms are available that someone might read in a reasonable length of time in order to better understand the Catholic faith. I hope that this work will provide a readable, reliable catechism of the Catholic faith that will lead to a deeper appreciation and understanding of Catholic Christianity. For those who desire a more thorough explanation of the Catholic faith than this compact catechism provides, I would recommend *The Teaching of Christ* by Ronald Lawler, O.F.M. Cap., Bishop Donald Wuerl, and Thomas Comerford Lawler; *The Catholic Catechism* by John Hardon, S.J.; or the three volume *Fundamentals of Catholicism* by Fr. Kenneth Baker.

A more important reason for this catechism is a concern for truth. A story is told about a biochemist who was approached by a beer company which had to throw away thousands of gallons of beer because the leaven fermenting it had gone bad. The biochemist had to work long hours in the laboratory to purify the leaven so that it could produce good beer once again. The basic teaching of the church is like that leaven. If the basic teaching "goes bad" through distortion, the whole church is seriously harmed. We must recover the pure leaven of the teaching of the Catholic church if our church is to be pure, renewed, and pleasing to God.

There is a great deal of confusion, even within the Catholic world, about what the Catholic church truly teaches. One Catholic leader, Ralph Martin, speaks of a "crisis of truth" within the Catholic church. We are living in a time of moral and religious relativism, when even the concept of a clearly definable, objective truth in the religious or moral sphere appears unsophisticated, laughable, or repulsive to many people. We are reminded of Pontius Pilate's ironic question, "What is truth?" as the fullness of truth, Jesus Christ, stood before him. The words of St. Paul to Timothy are pertinent today:

> For the time is coming when people will not endure sound teaching, but having itching ears they will accumulate for themselves teachers to suit their own likings, and will turn away from listening to the truth and wander into myths. (2 Tm 4:3-4)

Out of this concern for sound doctrine, the 1985 Extraordinary Synod of Bishops called for the composition of a "universal catechism," or compendium of all Catholic doctrine regarding both faith and morals. I look forward to the appearance of this normative compendium of the Catholic faith.

How can we know that what the Catholic church teaches is true? Certainly faith is necessary, but it is not a blind faith. We can judge the Catholic church's teaching by its fruit. Unlike the novel teachings and trends which come and go, the truth proclaimed by the Catholic church has withstood the test of time, enduring for nearly two thousand years. The Catholic faith is embraced by more people than any other single, unified religious group—an estimated 830 million Catholics in 1985.

More importantly, the truth of Christianity has power to liberate and dignify the human person and the human spirit in a way that no other religion, political system, military force, or worldly ideology can do. Jesus said, "If you continue in my word, you are truly my disciples, and you will know the truth, and the truth will make you free" (Jn 8:31-32). The only way to verify truth is to believe in it and live it. Accept the word of God as faithfully guarded and handed on in the Catholic church, become a committed disciple or follower of Jesus Christ, and "you will know the truth, and the truth will make you free." Neither death nor the fear of death will have power over you (1 Cor 15:55-57).

ONE

God, His Creation, and Man's Rebellion

In the beginning God created the heavens and the earth. . . . (Gn 1:1)

IN OUR STUDY OF THE CATHOLIC FAITH, it is appropriate to look first at our beginnings. Although the Book of Genesis was not the first book of the Bible to be written, it is placed first in the Hebrew Scriptures (or Old Testament) because it tells of the genesis, the beginning, of God's work of creation and salvation. This revelation of God about our beginnings is the foundation of the Catholic and Christian faith. If the basic truth presented in the Book of Genesis is distorted or misunderstood, so too will be the rest of the teachings of the Bible or Christianity. Genesis is the foundation; if the foundation is not sound, the whole building eventually collapses.

Interpreting Genesis

How is the Book of Genesis to be properly interpreted? Many people today, even some Christians, consider Genesis a fascinating story springing from the mythology of the primitive people. Every primitive people, they say, developed some story about the origin of the universe and the human race. Naturally, then, the Book of Genesis resembles other ancient stories, such as the Babylonian myths, the "Epic of Gilgamesh" or *Enuma Elish*.

The Catholic church, along with many other Christian churches, acknowledges that the Book of Genesis is presented in the form of a story or a myth that is similar to other such stories in the ancient world. However, Catholics insist that the content of Genesis, properly understood, contains the absolute and unfailing truth about God's action and plan in creating the universe and the human race. Why? Because Genesis is part of the collection of books, known as the Bible or the sacred Scriptures, that has been inspired and preserved in truth by the author of the universe, God himself. The Catholic church has affirmed in the Dogmatic Constitution on Divine Revelation of the Second Vatican Council that:

> ... the books of Scripture must be acknowledged as teaching firmly, faithfully, and without error that truth which God wanted to put into the sacred writings for the sake of our salvation. (no. 11)
>
> and
>
> ... the books of the Old Testament, in accordance with the state of mankind before the time of salvation established by Christ, reveal to all men the knowledge of God and of man and the ways in which God, just and merciful, deals with men. ... (no. 15)

It is important to understand that the Book of Genesis is more than an interesting ancient story. It teaches essential truths about God, his creation, and the beginnings of humanity.

The purpose of this chapter is to present the basic truth about the beginning of things that God reveals through the Bible, especially the Book of Genesis. The Catholic church affirms that God has inspired the authors of the Bible. By this we understand that the statements they made, "for the sake of our salvation," about God, his plan of salvation, and his relationship with his creation (including the human race) are infallibly true. Although the entire Bible is inspired in this sense, not every aspect of the Bible is directly concerned with mankind's salvation. Catholics, for example, are not bound to believe that God guarantees the scientific or historical accuracy of every statement in the Bible, because we believe this was not his primary intention in inspiring the authors of sacred Scripture. (Note that the Bible may be largely or entirely accurate in terms of science or history, but not necessarily because of God's inspiration of the authors with regard to those matters.) Catholics look at Genesis and the other writings of the Bible as theological (God-centered) works that God has inspired in order to reveal the truth about himself, his will and plan, and his relationship and dealings with his creatures (including humanity). The Catholic understanding of the Bible differs from that of some other Christians in this regard.

The Existence of God

Before asserting that God "created the heavens and the earth" in the beginning, we must ask some more fundamental questions: "How do we know there is a God?" and "If there is a God, what is he like?"

The Catholic tradition basically recognizes two ways that we can come to know that God exists, and what he is like. The first way is through observing and thinking about the universe, in order to discover the God behind it. This is sometimes called natural revelation—God revealing himself through nature or the universe. "The heavens are telling the glory of God . . ." the psalmist proclaims (Ps 19:1). St. Paul taught that, "Ever since the creation of the world his [God's] invisible nature, namely, his eternal power and deity, has been clearly perceived in the things that have been made" (Rom 1:20).

In the Middle Ages, St. Thomas Aquinas developed five celebrated proofs for the existence of God, based on reasoning about the universe. Aquinas argued that since everything has a cause, there must be a "first cause" that brought the material universe into being, and an "unmoved mover" that set it in motion. The magnificent order and beauty of the universe implies the existence of a great intelligent artist who designed it. For Aquinas, the existence of matter and of the universe points to the existence of a superior power and intelligence, God, who created it and set it in motion.

This philosophical approach does not conflict with most scientific theories about the origin of the universe. A current theory proposes that the universe began with a "big bang"—a primordial explosion producing matter and energy. Yet, science has not yet determined where the matter exploded in the big bang came from. Christians answer that God is ultimately the source of the universe coming into being, however or whenever this occurred. Catholics may accept any scientific theory of the origin of the cosmos, as long as it does not deny that God is finally and ultimately the source and creator of whatever exists. However, science is incapable of answering the basic philosophic questions about the universe, such as, "Why is it there?" and "Why is there something rather than nothing?" Christian doctrine answers these questions by claiming that the universe itself points to the existence of a God who created it.[1]

God Has Revealed Himself

If all we had to rely upon was natural revelation—the existence of the universe pointing to God—we would know God existed, but not much about him and what he is like. So, God has provided a second and more complete way of coming to know him. After speaking about the ability to know God by reflecting on created things, the First Vatican Council (1870) added:

> Yet it pleased His (God's) wisdom and goodness to reveal Himself and the eternal decrees of His will to mankind in another, supernatural manner. As the Apostles say: "In many and various ways God spoke of old to our fathers by the prophets; but in these last days He has spoken to us by His Son." (Heb 1:1-2)
>
> Because of this divine revelation, all men are able . . . to know with readiness, with firm certitude, and without admixture of error, whatever in divine matters is not of itself beyond the grasp of human reason.[2]

This constitution explains that divine revelation is contained "in the written books (of the Old and of the New Testament) and in the unwritten traditions, which have been received by the apostles from the mouth of Christ himself, or from the apostles themselves, at the dictation of the Holy Spirit, [and] have come down even to us, transmitted as it were, from hand to hand. . . ."[3]

Thus, God has revealed himself and his mind to us through the Scriptures, the apostles, and those who have faithfully recorded and handed on their teaching down through the centuries.

How do we know that God had spoken or revealed himself to the human race in this way? Such a claim cannot be proved by reason or scientific experimentation. Ultimately, we only know with assurance that God has spoken and revealed himself to us through *faith*. We believe the writings and witnesses who testify that God has spoken and made himself known.

However, this assurance is not a result of "blind faith." The truth has a way of proving itself to the human heart without rational or scientific demonstration. One Christian author, J.B. Phillips, wrote that the Bible is convincing, even to nonbelievers, because it has that "ring of truth"[4]—it rings true with our human experience. As the Letter to the Hebrews describes it:

> For the word of God is living and active, sharper than any two-edged sword, piercing to the division of soul and spirit, of joints and marrow, and discerning the thoughts and intentions of the heart. (Heb 4:12)

Faith in God's revelation is a light that illumines God and his presence among us. Just as scientific observation and experimentation is the light, or medium, that enables us to see and know about electrons and distant stars, faith in the truth God reveals is the light or medium that enables us to see and know God, and spiritual reality.

The One, True God

It is possible, through natural and divine revelation, to come to know that there is a God, and what he is like. What do we know about God through these sources? The foundational affirmation about God, which for centuries distinguished the Jews from their polytheistic neighbors, is that there is one, and only one, God. No other people in the ancient world spoke of only one God. The traditional daily prayer of the Jewish people, the *Shema,* begins, "Hear, O Israel: The LORD our God is one Lord . . ." (Dt 6:4). Christians, too, reject the belief in many gods (polytheism), based on Jesus' clear teaching (Mk 12:29).[5]

Today we might be tempted to laugh at primitive people who believed in many gods. Yet, the truth is that even today, in modern Western societies, those who do not really know the one, true God pay homage to other gods, whether consciously or not. Most don't worship the earth, the stars, or graven images made of stone or metal. The gods of modern Western society are economic, psychological, social, or historical laws;

self, money, pleasure, popularity, power; Wall Street, the banking and marketing system, military might, the mass media, multinational corporations, governments; or secular ideologies held to be ultimate and inviolable—whether it be capitalism, socialism, Marxism, or feminism. Though some of these things might not be evil in themselves, for many Western men and women these are the forces (the gods) that dominate or rule their lives and decisions, instead of faith and life in the one, true God. Salvation, as we shall see, is not only a matter of the next life, but of being freed in this life from the domination of every god—freed to serve the one, true God.

Some people turn to other gods because they consciously reject the existence of God. Atheism, the denial of God's existence, has been designated by the Second Vatican Council as "among the most serious problems of this age" (GS, no. 19). The Council discussed the various forms and causes of atheism, and noted that atheism can emerge from the failure of believers in God to live according to their beliefs:

> ... believers can have more than a little to do with the birth of atheism. To the extent that they neglect their own training in the faith, or teach erroneous doctrine, or are deficient in their religious, moral, or social life, they must be said to conceal rather than reveal the authentic face of God and religion. (GS, no. 19)

However, those who deny the existence of God finally bear the responsibility for their choice, for as Psalm 53 tells us, only the fool says, "There is no God" (Ps 53:1).

Another category of nonbelievers are agnostics, those who claim that it is impossible to know for certain whether or not God exists. Sometimes it is effective to ask such people (if they are serious about finding out whether God exists) to attempt an experiment. Ask them to go off by themselves sometime and earnestly ask God, if he is there, to reveal himself to them in some way that they will know that it is he. This may sound like putting God to the test or seeking a sign, but if the person is truly seeking God, Christians have good reason to believe that God will answer. St. James wrote, "Draw near to God and he will draw near to you" (Jas 4:8). The Book of Revelation says "Behold, I stand at the door and knock; if any one hears my voice and opens the door, I will come in to him and eat with him, and he with me" (Rv 3:20). Jesus, during his life on earth, insisted, "And I tell you, Ask, and it will be given you; seek, and you will find; knock, and it will be opened to you. For every one who asks receives, and he who seeks finds, and to him who knocks it will be opened" (Lk 11:9, 10).

God is not trying to hide himself from the human race nor from any individual—just the opposite is true. God desires each person to come to know him and to receive his abundant life in this world and in eternity (1 Tm 2:3, 4; Jn 10:10). As Francis Thompson described so beautifully in his famous poem, God is "the hound of heaven" who does not rest from his pursuit of us until we are "caught" through accepting him.[6]

Specifically, as Christians, we know that God so desired to reveal himself to humanity and to show his love for each person, that he actually became a man, Jesus Christ, and loved us to the extent of accepting an unjust and horrible death in order to free us from our sin and rebellion against him. What more could God have done to reveal to us his existence and his love, without overpowering us or otherwise violating our freedom?

All people strive to find the ultimate meaning or purpose of their lives and of human existence. Christians know that this ultimate meaning can be found only in the one, true God. We have been created to find our fulfillment and peace only in knowing, loving, and serving God. It is a plain fact of experience that human beings will be restless and searching until they have surrendered their lives totally to God. We have been created with a God-shaped hole, or vacuum, in our hearts, which can only be filled by him. It simply won't work to find true happiness and fulfillment in anything or anyone else. St. Augustine tried it for years, but finally told God in his *Confessions,* "You have made us for Yourself, and our hearts are restless until they rest in You."[7]

God Is Spirit

Who is this one God, whom Jews and Christians can so confidently claim is the fulfillment of all human needs and desires? Even believers sometimes yield to the scepticism of those who doubt God's existence because he cannot be observed. Soviet cosmonauts triumphantly announced on their first space flight that God was nowhere to be seen, instead of praising the beauty of God's creation. They failed to understand that God belongs to a different order of being. Jesus told the Samaritan woman near Jacob's well in Sachar, "God is spirit" (Jn 4:24). "Spirit" is a form of being that is non-material but that possesses intellect and free will—the ability to think and reason, to choose and decide. Pope John Paul II, in a general audience on September 11, 1986, summarized the basic Catholic teaching on God's nature as defined by the First Vatican Council:

> "God is a unique spiritual *substance,* utterly simple and immutable"; and again, "God is infinite in *intellect, will, and in every perfection....*"
>
> The Divine Being is by its own essence absolutely spiritual. Spirituality signifies intellect and free will. God is *Intelligence, Will, and Liberty* in an infinite degree, just as He is also *all perfection* in an infinite degree.[8]

To attempt to explain the concept of spirit fully would be impossible here. The most difficult thing for most modern people to accept or grasp is that there is a realm of existence that is not material; they tend to think that intelligence and will are dependent upon the existence of a material or biological organ, like the human brain. Yet, God does not have a brain, nor any other material part. He is pure, infinite, unbounded spirit. St. Anselm simply said God was "something . . . than which a greater cannot be conceived."[9] In other words, God is greater than the greatest thing we can conceive of, whether it be love, truth, justice, beauty, or goodness. Since these are not material things, we can gain some idea why the Judaeo-Christian tradition claims that God is not material. The best description of God that has positive content (expressing what he *is,* and not what he is not), is to say God is omnipotent (all-powerful); omniscient (all-knowing) and all-wise; eternal (having no beginning and no end); omnipresent (present everywhere simultaneously); immutable (unchanging in his being); all-loving; and perfect in goodness, beauty, truth, justice, mercy, and so on.

Some people object that this view of God is merely a projection of humanity's highest ideals. However, from where did human beings get these ideals? Did they produce them? No! God is not mankind's projection. If anything, the human person is God's projection. Our highest ideals—even our very being and nature—is a reflection of God, the creator, who is the source of all existence and ideals. The only reason humanity can have some idea of God at all is because human beings are not merely material or physical, but also possess a spiritual nature which is similar to God's nature as a pure spirit.

A Personal God

Envisioning God as spirit could leave us thinking of God as a vast, impersonal force pervading the universe, like cosmic energy or electricity. Fortunately, God has revealed not only ***what*** he is, spirit, but also *who* he is. God is neither a human invention nor a cosmic force; God is a personal being.

We all have some idea of what a person is because each of us is one. God is the ultimate source and model of personhood; he defines what a person is. We are called persons only because we reflect the personhood of God. The Bible says we are made in God's "image" and "likeness" (Gn 1:26).

There is one word in the Bible, both in the Old and New Testaments, that is most often used to describe God as a person. That word is "father."[10] God is the Father of the universe, of the human race, of his chosen people, and of each individual human person. The word "father" refers to God as both the origin or source of all that is, and also to his fatherly care as protector and provider for all beings.

The Trinity

The Bible also reveals something about God's personhood that is surprising. The first and fundamental belief of Jews and Christians about God is that God is one; there is only one God. As we have just seen, the Hebrew people often referred to this one God as father. However, the New Testament completes the Old Testament revelation of God by stating clearly, through Jesus Christ, that the one God is actually three persons: the Father, the Son (or the Word), and the Holy Spirit. Christians have traditionally called this mystery of three persons in one God, the Trinity.

It is easy to misunderstand this doctrine. People ask, "Is God one, or is he three?" or "Don't Christians pray to three Gods: Father, Son, and Holy Spirit?" The key to resolving this is to consider in what sense God is one, and in what sense, three. Christian theology has clarified this by the use of the terms "nature" and "person." God is one because he possesses a single divine nature, the nature of God. Nature, in this sense, is what makes something what it is. As Pope John Paul II has explained:

> Nature (essence) is all that whereby that which concretely exists is what it is. Thus, for example, when we speak of "human nature," we indicate what makes a man a man, with his essential components and his properties.
>
> Applying this distinction to God, we recognize the unity of nature, the unity of the Divinity, which belongs in an absolute and exclusive way to Him Who exists as God.[11]

The one God exists as three persons who are distinct but undivided, since each person fully possesses the same divine nature, the nature of God. A human person "is he or she who exists as a concrete human being, as an individual possessing humanity, that is, human nature."[12] In God, the persons are distinct, and yet are united in a far deeper way than any human persons because of the perfection and integrity (unity) of the divine nature, the being of God. The unity of the three persons of God is so great and profound that it is incorrect to say they are divided in any way.

How, then, are the three persons of God related to each other? Theologians speak of the "relations" among the three persons of the Trinity as the only thing that distinguishes them; the fact that they are not identical is proven because they are in relation to each other.[13] We only know this because God chose to reveal to us the secrets of his inner life through Jesus Christ, especially in the great Trinitarian passages in the Gospel of John (see Jn 10:30; 14:10, 11; 15:26).

Much more could be said about the development of the Christian understanding of the Trinity, but as Pope John Paul II has said:

> . . . even after Revelation it remains the Most profound mystery of faith, which the intellect by itself can neither comprehend nor penetrate . . .
>
> The intellect, however, enlightened by faith, can in a certain way grasp and explain the meaning of the dogma.

Thus it can bring close to man the mystery of the inmost life of the Triune God.[14]

Through the study of the Bible and the creeds of the early church, Catholics can come to a fuller appreciation and understanding of the mystery of the Trinity. Through faith, we can hold onto this truth about God as He has revealed it to us. For example, the *Quicumque* Creed of the fifth century proclaims, "Such as the Father is, such likewise is the Son, and such also is the Holy Spirit." That "such" is explained by the words of the *Quicumque* which follow, referring to God as "uncreated, immense, eternal, omnipotent . . . not three omnipotents, but only one omnipotent: thus God the Father, God the Son, God the Holy Spirit. . . . There do not exist three Gods, but only one God."

God Is Love

God has a personal nature, and therefore personal qualities. Perhaps the greatest personal attribute of God is love. The First Letter of John simply says: "love is of God" (1 Jn 4:7). The Bible repeatedly testifies that the inner life of God—the Father, Son, and Holy Spirit—is especially characterized by their mutual love. Jesus, the Son, is constantly honoring the Father who sent him (e.g., Jn 12:27, 28, 49, 50). God the Father cries out, "This is my beloved Son" (Mt 3:17). The Holy Spirit also glorifies Jesus: "He (the Holy Spirit) will glorify me, for he will take what is mine and declare it to you" (Jn 16:14). The Spirit points to Jesus' true identity: ". . . no one can say 'Jesus is Lord' except by the Holy Spirit" (1 Cor 12:3). The Father and the Son send the Holy Spirit to us, giving us a share in their perfect, mutual love: "God's love has been poured into our hearts through the Holy Spirit which has been given to us" (Rom 5:5). These texts should lead us to understand that the persons of the Trinity, because of their perfect mutual love and unity, constantly exalt and glorify each other.

The love of God must be understood rightly. God's love is not a passing emotion or feeling, nor is it a love that allows unrepented injustice, sin, or rebellion to go unpunished. God's merciful love does not deny or contradict his justice. To understand what love truly is, we should study how God acts and relates to his creatures. The Bible speaks constantly of God's love:

> The steadfast love of the Lord never ceases,
> his mercies never come to an end;
> they are new every morning;
> great is thy faithfulness. (Lam 3:22, 23)

Jesus shows that love involves obedience, as he was obedient to his Father's will, even accepting death as the greatest expression of God's love for us.

> In this is love, not that we loved God but that he loved us and sent his Son to be the expiation for our sins. (1 Jn 4:10)

The psalms especially resound with praise of God for his love and all his other perfections. Psalm 117 is one example:

> Praise the Lord, all nations! / Extol him, all peoples! / For great is his steadfast love toward us; / and the faithfulness of the LORD endures forever. / Praise the LORD! (Ps 117:1, 2)

Creation—an Expression of God's Love

Christians believe that God's love is demonstrated by the very existence of the cosmos. Sometimes we forget that the universe need not exist. Christians believe that there was a time before anything existed, except God. Even then, God was not deficient in any way; he was perfectly complete and happy (to use inadequate human concepts).

Why, then, did God create the universe?—Because God is love. It is the nature of love to express itself, to give of itself. Love is naturally generous and creative. Christians believe that the universe—so incredibly vast, diverse, majestic, and beautiful—came into being from God's desire to express himself, to give of himself, out of sheer love.[15]

Some people feel threatened by the immensity of the universe, overwhelmed by a sense of their own insignificance and frailty. A healthy humility should arise from the fact of our limited human lives. Psalm 144 observes, "Man is like a breath, / his days are like a passing shadow" (Ps 144:4). Catholics are marked with ashes each year on Ash Wednesday to remind us of the shortness of our lives, "Remember, man, that you are dust, and unto dust you shall return."

Without God this reflection can lead to despair or existential *angst* (fear). Knowing God should enable us to realize our utter and absolute dependence on him. ". . . 'Thou art my God.' My times are in thy hand . . ." (Ps 31:15, 16). Only in realizing our insignificance and weakness can we appreciate God's love. God not only created the universe in the beginning out of love, but he sustains the universe and each one of us in existence at every moment. If God were to forget us, we would cease to exist.

Yet God does not forget us. He loves and cares for each of his creatures, individually and personally. How foolish it is when human beings try to deny or avoid God! First, it is impossible to hide from God. Psalm 139 beautifully recounts how God formed each one of us in the womb, knows everything about us, and is present everywhere we could go. Take a moment to read this psalm and reflect on it. Second, why should we want to hide from the God who created us, sustains our existence, and loves us so totally? St. Paul told the Athenians, "In him we live and move and have our being" (Acts 17:28). God's deepest desire is for every person to come to know his personal love for them, to accept that love, and to love and obey him in return. In doing this, human nature is perfected; we reach the destiny that God has prepared for us: everlasting life and happiness in his presence. Paul also wrote, "For the creation waits with eager longing for the revealing of the sons of God . . ." (Rom 8:19). He teaches that even the creation itself "will be set free from its bondage to decay and obtain the glorious liberty of the children of God" (Rom 8:21). God created the world out of love, and he will reveal his love once again by renewing the creation and bringing it to fulfillment in him (see Col 1:15-20).

The Creation

What do we mean by "creation," or the "created universe"? To create means to produce something out of nothing, to bring forth being (whether material or spiritual) that previously did not exist. Pope John Paul II has written: "The truth of creation expresses the thought that everything existing outside of God has been called into existence by Him . . . 'Creation' therefore means: to make from nothing; to call into existence, that is, to form a being from nothing."[16] The first verse of the Bible states that before the creation of the material universe, only God and other purely spiritual beings existed. God created all things, matter and energy, and even the medium (time) that is used to measure their duration and change.

The material universe was not the first of God's creations. God also created beings who are pure spirits, like himself, possessing understanding and free will: the angels. The Greek word, *angelos,* means "messenger." The Bible records that God often sent these spirits as messengers to humanity, bearing important truths or commands. Before time began, before the universe was created, angels gave glory to God, their creator (Heb 1:6), and served God's will and purposes (Heb 1:14).

However, God has revealed to us a tragedy of cosmic proportions that came to affect the history of the human race. Although God created all of the angels in his own image, perfectly good and loving, some of the angels used their free will to rebel against God. The leader of this rebellion has been called by various names in the Bible and Christian tradition: Lucifer, Satan, the devil. The basic sin attributed to Satan is pride, desiring to be God or God's equal. The prophet Isaiah laments:

> "How you are fallen from heaven,
> O Day Star, son of Dawn! . . .
> You said in your heart,
> 'I will ascend to heaven;
> above the stars of God
> I will set my throne on high. . . .
> I will make myself like the Most High.'
> But you are brought down to Sheol,
> to the depths of the Pit." (Is 14:12-15)

The Letter of Jude says that "the angels that did not keep their own position but left their proper dwelling have been kept by him [God] in eternal chains in the nether gloom . . ." (Jude 6). The Book of Revelation describes the fall of Lucifer, or Satan, more graphically, picturing the angels obedient to God, led by Michael, defeating and casting down Satan and the rebellious angels who followed him:

> Now war arose in heaven, Michael and his angels fighting against the dragon; and the dragon and his angels fought, but they were defeated and there was no longer any place for them in heaven. And the great dragon was thrown down, that ancient serpent, who is called the Devil and Satan, the deceiver of the whole world—he was thrown down to the

earth, and his angels were thrown down with him. (Rv 12:7-9)

Thus the angels obedient to God are forever united with him in the joy of heaven, the "dwelling place" of God, while the rebellious angels (or demons) are destined to eternal separation from God as a consequence of their own free choice.

The Origin of Evil

The ultimate origin of evil is rebellion of powerful spiritual beings against God. Evil may be defined as any rebellion against God, his will, and any consequence of that rebellion.

God does not actively will evil (Jas 1:13-15). Even the idea involves a contradiction—why would God rebel against himself or his own purposes? God is totally good and desires only the perfect harmony and happiness of his creation. The Book of Genesis observes, "God saw everything that he had made, and behold, it was very good" (Gn 1:31). God did not create evil. Evil has no existence of its own; it is a distortion or corruption of the good that comes from God.

God created beings with genuinely free will. In doing so, he took a great risk. He so highly valued the existence of creatures with freedom of choice that he introduced the possibility of these creatures using their free will to rebel against him. Satan and the angels who followed him chose this path. God did not destroy these spirits, who are eternal by nature, but allowed them to receive the inevitable result of their own free choice. They were eternally separated from God and his favor. Their situation is, literally, hell—a condition of eternal torment—for apart from God there is no real happiness or peace.

Is God unjust in allowing Satan and his angelic followers to suffer forever? He is just, for he is giving them what they freely chose. The more difficult question is how God is loving and merciful in allowing this. There is a mystery involved here, but we must realize that Satan and the fallen angels, with their great intelligence, fully realized the possible consequences of their action. They freely chose to rebel against God. God is fully loving and merciful, but it must be understood that he does not impose his love and mercy on any free creature. Since God created beings who are genuinely free, it is certainly possible that some would choose not to accept and obey God. Thus, they separate themselves from his love and mercy.

Finally, good and evil are not equally powerful. There are religions which teach that good and evil are two equally potent cosmic forces (or gods) at war with one another, with the outcome of the struggle still in question. This is called dualism. St. Augustine believed this during his ten years as a Manichee, before his conversion to Christianity. Christianity teaches that the one God, who is totally good, is ultimately victorious.

The Creation of Mankind

The Book of Genesis begins with two interwoven accounts of God's creation of the material universe, including the human race. Despite some differences in detail in the Yahwist and Priestly accounts, they both affirm that God created all things, and that the climax of the creation of the world was man (Hebrew: *adam*).[17]

> Then God said, "Let us make man in our image, after our likeness; and let them have dominion over [the earth's creatures]." . . . God created man in his own image, in the image of God he created him; male and female he created them. And God blessed them, and God said to them, "Be fruitful and multiply, and fill the earth and subdue it. . . ." (Gn 1:26-28)

The fact that human beings are made in God's "image and likeness" primarily indicates that God created them to exist in a relationship with him. It also indicates that humanity possesses a spiritual nature like God, as well as intelligence, free will, and other God-like qualities and virtues.

The Genesis account accentuates God's special love for the man and woman he created, and his friendship with them. As Pope John Paul II teaches:

> Indeed man, thanks to his spiritual nature and to his capacity for intellectual knowledge and freedom of choice and action, is, *from the very beginning, in a special relationship with God.* The description of creation (cf. Gn 1-3) permits us to observe that the "image of God" is manifested above all in the relation of the human "I" to the divine "You." *Man knows God,* and his heart and will are capable of uniting themselves with God *(homo est capax Dei).* Man can say "yes" to God, but he can also say "no." He has the capacity to *accept* God and His holy will, but also the capacity to *oppose* it.[18]

The only prohibition on the couple was that they must not eat of the tree of knowledge of good and evil, lest they die (Gn 2:16, 17). Death, and even sickness, were apparently unknown to them, and all their needs were provided for (Gn 2:9). They enjoyed a full, rich human existence in complete harmony with God, nature, and each other. This state of humanity before the rebellion against God is called, in Catholic theology, the state of "original righteousness" or "original innocence."

The Temptation and Fall of Man

The Book of Revelation refers to "that ancient serpent, who is called the Devil and Satan, the deceiver of the whole world" (Rv 12:9). The one whom Jesus called "a liar and the father of lies" (Jn 8:44) appears in Genesis 3 in the form of a serpent. He convinces the first woman, Eve, to disobey God's command not to eat of the fruit of that particular tree: ". . . God knows that when you eat of it your eyes will be opened, and you will be like God, knowing good and evil" (Gn 3:5). Thus, Satan lured the human race into his own sin of pride. He deceived them into wanting to be like God, on their own terms.

It should be noted that the image the Book of Genesis uses for the original sin of mankind—eating the fruit of the tree of knowledge of good and evil—may be interpreted in a symbolic way. The original sin was not eating an apple or having sexual relations (which is a gift of God to married couples), but prideful rebellion against God. Satan tempted Eve by telling her that what God commanded was not true, and that she would actually become like God by disobeying him. Rebellion against God and pride are at the heart of humanity's primordial sin.

When Eve and Adam sinned, they received part of what Satan promised. They knew good and evil because for the first time they had done evil. This is what Catholics traditionally and rightly call "original sin"—the first sin of the human race. Adam and Eve had disobeyed the God who had loved them so perfectly, so they joined in Satan's rebellion.

Through this account, the Book of Genesis conveys the basic truth that humanity has turned away from God and his plan, like Satan, by free choice. This sin of our first parents was not only a rebellion with personal consequences, however. It affected the whole human race that would spring from them biologically. Original sin not only refers to the first human sin but to the condition of separation from God into which every human person is born.

From our own experience, we are aware of original sin and its effects. Human beings are not born naturally into a full knowledge of God and a real relationship with him. For example, what was evident to St. Augustine was not the natural innocence of children, but their selfishness and greed that needed constantly to be curbed.[19] He saw this as a sign of original sin. Another effect of original sin is that the human race endures suffering and death, and no longer possesses some other natural gifts that Adam and Eve enjoyed before their rebellion.

One does not need these theological reflections to affirm the reality of original sin. Newspapers and other media reports testify daily to the wretched human condition. St. Paul described the root of the problem in his Letter to the Romans: ". . . sin came into the world through one man and death through sin, and so death spread to all men because all men sinned" (Rom 5:12; see also Jas 4:1-4). In St. Paul's terminology, original sin is the "law of sin and death" (Rom 8:2) that every person[20] is subject to from the moment of conception as a result of the Fall of our first parents. We are forced to cry out with the psalmist, "Behold, I was brought forth in iniquity, / and in sin did my mother conceive me" (Ps 51:5).

The Catholic church teaches that original sin is not transmitted merely by example but through an actual corruption or distortion of our common human nature. God created our humanity "very good," in his own image and likeness, so it is incorrect to speak of "the total depravity of man," as do some Christian churches. Human nature is essentially good and God-like, but since the first or original rebellion of the human race, it is a fallen nature, distorted and corrupted by sin.

Original sin results in an inherited rebelliousness against God and his ways. St. Paul calls this "the flesh" (see Gal 5:19-21), not referring to our physical bodies, but to the intrinsic drive we all have to fulfill our desires and passions without regard for God or others. Each of us experiences this resistance to God fully ruling our lives and the tug of our passions urging us to satisfy their desires. As the Letter of James says:

> Let no one say when he is tempted, "I am tempted by God"; for God cannot be tempted with evil and he himself tempts

> no one; but each person is tempted when he is lured and enticed by his own desire. Then desire when it has conceived gives birth to sin; and sin when it is full-grown brings forth death. (Jas 1:13-15)

This is the experience and effect of original sin.

The Consequences of Sin

Adam and Eve used their free will to disobey God and his plan. As a result, they forfeited the intimate friendship with God they had previously enjoyed. The Book of Genesis speaks of our first parents being cast out of the Garden of Eden, with an angel barring their return, to signify the separation and alienation from God.

Alienation from God is the primary effect of sin, but there are also other consequences. Adam and Eve and their offspring also became subject to suffering and death. They were forced to survive on the earth through hard labor, and women brought forth children in pain as a result of original sin. Even the order and harmony of nature and other created things was disrupted by humanity's rebellion against God (Rom 8:19-22).

Again, there is a temptation to ask, How could a loving God permit this? In his love, God gave angels and men the great gift of free will. In his justice, God allowed angels and men to receive the consequences of their free choice. The great Puritan poet, John Milton, characterizes Satan's attitude: "Better to reign in Hell, than serve in Heav'n."[21] God, in his justice, gave him what he wished.

In justice, God also allowed Adam and Eve, and the whole human race, to experience the consequences of sin and rebellion against him. For humanity, this justice is not God's last word. Realizing its weakness and limited understanding, God decided to give the human race another chance, a hope of reconciliation with him. God has offered this second chance to us out of pure mercy and love. God gave Adam and Eve a foreshadowing of their deliverance when he told the serpent (Satan) who had just deceived them:

> "I will put enmity between you and the woman, / and between your seed and her seed; / he shall bruise your head, and you shall bruise his heel." (Gn 3:15)

This passage is known as the *proto-evangelium*—the first glimpse of the good news that an offspring of a woman of our race would strike at the head of the serpent, Satan, and ultimately defeat him. When and how this would happen was not clear to the author of Genesis, nor to Adam and Eve, nor to any other human being until the coming of the one who would fulfill this prophecy, the Savior, Jesus Christ. As Pope John Paul II has summarized salvation history:

> Thus the Bible begins absolutely with a first, and then with a second account of creation, where the origin of all from God, of things, of life, of man (Gn 1:2), is interwoven with the other sad chapter about the origin, this time of man, not without temptation of the devil, of sin and of evil (Gn 3). But God does not abandon His creatures. And so a tiny flame of hope is lit towards a future of a new creation freed from evil (the so-called *protoevangelium*, Gn 3:15; cf. 9:13). These three threads, God's creative and positive action, man's rebellion, and, already from the beginning, God's promise of a new world, form the texture of the history of salvation, by determining the global content of the Christian faith in creation.[22]

Conclusions

Since the Book of Genesis and the other biblical evidence regarding God and his creation is the foundation of Catholic and Christian faith, let us review some of the basic biblical truths presented in this chapter "for the sake of our salvation."

1. There is only one God—eternal, almighty, all-loving and all-wise—who created every spiritual being (such as angels) and the entire material universe out of nothing.

The Catholic church does allow different views of precisely how and when God created the universe, but insists that only God is the author of creation.

2. There is an angel known as the Devil or Satan whose rebellion against God is the ultimate origin of all evil.

Pope Paul VI addressed this issue in a general audience given on November 15, 1973. He said:

> What are the greatest needs of the church today? Do not let our answer surprise you as being over-simple or even superstitious and unreal: one of the greatest needs is defense from that evil which is called the Devil . . . it is not a question of one Devil, but of many, (as) is indicated by various passages in the gospel (Lk 11:17; Mk 5:9). But the principal one is Satan, which means the Adversary, the Enemy . . . So we know that this dark and disturbing spirit really exists, and that he still acts with treacherous cunning; he is the secret enemy that sows errors and misfortune in human history. . . .[23]

3. God created man, male and female, in his own image and likeness. Man is a creature composed of both spirit and matter, called by God to an eternal destiny of life with him.

The Catholic church does not officially teach either that the human race evolved from lower species or was created directly by God. To Catholics, the evolution versus creation debate concerning the origin of mankind involves an issue open to scientific investigation rather than a matter of faith necessary to salvation.

The Catholic church does insist, however, that the soul or

spiritual nature of man was directly infused by God into man and woman; it did not evolve. By this act of God, the infusion of the human soul, a distinctive race of human beings with moral responsibility and an eternal destiny was established by God.[24]

> *4. The first human beings, deceived by Satan, rebelled against God through pride and disobedience and were thereby separated from his friendship. This original sin also introduced suffering, death, and loss of certain gifts and abilities into the human condition.*

It is difficult for us to imagine human existence without struggle, pain, and death. These seem like biological necessities. Life without them sounds like a utopian fairy tale. But Christians believe that it is a fact that if humanity had not rebelled against God, we would enjoy all the gifts and blessings that the Book of Genesis says that Adam and Eve possessed in the Garden of Eden before their sin. We base this belief on God's word and on the supposition that all evil, including pain and death, is a result of sin. If there had been no original sin, there would be no human struggle, suffering, or death.

> *5. Each human person ever born (with the exception of Jesus and his mother) is subject to original sin and its effects. Human nature has been corrupted, though not destroyed or irreparably damaged, by original sin.*

The effect of original sin on the human condition is pervasive. Human beings cannot avoid doing evil without God's intervention and help. Man alone is powerless to overcome original sin and its effects. Few people have described so well the plight of man after the Fall as St. Paul in his Letter to the Romans:

> I do not understand my own actions. For I do not do what I want, but I do the very thing I hate.... So then it is no longer

I that do it, but sin which dwells in me. For I know that nothing good dwells in me, that is, in my flesh. I can will what is right, but I cannot do it. For I do not do the good I want, but the evil I do not want is what I do. . . .

Wretched man that I am! Who will deliver me from this body of death? (Rom 7:15, 17-19, 24)

6. In spite of man's rebellion against him, God gave humanity after the Fall of Adam and Eve a hope of reconciliation with himself.

Primitive man, though alienated from God and without knowledge of him, sought for God and for ways to please (or appease) him. For centuries, the true God remained hidden from the human race, awaiting the time to begin his great plan of reconciliation and restoration.

TWO

God's People of the Old Testament

THE FIRST CHAPTER HAS DESCRIBED the rebellion of our first parents against God who created them and loved them. Both their original sin and all the subsequent personal (or actual) sins of their offspring resulted in the estrangement of the human race from its Creator.

The plight of humanity at this point seemed hopeless. Man had used God's gift of free will to turn from God and to reject his plan for human life. Having rebelled, man found that it was beyond his power to reconcile himself to God and reestablish the loving relationship with his Creator that he had rejected. The effect of sin is like a person who digs himself into a pit, and then realizes that he has no way of getting out. Only someone outside of the pit can reach down and save him. Likewise, after the sin of Adam and Eve, only God could save the human race and draw it back into right relationship with himself.

God's love and mercy is demonstrated by his desire to reconcile humanity with himself—to rescue us from our sin and its effects. This salvation is totally gratuitous—a free, undeserved gift. If God would act strictly according to justice, the human race clearly deserves to experience all of the terrible consequences of the sin it chose, the ultimate consequence being death. Instead, God has offered the human race a second chance—an opportunity to be freed from sin and all its effects.

This chapter will describe some major aspects of the first stage of God's plan to save humanity from sin and death. God did not do this in a single act; he prepared the human race over the course of many centuries for the full work of his salvation. This long preparation was necessary due to both the magnitude of the work God had in mind and to humanity's stubborn resistance to God's work.

This process of God calling us back to himself is often called salvation history. Let us recall some of the events of this history of God's saving plan that paved the way for his full deliverance of the human race in Jesus Christ.

God's Plan of Salvation

Conceivably, God could have forgiven man's sin and reconciled humanity to himself simply by decreeing it: "I forgive." However, would this have conveyed to us the seriousness of our offense against God? Would it have been totally just for God simply to overlook the choice mankind had freely made? Would not such a decree, imposing God's forgiveness upon us, violate our free will?

God takes seriously our freedom; he refuses to obstruct even our wrong choices. God desires to forgive and save the human race, but he refuses to impose forgiveness or reconciliation on anyone. Each person must desire, must choose, to be reconciled to God.

In his consummate wisdom, God has a perfect plan for drawing the human race back into right relationship with himself. It depends both on God's merciful offer of forgiveness, and on man's free response to this offer based on faith and trust in God. The initial stage of God's plan was to form a specific people who would learn to know God and to live according to his will. Through this people, other peoples and eventually the whole human race would come to know who God is, and would learn to love and obey him. Also, from the midst of this specific people would emerge the one person who would bring God's salvation fully to the human race, a Savior for the whole world.

The Covenant Relationship

This grandiose scheme actually had very unlikely and humble beginnings. In fact, at first it looked as if it would never have a chance to begin. Adam and Eve initially violated the covenant relationship of love and trust that God had established between him and them. They disbelieved God's word and his faithfulness and so disobeyed his command. Later, after the Fall, the Book of Genesis records that the wickedness of their descendants was so great that God decided to destroy the human race through a great flood. However, there was one righteous man, Noah, to whom God offered the possibility of salvation. If Noah would hear and obey God's instruction to build a huge ark, then he and his family (along with pairs of every living creature) would be saved from the flood. Unlike Adam and Eve, Noah believed what God had spoken to him and obeyed his instruction. As a result, God spared Noah and his family and made his first great covenant with them after the original sin of Adam and Eve.

The term "covenant" is essential in understanding God's plan for relating to and saving the human race. The word "covenant" was used in the ancient Near East to describe any solemn agreement between two (or more) parties. The Judaeo-Christian tradition believes that God himself initiated a series of covenants with mankind, which became the basis of the relationship between God and a particular people.

The terms of the covenant with Noah were simply that God solemnly agreed never again to attempt to destroy the human race by a flood (see Gn 9:9-11), and God set the rainbow in the sky as a "sign of the covenant between me and the earth" (Gn 9:13). This story illustrates certain important points about all of God's covenants with man. First, God alone initiates the covenant, but man must accept the covenant and cooperate with it. As Pope John Paul II has stated, the covenant "is a completely sovereign initiative of God the Creator," and that, "Man is the suitable subject for the Covenant, because he was created 'in the image' of God, capable of knowledge and freedom."[1] Second, God's covenants have a saving purpose, in this case to preserve the human race from future destruction. Thirdly, there is often an outward sign (or signs) of the covenant, in this case the rainbow, which symbolizes and calls to mind the covenant between God and humanity.

The Covenant with Abraham

God's first covenant through Noah foreshadows the great covenant by which God set apart a people to be his own, through which the human race might be restored to God's friendship. The Book of Genesis reports that God revealed himself to a man named Abram, saying:

> "Go from your country and your kindred and your father's house to the land that I will show you. And I will make of you a great nation, and I will bless you, and make your name great, so that you will be a blessing. . . . and by you all the families of the earth shall bless themselves." So Abram went, as the LORD had told him. . . .(Gn 12:1-4)

Many years later, God spoke to Abram of a covenant:

> "Behold, my covenant is with you, and you shall be the father of a multitude of nations. No longer shall your name be Abram, but your name shall be Abraham; for I have made you the father of a multitude of nations. . . . I will establish

> my covenant between me and you and your descendants after you throughout their generations for an everlasting covenant, to be God to you and to your descendants after you." (Gn 17:4, 5, 7)

The sign of this covenant was that "every male among you shall be circumcised" (Gn 17:10).

The call of God to Abram set in motion God's salvific plan. God desired to set apart a people, the descendants of Abraham, to be a nation under God's particular care. Through this people, known at first as the Hebrews, God would eventually bring the blessing of salvation to all mankind.

The Cost of the Covenant

Although this covenant was initiated by God, it required Abraham's full response. Abraham heard and obeyed the call of God to leave his homeland and kinfolk, and settle in a new land, Canaan (Gn 12:4-6). Later, he had to move to Egypt for a time because of famine. Abraham believed God when God told him that his elderly, barren wife, Sarah, would bear a son, thus fulfilling God's promise that Abraham would be the father of many nations. Then Abraham had to face the severest test of his faith. God asked Abraham to kill his only son, Isaac, as a sacrifice to God, even though Isaac was the key to the fulfillment of God's promise of descendants for Abraham. God sent his angel to stop Abraham's knife-poised hand at the last minute.

Through all these many trials and tests, Abraham remained steadfastly faithful to God: "And he believed the LORD; and he reckoned it to him as righteousness" (Gn 15:6). Abraham, like Noah, believed in God and his promises, and obeyed God, regardless of the cost. It was through this sort of faith and obedience that God was able to act in history, to reverse the lack of faith and disobedience of Adam and Eve. To this day,

Christians, as well as Jews, recognize Abraham as our father in faith (see Rom 4; Gal 3; Heb 11:8-10, 17-19).

This covenant of God with the descendants of Abraham, the Hebrew people, endured for centuries. The content of the covenant was clear and simple: believe in and obey the one God who has revealed himself to Abraham. Circumcise all males as a sign of the covenant, and follow whatever other commands or directives God gives.

Moses and the Covenant at Sinai

Abraham's son, Isaac, fathered two sons, Esau and Jacob, also called Israel. Israel had twelve sons, patriarchs of the twelve tribes of Israel. Jacob's second youngest son, Joseph, was sold into slavery by his brothers and dwelt in Egypt where he rose from slavery to the highest position in government next to Pharaoh. When a famine struck the land of Canaan, the other sons of Jacob moved with their families to Egypt where they prospered for many years due to Joseph's influence. Then a new king "who did not know Joseph" (Ex 1:8) came to power; he began to oppress the Israelites with forced labor and even ordered the midwives to the Hebrews to kill their male children. One of these children, Moses, was rescued and adopted by Pharaoh's daughter. When Moses grew up, though, he killed an Egyptian and was forced to flee to the wilderness of Midian, where he married the daughter of Jethro and became a shepherd of his flocks.

This brief summary is designed to set the stage for one of the most seminal periods in the history of God's plan of salvation. The first key event was God's revelation of himself and his name to Moses. God spoke to Moses from a burning bush, saying:

> "I am the God of your Father, the God of Abraham, the God of Isaac, and the God of Jacob. . . . I have seen the affliction of

> my people who are in Egypt . . . and I have come down to deliver them out of the hand of the Egyptians, and to bring them up out of that land to a good and broad land, a land flowing with milk and honey. . . . Come, I will send you to Pharaoh that you may bring forth my people, the sons of Israel, out of Egypt." (Ex 3:6-10)

Moses was unwilling at first, objecting that he would need to know God's name to prove to Pharaoh that he had truly been sent by God. "God said to Moses, 'I AM WHO I AM.' And he said, 'Say this to the people of Israel, "I AM has sent me to you."'" (Ex 3:14). This utterance of God is the source of the word YHWH (Yahweh), the personal name of the God of Israel. The name is considered so sacred by the Jewish people that it is not even pronounced. Substitutes like *Adonai* ("my Lord") are spoken instead. Books have been written about the precise meaning of this sacred tetragrammaton, YHWH, but the primary point is that God reveals himself as the one who is: he is God. In the ancient Near East, to know a person's name was thought to provide some influence over the person. It is significant that God would reveal his proper name to Moses. It signifies a major step forward in their relationship and the relationship between God and his Old Covenant people, the Jews.

God demonstrated his love and providential care for his people through concrete historical events. Nothing has shown God's love and care for the Hebrew people more clearly than the series of events that resulted from God's summons to Moses. God sent Moses to Pharaoh, king of Egypt, to demand that he allow the Jews to stop work and worship God in the wilderness. Pharaoh refused, and God sent the plagues upon the Egyptians in an attempt to convince them to heed Moses' request. Finally, Pharaoh relented when an angel of death killed all the first-born males of the Egyptians, both man and beast, while he "passed over" the homes of the Jews and spared their children.

The meal that the Jews ate in haste as they prepared to flee to Egypt is called the Passover meal. It is celebrated annually by the Jewish people to commemorate God's mighty act of leading them out of captivity in Egypt through the miraculous parting of the Red Sea (or Sea of Reeds) when the Egyptians were in hot pursuit.[2] This Passover of the Jewish people from captivity to freedom has been remembered by them as the most important event illustrating God's salvation and protection of his people. The "Song of Moses" in Exodus 15 and a number of the psalms (66, 78, 105, 106, 136) recall this event and praise God for his mighty acts.

For Christians, God's liberation of the Jewish people from political captivity in Egypt is a great symbol and foreshadowing of God's liberation of humanity from the spiritual captivity of sin and death, accomplished through the dying and rising of Jesus Christ.

The Commandments

Before Moses, God's covenant with the Hebrew people required their faith in God and obedience to him, but there was no explicitly defined law that governed the life of this people. After the crossing of the Red Sea, the Hebrews wandered into the desert until they reached Mount Sinai, or Horeb, a large peak in the midst of the mountains in the southern Sinai Peninsula. At this mountain, God revealed himself once again to Moses, instructing him to tell the Israelites:

> ". . . if you will obey my voice and keep my covenant, you shall be my own possession among all peoples; for all the earth is mine, and you shall be to me a kingdom of priests and a holy nation." (Ex 19:5, 6)

Later, the Lord gave Moses ten commandments or words that were to be the norm of their conduct. These commandments, in summary, are:

1. "I am the Lord your God. . . . You shall have no other gods before me." (Dt 5:6, 7)
2. "You shall not take the name of the LORD your God in vain." (Dt 5:11)
3. "Observe the sabbath day, to keep it holy, as the LORD, your God commanded you. Six days you shall labor, and do all your work; but the seventh day is a sabbath to the LORD your God. . . ." (Dt 5:12-14)
4. "Honor your father and your mother, as the LORD your God commanded you, that your days may be prolonged. . . ." (Dt 5:16)
5. "You shall not kill." (Dt 5:17)
6. "Neither shall you commit adultery." (Dt 5:18)
7. "Neither shall you steal." (Dt 5:19)
8. "Neither shall you bear false witness against your neighbor." (Ex 5:20)
9. "Neither shall you covet your neighbor's wife." (Dt 5:21)
10. "You shall not desire your neighbor's house, his field, . . . or anything else that is your neighbor's." (Dt 5:21)

God's announcement of the Ten Commandments, or Decalogue, is another landmark event in salvation history. God's formation of Israel is similar to parents raising a child. At first, it was enough to expect the Hebrews to believe in one God and obey God as he sovereignly directed them in specific circumstances. Now Israel had matured to the point that God could reveal his will more fully, through his Law.

It is important to understand that God's commandments, the Mosaic Law, are not a set of arbitrary, externally imposed regulations. Rather, they codify some of the ways that God had originally created human beings to relate to him and to each other. This is why Jesus says of these commandments:

> . . . not an iota, not a dot, will pass from the law until all is accomplished. Whoever then relaxes one of the least of these commandments and teaches men so, shall be called least in

> the kingdom of heaven; but he who does them and teaches them shall be called great in the kingdom of heaven. (Mt 5:18-19)

It is a disturbing fact that many Catholics today do not even know the Ten Commandments. These commandments are not outdated. Certainly Jesus taught the Jewish people in his day how to interpret these commandments correctly and how to live them more radically, but first he insisted that they be obeyed. When a man questioned Jesus about what he had to do to gain eternal life, Jesus' immediate response was, "If you would enter life, keep the commandments" (Mt 19:17). When the man asked, "Which ones?" Jesus proceeded to list a number of the Ten Commandments (Mt 19:18, 19).

John, in his First Letter, states the importance of this very directly: "For this is the love of God, that we keep his commandments. And his commandments are not burdensome" (1 Jn 5:3). Those who know God and who want to love him keep his commandments:

> And by this we may be sure that we know him, if we keep his commandments. He who says, "I know him" but disobeys his commandments is a liar . . . but whoever keeps his word, in him truly love for God is perfected. (1 Jn 2:3-5)

Israel's Disobedience and God's Steadfast Love

God has given his people guidance for their lives in his Law or commandments, and yet the Hebrews failed to obey it faithfully. No sooner had Moses delivered the Law than the Israelites violated the first commandment by making and worshiping a golden calf. The subsequent history of Israel is a continuous repetition or cycle of a basic pattern of events:

1. The people sin, violating God's commandments;
2. God allows them to suffer the just punishment of their rebellion;
3. The people cry out to God for mercy and forgiveness;
4. The Lord has compassion, removing the punishment and offering forgiveness;
5. The people repent: turning away from their wrongdoing and returning to obedience to God.

A good example of this cycle is presented by the Book of Judges 2:6-23.

The truth that stands out in the history of Israel is the tremendous faithfulness of God to his chosen people in spite of their infidelity. The Hebrew Scriptures repeatedly extol God's steadfast love, *emet*:

> I will sing of thy steadfast love, O Lord, forever; / ... For thy steadfast love was established forever, / thy faithfulness is firm as the heavens. (Ps 89:1-2)

Psalm 89 goes on to proclaim that God's love and faithfulness are based on his covenant relationship with Israel. Because of this covenant, God always stands ready to forgive and renew his mercy, regardless of the seriousness of Israel's sin and rebellion against him. God is truly portrayed in the Old Testament as both a just and a merciful God, a loving father, a God of steadfast love and faithfulness.

Kings and Prophets

One sign of God's love for Israel was the fulfillment of many of their desires. After Joshua had led the people out of the Sinai desert and back into the land God had promised to give them, they were ruled by a series of judges. Still, Israel desired a king, like the other nations, so God sent the prophet Samuel to anoint Saul as the first king of Israel. Saul was succeeded by the greatest king of the Old Covenant, David, followed by his son, Solomon, who built the first temple in Jerusalem.

Despite God's blessings, the Hebrew people often violated their covenant with God through sin. God responded by raising up the prophets, whose mission was to call the people to repent, to change their evil ways, and turn back to faithfulness to the covenant. The task of the prophet is not so much to foretell the future, although prophets may do this through God's inspiration. The prophet is primarily called by God and sent out to challenge God's people to change their lives and return to faithfulness to God and their covenant with him. The message of the prophets is sometimes a harsh word of conviction for sin (for violation of the covenant), but at other times it is a message of hope and consolation in times of hardship or affliction resulting from the peoples' sin and infidelity. The true prophet speaks not his own word but God's word, through the inspiration of the Holy Spirit. The Old Testament canon contains the longer writings of the "major prophets" Isaiah, Ezekiel, and Jeremiah; and the shorter accounts of the "minor prophets" Hosea, Joel, Amos, Obadiah, Micah, Nahum, Habakkuk, Zephaniah, Haggai, Zechariah, Malachi, Daniel, Baruch, and the Book of Lamentations. Jonah is also sometimes considered a prophetic book.

The Messianic Prophecies

Another important role of the prophets was to foretell and prepare the people for one who would deliver God's people from all of its bondage—the offspring of Eve whom the Book of Genesis said would crush the head of the serpent. Thus, we find that a number of the writings of the prophets contain messianic prophecies, prophecies foretelling the Messiah or anointed one who would deliver Israel from all its captivity.[3]

One of the foundational messianic prophecies was delivered by the prophet Nathan to King David:

> Moreover the LORD declares to you that the LORD will make you a house. When your days are fulfilled and you lie down with your fathers, I will raise up your offspring after you, who shall come forth from your body, and I will establish his kingdom. He shall build a house for my name, and I will establish the throne of his kingdom forever. I will be his father, and he shall be my son. (2 Sm 7:11-14)

As with many prophecies, this one has a dual fulfillment. The immediate fulfillment was in David's son, Solomon, who built a house for the Lord, the first great temple in Jerusalem. The deeper fulfillment of the prophecy was the coming of the Messiah, whose rule would last forever, and who is Son of the Father (God) in the fullest sense, sharing the Father's very own nature.

Christians believe that God spoke through many of the prophets of the Old Testament to point to and prepare the way for the coming of the true Messiah, Jesus Christ. Jesus is the only one who ultimately fulfills all of the prophecies of the Messiah in the Hebrew Scriptures. There are many such prophecies speaking of such things as the Messiah's birth of a virgin (Is 7:10-14), the place of his birth (Mi 5:1-3), and of the Messiah himself as "one like a son of man" coming on "the clouds of heaven" (Dn 7:13, 14).

There are also Old Testament prophecies that speak of a suffering servant of God, who would endure pain, hardship, and even death for the sake of the people (see Is 52:13-15; Is 53; Ps 22). Few of the Jewish people at the time of Jesus understood these latter prophecies as messianic because they appeared to contradict their image of the Messiah as a great triumphant warrior or a magnificent king. Only in the person of Jesus of Nazareth, who both suffered as a man and was glorified as king by his Father, are these two types of prophecies reconciled and perfectly fulfilled.

Prophecies of the New Covenant

Besides foretelling the coming of a Messiah for Israel, the prophets also spoke of God establishing a new covenant with Israel, a covenant that would fulfill and even exceed the promises of God in the former covenant. The prophet Jeremiah announced:

> "Behold, the days are coming, says the LORD, when I will make a new covenant with the house of Israel and the house of Judah, not like the covenant which I made with their fathers when I took them by the hand to bring them out of the land of Egypt.... But this is the covenant which I will make with the house of Israel after those days, says the Lord: I will put my law within them, and I will write it upon their hearts; and I will be their God, and they shall be my people. And no longer shall each man teach his neighbor and each his brother, saying 'Know the Lord,' for they shall all know me, from the least of them to the greatest, says the LORD; for I will forgive their iniquity, and I will remember their sin no more." (Jer 31:31-34)

A sign of this New Covenant would be the sending of God's spirit in a new and more powerful way upon the people. The prophet Ezekiel compared Israel with an enormous pile of dry bones in the middle of a plain. When God breathed his spirit into them, though, "they lived, and stood upon their feet, an exceedingly great host" (Ez 37:10). As Psalm 104 says, "... when thou takest away their breath, they die, / and return to their dust. / When thou sendest forth thy Spirit, they are created; / and thou renewest the face of the ground" (Ps 104:29, 30).

The sending of the Holy Spirit in a new and more powerful way is part of the promise of the New Covenant. In the Old

Covenant, only particular people, like prophets and kings, received the spirit of God. But in the New Covenant, as God says through the prophet Joel:

> ". . . I will pour out my spirit upon all flesh; / your sons and daughters shall prophesy, / your old men shall dream dreams, / and your young men shall see visions. / Even upon the men-servants and maidservants / in those days, I will pour out my spirit." (Jl 3:1-2)

The abundant outpouring of the Holy Spirit of God is a sign of the New Covenant predicted by the prophets.

The Relationship of the Old and New Covenant

Pope John Paul II noted that the Old Covenant remained "unchanged throughout the history of salvation, until the definitive and eternal Covenant which God will make (and now has made) with mankind in Jesus Christ."[4]

It is the Messiah, the Savior of Israel, who would come to establish this New Covenant. God's intention in establishing a New Covenant did not necessarily mean totally abandoning his chosen people of the Old Covenant. In fact, the Hebrew people, Israel, were intended to be the principal recipients and beneficiaries of the New Covenant. However, since God does not impose his designs on anyone, even his chosen people were free to reject the New Covenant. Christians are saddened by the fact that relatively few of God's people of the first covenant accepted the New Covenant that God was offering them. Only a portion or a remnant of the Jewish people accepted Jesus as the Messiah and entered into the New Covenant he established and offered them.

This notion of a faithful remnant of the Jewish people who recognize God's work and remain faithful to it is a familiar theme in the Hebrew Scriptures. Each time the Jewish people were taken into captivity, or each time that God sent a prophet, a remnant (or a part) of the people remained faithful to God and moved ahead with God's plan.

Since many of the Jewish people, even today, have not responded to God's invitation to the New Covenant relationship, Christians have the responsibility to continue to announce to them the message of salvation. The section devoted to the Jewish people in the Declaration on Non-Christian Religions (*Nostra Aetate*) of the Second Vatican Council ends by exhorting Catholics to fulfill their duty to preach and proclaim the cross of Christ:

> It is, therefore, the duty of the church's preaching to proclaim the cross of Christ as the sign of God's all-embracing love and as the fountain from which every grace flows. (no. 4)

Nonetheless, the council also teaches that Christians must proclaim the gospel of Christ with love and deep respect for this people (the Jews) who remain ". . . beloved [by God] for the sake of their forefathers. For the gifts and the call of God are irrevocable" (Rom 11:28-29). The Catholic church vigorously condemns anti-Semitism—any bitterness, discrimination, or persecution directed against the Jewish people. Nevertheless, Christians continue to proclaim to God's people of the first covenant that God has a fuller plan in mind for them that they are always welcome to accept. The Messiah has now come, fulfilling the message of the Law and the prophets, and bringing a New Covenant of life, power, and salvation to all mankind.

The Value of the Old Testament for Christians

The Catholic church has always valued the Old Testament. We are a people with a history, and our history can be traced back centuries, even millennia, to when God first created us and then formed a people with whom he established a covenant relationship. The history of the Hebrew people and God's revelation to them is part of our history as Christians. God was at work among them, revealing himself, guiding them, and preparing for the coming of the Messiah. Without this preparation, no one could have recognized or accepted the Savior of the world when he came.

Much that God has revealed about himself and his will is recorded in the sacred Scriptures of the Hebrew people, the Old Testament. We find recorded in them the initial covenants of God with mankind, the history of God's mighty acts of salvation and deliverance, the prophetic word that continues to call us back to faithfulness to God, and much practical wisdom of God for our lives, as is recorded in the wisdom literature of the Hebrew Scripture. Thus, the Old Testament is an essential part of God's revealed truth, part of "the truth that sets us free" (see Jn 8:32).

For Christians the Old Testament must be read in light of the New Testament. Jesus of Nazareth, the Messiah, came to fulfill the Hebrew Scriptures and to interpret it authoritatively. Also, there are some elements of the Old Testament revelation that were intended by God to be relevant and meaningful only for a particular time, but are now no longer binding in light of God's revelation in the New Testament. The dietary laws of the Old Testament are an example of this. Even some moral practices and outlooks found in the Old Testament, such as polygamy or indiscriminate killing through holy wars, are not considered by Christians to be God's law but a concession to the weakness of the people. God forming a people is like parents raising a child. There are some things that God permitted or overlooked in the infancy and childhood of his people that he later prohibited or changed because of their increasing maturity. For example, when the Pharisees referred to Moses' practice of allowing divorce, Jesus replied: "For your hardness of heart Moses allowed you to divorce your wives, but from the beginning it was not so. And I say to you: whoever divorces his wife, except for unchastity, and marries another, commits adultery" (Mt 19:8, 9).

All of these changes brought about by Jesus through the New Covenant are intended to lead God's people to become increasingly more conformed to God and his will, more holy and righteous. The goal of the Christian life is not simply to keep God's law, but to "be perfect, as your heavenly Father is perfect" (Mt 5:48).

The value of the Old Testament for Catholics is, perhaps, best summarized by the bishops of the Second Vatican Council, in paragraphs 15 and 16 of the Dogmatic Constitution on Divine Revelation:

> 15. The principal purpose to which the plan of the Old Covenant was directed was to prepare for the coming both of Christ, the universal Redeemer, and of the messianic kingdom, to announce this coming by prophecy (see Lk 24:44; Jn 5:39; 1 Pt 1:10), and to indicate its meaning through various types (see 1 Cor 10:11). Now the books of the Old Testament, in accordance with the state of mankind before the time of salvation established by Christ, reveal to all men the knowledge of God and of man and the ways in which God, just and merciful, deals with men. These books, though they also contain some things which are incomplete and temporary, nevertheless show us true divine pedagogy. These same books, then give expression to a lively sense of God, contain a store of sublime teachings about God, sound wisdom about human life, and a wonderful treasury of prayers, and in them the mystery of our salvation is present in a hidden way. Christians should receive them with reverence.
>
> 16. God, the inspirer and author of both testaments, wisely arranged that the New Testament be hidden in the Old and the Old be made manifest in the New. For, though Christ established the New Covenant in His blood (see Lk 22:20; 1

Cor 11:25), still the books of the Old Testament with all their parts, caught up into the proclamation of the gospel, acquire and show forth their full meaning in the New Testament (see Mt 5:17; Lk 24:27; Rom 16:25-26; 2 Cor 3:14-16) and in turn shed light on it and explain it.

THREE

Jesus Christ and the New Covenant

"WHO DO MEN SAY THAT I AM?" (Mk 8:27). This question posed by Jesus almost two thousand years ago has become one of the most controversial issues in human history. Why? Because Christianity is based primarily on the person and identity of Jesus. Christianity is not, at its root, a philosophy of God, nor an ethical system, nor a set of religious practices or devotions. Christianity is based on belief in Jesus of Nazareth and on a living relationship with him. For Christians, the question Jesus asked his disciples, "But who do you say that I am?" (Mk 8:29), is the one question of ultimate importance that confronts each person.

Who Is Jesus?

What responses have people made to Jesus' question about his identity? Many of Jesus' contemporaries identified him as one of the great prophets of Israel, either of the past, such as Elijah, or of the present, such as his cousin John the Baptist (see Mk 8:28).

Today we see similar attempts to identify Jesus. Practically everyone agrees that Jesus was a great man. The reason for his greatness, though, is debated. Some say he was an unmatched teacher or moralist; others think of him as a profound mystic, still others as a pioneering social critic or reformer. Jesus, for some, is the great teacher of love, or the man born to serve others.

The difficulty with all of these answers is not that they are entirely wrong but that they are incomplete. Jesus' identity and mission is far more radical and unique than any of these explanations indicate. In order to discover Jesus' true identity, we must examine the only set of documents that thoroughly records Jesus' life, the New Testament and especially the four Gospels.

Approaching the New Testament

Before we look at the accounts of Jesus' life in the New Testament, we must ascertain what type of documents they are. The New Testament is basically the proclamation (*kerygma* in Greek) of the apostles and the early Christian church of their faith or belief in Jesus. Specifically, the New Testament proclaims their belief that Jesus of Nazareth is the long-awaited Messiah or Savior of Israel, and that he is the only divine Son of God the Father. Therefore, the accounts of Jesus in the New Testament are not neutral or purely objective, but present Jesus through the perspective of their faith in him.[1]

The authors of the New Testament were interested in more than just the bare facts about Jesus, but we must beware of those who claim that these authors distorted or falsified history. For example, some biblical scholars attempt to produce purely naturalistic explanations of Jesus' miracles, such as his healings or multiplication of food, or deny that Jesus literally expelled demons from people. They even question whether the resurrection of Jesus was an historical event. Much of this theorizing—such as rejection of the possibility of miracles (meaning the direct intervention of God in human history), or denial of the existence of the devil, of demons, or of any spiritual realm—is based on modern presuppositions and prejudices that began with the Enlightenment.

The Catholic church does not deny the value of much modern biblical research regarding the identity of Christ, and even praises sound scholarship. We acknowledge that the authors of Scripture did shape their presentation of the events of Jesus' life according to their own interests, understanding, and audience. Nevertheless, the Catholic church officially teaches that the New Testament is a proclamation of faith in Jesus based on reliable historical facts about what Jesus of Nazareth actually did and said. The Dogmatic Constitution on Divine Revelation of the Second Vatican Council unequivocally states:

> Holy Mother Church has firmly and with absolute constancy held, and continues to hold, that the four Gospels . . . , whose historical character the church unhesitatingly asserts, faithfully handed on what Jesus Christ, while living among men, really did and taught for their eternal salvation until the day he was taken up into heaven (see Acts 1:1-2). . . .
>
> The sacred authors wrote the four Gospels, selecting some things from the many which had been handed down by word of mouth or in writing, reducing some of them to a synthesis, explicating some things in view of the situation of their churches, and preserving the form of proclamation, but always in such a fashion that they told us the honest truth about Jesus. (no. 19)

Recognizing the New Testament as an historically reliable set of documents, let us proceed to examine what it teaches, and what the Catholic church professes, about the person and work of Jesus.

In the Beginning Was the Word

Before Jesus walked the earth as a man, the eternal Son or Word of God existed and was God. As the Second Person of the Blessed Trinity and the Son of the eternal Father, Jesus was able to announce, "... before Abraham was, I am" (Jn 8:58), echoing God's revelation of his identity to Moses. The prologue of the Gospel of John states: "In the beginning was the Word, and the Word was with God, and the Word was God" (Jn 1:1). The Letter to the Hebrews explains: "He reflects the glory of God and bears the very stamp of his nature. ..." (Heb 1:3).

At the Council of Constantinople in A.D. 381, the bishops of the early church formulated a creed or profession of faith to clarify exactly what Christians believe about Jesus as the preexistent Son or Word of God. Catholics profess this Nicene Creed every week at Mass, saying: "We believe in one Lord, Jesus Christ, the only Son of God, eternally begotten of the Father, God from God, Light from Light, true God from true God, begotten, not made, one in being with the Father...."

This part of the Nicene Creed was written to refute the heresy of Arius, who claimed that the Son was not God but only the highest creature of God. The Creed answers this claim by asserting that the Son of God was begotten, or born, of God, not "made" or created. The Son is, therefore, "God from God, Light from Light, true God from true God." Another way that this Creed affirms that the Son is fully God is the statement that the Son is "one in being" (Greek: *homoousios*) with the Father. Whatever type of being the Father is, so is the Son. Since the Father is God, so is the Son.

When we hear that the Son of God is born or begotten of the Father, it is natural to ask when he was born. Arius reasoned that since the Son is born of God, there must be a time when the Son was not—a time before the Son existed. The Creed says that the Son is "eternally begotten" of the Father, which means that there was never a time when the Son, or Word, of God did not exist. The fact that there is no beginning of the Son's existence challenges us to remember that the Son, because he is God, is eternal, even though he is in some way dependent on the Father for his life within the Trinity.

Finally, the Bible and the Creed affirm that with the Father, the Son of God created all that has been made. The Nicene Creed states: "Through him (the Son) all things were made." The Bible also teaches this: ". . . all things were made through him, and without him was not anything made that was made" (Jn 1:3; see also Col 1:16-17; Heb 1:2). The Son of God brought the universe and each of us into existence, and holds us in existence, for "in him all things hold together" (Col 1:17).

The Word Became Flesh

The greatest event in human history was inaugurated with the birth of the eternal Word of God into our human condition. God himself became man. This event is called the incarnation of the Word: "the Word became flesh and dwelt among us. . . ." (Jn 1:14), or as St. Paul taught, ". . . when the time had fully come, God sent forth his Son, born of woman, born under the law. . ." (Gal 4:4).

Why did the Son of God become a man, taking on the limitations and pains of our human condition? It was the key to God's plan to redeem the human race from sin and rebellion against him, and to restore us to his friendship:

> For God so loved the world that he gave his only Son, that whoever believes in him should not perish but have eternal life. For God sent the Son into the world, not to condemn the world, but that the world might be saved through him. (Jn 3:16-17)

This is the heart of the good news! God has loved the human race so much that he has not merely sent angels, prophets, and other messengers to lead us back to himself, but he personally entered into human history to save us from our sin and rebellion against him. What a free, unmerited gift! Who could have imagined that God would have gone to this extreme to show his love and to overcome the sin of the whole human race? Christ has not come to save humanity in general but to show his love for each one of us individually, to free each individual from the bondage of his sin. God has come in person, in the flesh, which is the meaning of "incarnation." In this mystery, the depth of God's love and humility is revealed. The primitive Christian hymn about the Son that Paul includes in his Letter to the Philippians expresses this most beautifully:

> ... though he was in the form of God, did not count equality with God a thing to be grasped, but emptied himself, taking the form of a servant, being born in the likeness of men. (Phil 2:6-7)

Born of a Virgin

In fulfillment of Isaiah's prophecy, the Son of God became man by his birth "... to a virgin betrothed to a man whose name was Joseph, of the house of David; and the virgin's name was Mary" (Lk 1:27). Jesus had no human father. Joseph is honored by Christians as the guardian, protector, and foster father of Jesus, and head of the Holy Family. Mary conceived the Son of God in her womb solely by the power of the Holy Spirit (Lk 1:31, 35). Mary is the true, natural mother of Jesus, and so she has been honored for centuries by Christians as the "Mother of God." This title was defended and confirmed at the Council of Ephesus in A.D. 431 because it attests to the facts that Jesus was truly God and that Mary really bore God himself in her womb.

Truly God, Truly Man

The Catholic church has always vigorously affirmed the truth of both Jesus' full divinity and full humanity. Jesus is truly God and truly man. This truth was authoritatively stated by the

Council of Chalcedon in A.D. 451. The council declared that Jesus ". . . is perfect both in his divinity and in his humanity, truly God and truly man composed of body and rational soul; that he is the same substance (*homoousios*) with the Father in his divinity, of the same substance (*homoousios*) with us in his humanity, like us in every respect except for sin (see Heb 4:15)."[2] Jesus possesses two distinct but inseparable natures, the divine and the human, united in one person. Chalcedon's definition leaves one question unanswered: *how* are these two natures perfectly joined into one person? This remains a mystery; Chalcedon only could declare that they *are* joined, not how. Creeds and theological definitions about God or Jesus can distinguish what is true and what is false, but they can never exhaust the mystery of the reality of God and his plan.

When we speak of Jesus' two natures, it would be easy to think of Jesus behaving like a split-personality—at one moment doing something human, the next moment doing something that only God could do. Those who followed Jesus did not perceive him in this way because these two natures in Jesus worked together in perfect harmony. John Calvin proposed that Jesus' two natures functioned together like our two eyes: each eye is distinct, yet they work together in such perfect unison that our vision is one. Likewise, Jesus' human nature and human will were so conformed to his divine nature and divine will that the two were joined into an inseparable harmony so that we can truly say that Jesus was one person, not two, but composed of a divine and a human nature.

We can appreciate this truth more fully by reflecting on our own nature. Although we are single, unified persons, we are at the same time both spiritual and physical beings. When we act or decide, it is not just our soul or mind that acts, but *us*, as whole persons. My human nature does not decide or do something, I do. In the same way, Jesus acted as a single, unified person, even though he is both God and man. It is a person who acts, not a nature. Thus, the *person* of Jesus was the principle of all his actions, not one or the other nature.[3]

The divine nature of Jesus Christ is perceived by us only as it is reflected through the fullness and perfection of his human nature. As a man, Jesus came only to do the will of his Father, God. As the Son of God, he alone was capable of doing this perfectly, being the only-begotten divine person, the Son of God incarnate.

Jesus' Ministry Begins

Jesus was the Son of God from the moment of his conception in Mary's womb. He was not adopted by God at some point. It is amazing to think that for the first thirty years of his life, Jesus, the Son of God, lived in relative obscurity as a carpenter's son, residing in the small Galilean town of Nazareth. We know that the Gospels are not modern biographies of Jesus because they tell us relatively little about his early life, before his public ministry.

When Jesus was near thirty years old, his kinsman, John, began to call the Jewish people to repent, to turn from their sins, and to baptize them in the waters of the Jordan River as a sign of their repentance. John the Baptist was recognized by many of the Jews as a great prophet, and some even claimed he was the Messiah. But John declared, "I baptize you with water; but he who is mightier than I is coming . . . he will baptize you with the Holy Spirit and with fire" (Lk 3:16).

One day, Jesus came to receive John's baptism. The Gospels record that at the moment of his baptism, the Spirit of God descended like a dove and hovered over Jesus and a voice from the heavens said, "This is my beloved Son, with whom I am well pleased" (Mt 3:17). John then recognized Jesus as the long-awaited Messiah, the "Lamb of God, who takes away the sin of the world" (Jn 1:29). God began to reveal Jesus' identity even as his public ministry was about to unfold.

Jesus immediately went out into the desert to pray and fast, and there was tempted by Satan. Jesus defeated the devil by ignoring his lies and false promises, and by quoting the Hebrew Scripture, particularly the Book of Deuteronomy, to refute him. After this, Jesus "came into Galilee, preaching the gospel of God, and saying, 'The time is fulfilled, and the kingdom of God is at hand; repent, and believe in the gospel [good news]'" (Mk 1:14-15). The public ministry of Jesus had begun.

The Message of the Kingdom

The heart of Jesus' teaching, his good news, is about the reign of God. For centuries, the Jewish people had awaited the Messiah who would fulfill God's promise to establish a kingdom that would overcome all its foes and would endure forever. Jesus electrified his hearers by announcing, "The time is fulfilled. The kingdom of God is at hand!" This implied that he was the one sent by God to establish the kingdom of God!

However, most of the Jews of Jesus' time did not comprehend what Jesus meant by the kingdom of God. Most of them understood the kingdom of God in purely political terms. Jesus never defined what the kingdom was; instead he told numerous parables or stories relating what it was like. The essence of Jesus' understanding of the kingdom of God is that it is the reign or rule of God over people's hearts and lives. God sent his Son, Jesus, to set people free from anything that would prevent God from ruling over their lives. Jesus exhorted his hearers to do two things to prepare for the coming of God's kingdom: repent (reform your lives; turn away from all sin and wrongdoing) and believe the good news that Jesus had come to establish God's reign (see Mk 1:14).

The Reign of God: Present in Jesus

When Jesus said that the reign of God was "at hand," did he mean that it was beginning now, or was it to come in the future? The New Testament indicates that the reign of God began with Jesus' own teaching and ministry.

How do we know this? Jesus' ministry was marked by the full power and authority of God. First Corinthians 4:20 says that the reign of God does not consist in talk, but in power. Jesus manifested the power of God's reign in a number of ways. First, Jesus taught with authority. There was power, spiritual power, in his very words. The people recognized that Jesus was unlike the other rabbis or teachers of his day because "he taught them as one with authority, and not as their scribes" (Mt 7:29). Jesus attracted crowds of hundreds and thousands who came to him just to hear his word.

Second, Jesus demonstrated his power over Satan and evil spirits. The Jews recognized that Jesus had the power to cast out demons (exorcism). Some claimed that he did so by the power of the evil one, Beelzebub. Jesus retorted that this made no sense unless Satan were divided against himself. Jesus' power to exorcise must be from God: ". . . if it is by the finger of God that I cast out demons, then the kingdom of God has come upon you" (Lk 11:20).[4]

Finally, Jesus' mighty works of healing, raising the dead, stilling storms, multiplying food, and other works, were signs that God's kingdom had begun. John the Baptist sent his disciples to ask Jesus, "Are you he who is to come [the Messiah] or shall we look for another?" Jesus replied, "Go and tell John what you hear and see: the blind receive their sight and the lame walk, lepers are cleansed and the deaf hear, and the dead are raised up, and the poor have good news preached to them" (Mt 11:3-5). These are definite indications of the presence of God's kingdom. In the Gospel of John, Jesus insists that even if people don't believe his words, they should believe in him because of his "works" (see Jn 10:24-25, 37-38). If Jesus performed no miracles or mighty works, as some modern scholars claim, this reference in John's Gospel would make no sense. We know that Jesus performed miracles. On Pentecost, Peter began his speech, addressed to those who had known Jesus and had witnessed his crucifixion, with these words: "... Jesus of Nazareth, a man attested to you by God with mighty works and wonders and signs which God did through him in your midst, as you yourselves know..." (Acts 2:22). The power of Jesus' ministry was no secret; it was the growing jealousy and fear of the Jewish leaders concerning Jesus' evident power that finally led to his death.[5]

The reign of God is inaugurated with Jesus' public ministry. In Jesus himself the kingdom of God is present, at least in its initial form. This is what Jesus meant when he told the Pharisees, "'The kingdom of God is not coming with signs to be observed; nor will they say, "Lo, here it is!" or "There!" for behold, the kingdom of God is in the midst of you.'" (Lk 17:20-21). However, the completion or fulfillment of God's kingdom, when his reign will be evident to all, will not occur until Jesus returns to earth in glory as its king and judge.

Jesus' Teaching

In addition to his mighty works, Jesus revealed the nature and truths of the kingdom of God in his teaching. Jesus taught in two modes: in parables and directly. Jesus' parables are original analogies and stories that challenged his hearers. The parables of Jesus covered a wide variety of topics, but all were in some way related to the kingdom of God. Some spoke about it directly: "The kingdom of heaven is like a grain of mustard seed..." (Mt 13:31). Other parables told of the kind of conduct required of those living under God's rule, such as the parable of the Good Samaritan (Lk 10:25-37).

Jesus also taught directly, and much of this teaching, too, dealt with the kingdom of God. For example, Jesus' beatitudes

(Mt 5:1-12; Lk 6:20-26) are a charter for living with God and his will fully ruling one's life.

Prayer is essential for living under the reign of God, and Jesus taught his followers how to pray, how to relate to God. He instructs us in the proper motives and attitudes for prayer, and he even left us his own words of prayer by which we can address God as "our Father" (Mt 6:9-13; Lk 11:2-4).

The wisdom and insight of Jesus' teaching is recognized by almost everyone. It is original, fresh, and marked by genius. It's also a message so radical and challenging that only with strong faith and the grace of God can anyone hope to put it fully into practice. Jesus promises this help to all who decide to take his teaching seriously, who are willing to leave everything to follow him.

Jesus Reveals God

One radical aspect of Jesus' teaching was his claim to know God in an intimate, personal way. Jesus addressed the omnipotent God as Abba, the Aramaic equivalent of the English "dear Father" or "Papa." While Jews of that time would not even pronounce the proper name of God (YHWH) out of respect and reverence, Jesus called God his "dear Father." Not only did Jesus speak to God with this amazing intimacy and familiarity, but he taught his followers to address God in the same way. He instructed them to turn to the Father at all times in prayer, as he himself did.

What did Jesus teach about God, his Father? First, he taught that the Father loves Jesus' followers so much that he desires to care for them and to provide for them in all circumstances (see the parable of the lilies of the field in Mt 6:25-34). In teaching us to address God as Father, Jesus revealed that we are sons and daughters of God, and heirs of his kingdom—if we choose to allow God to rule over our lives. However, for those who choose to reject God and his kingdom and decide not to live as his sons and daughters, God is also a just Father who permits us to chart our own destiny freely. Sometimes it means that we must suffer the consequences of rebellion against him. Jesus, as God the Son, perfectly reflects his Father's joy over those who accept the kingdom of God (Lk 15:3-7); his sorrow and grief over those who reject it or do not recognize it (Lk 19:41-44); and his anger at those who prevent others from entering the kingdom by their hypocrisy, pride, or false teaching (see Mt 23).

Jesus revealed another essential fact about God's identity. Besides God being Father, with Jesus as his unique divine Son, Jesus also revealed that God is Holy Spirit. Jesus promised that he and the Father would send this Holy Spirit to his disciples in order to lead them into all truth (see Jn 14:15-17, 25-26; 16:7-15) and to fill them with the power of God (see Acts 1:8; 2). The Holy Spirit teaches us how to pray as we ought (Rom 8:16, 26, 27) and enables us to recognize that Jesus is Lord (1 Cor 12:3) and that God is our Father (Rom 8:15; Gal 4:6).

The Way of Discipleship

Another radical aspect of Jesus' teaching is what he expected of those who believed in his message. "Disciple" literally means a student or follower. To be a follower of Jesus, it is necessary both to know what he says and to put it into practice. Jesus sternly warns his disciples of the dire consequences of failing to put his teaching into practice (see Mt 7:21-26).

Jesus' first concern in his public ministry was to invite people to follow after him. Why? So they could be formed, taught, and trained by Jesus in the ways of God and his reign. This demanded a radical and complete commitment. Simon, Andrew, James, and John immediately left their nets and fishing boats, and Matthew his tax booth, to follow Jesus (Mt 4:18-22). Jesus told a certain young man that in order to be perfect, he had to sell his possessions, give the proceeds to the poor, and follow him (Lk 18:18-22).

Jesus continues even today to call us to discipleship. Being a Christian requires a radical commitment. Nothing in our lives can be more important than following Jesus and living according to his teaching. We may not necessarily have to leave our home or occupation to become a Christian, but it could involve that. Jesus warned: "Enter by the narrow gate; for the gate is wide and the way is easy, that leads to destruction, and those who enter by it are many. For the gate is narrow and the way is hard that leads to life, and those who find it are few" (Mt 7:13). What is this "narrow way"? Jesus said, "I am the door; if anyone enters by me, he will be saved" (Jn 10:9).

What is the road or way that leads to eternal life? Jesus said, "I am the way, and the truth, and the life; no one comes to the Father, but by me" (Jn 14:6). The only sure way or road to eternal life is the way of discipleship in Jesus Christ. As we shall see, discipleship involves both joy and suffering, glory and the cross. Christians are not perfect, but they are the people who have discovered the One who can save them from their sins and who shows them the true way to life—Jesus Christ. He is the "pearl of great value" (see Mt 13:44-46) for which we must abandon all else to obtain.

It is important for us to realize that Jesus Christ is not just a figure of the past or a theological problem but a living person who is calling each of us into a vital, intimate relationship with himself. Jesus wants us to come to know him and love him with all of our hearts, so that his call to each of us to "Come, follow me" is not just a duty or a burden but the greatest joy of our life. The Jesus whom we read about in the Gospels, who profoundly touched and changed the lives of all who responded to his invitation, is the same Jesus who longs to touch each of us with his life, love, and power—if we will only let him! Then the affirmations that Jesus is Lord or Savior will not just be dry doctrinal statements but heartfelt professions of how we actually relate to and experience Jesus in our lives.

Salvation without Discipleship?

What about the salvation of those who do not know, believe in, or follow Jesus Christ? There is much theological speculation today about the salvation of non-Christians. Many people are very optimistic about the possibility of their salvation. Catholics do not claim to know the eternal destiny of any individual, but do affirm certain things. First, we know that Jesus Christ is the only Savior. Acts 4:12 teaches, "there is salvation in no one else, for there is no other name under heaven given among men by which we must be saved." Second, the ordinary way for one to attain salvation through Jesus Christ is through faith, baptism, and a life of discipleship, that is, faithful obedience to Jesus and his teaching. Mark 16:15-16 records Jesus' words in a post-resurrection appearance: "Go into all the world and preach the gospel to the whole creation. He who believes and is baptized will be saved; but he who does not believe will be condemned." We have already noted what Jesus says about those who hear his word, believe in it, and yet do not put it into practice. Obedience to Jesus, as well as faith and baptism, are normally necessary for salvation.

Third, in God's mercy it is possible for those who are not Christians to be saved through the grace of Jesus Christ. There are certain biblical texts, such as the last judgment scene in Matthew 25 and Paul's Letter to the Romans, 2:12-16, that indicate that some will be saved by Christ on account of their charity, or through having followed the dictates of their conscience. The Second Vatican Council's Dogmatic Constitution on the Church affirms this:

> Those also can attain to everlasting salvation who through no fault of their own do not know the gospel of Christ or His church, yet sincerely seek God and, moved by grace, strive by their deeds to do His will as it is known to them through the dictates of conscience. Nor does divine Providence deny the necessary help for salvation to those who, without blame on their part, have not yet arrived at an explicit knowledge of God, but who strive to live a good life, thanks to His grace. Whatever goodness or truth is found among them is looked upon by the church as a preparation for the gospel. (no. 16)

This passage refers to the possibility of salvation of those who have not accepted the gospel through no fault of their own, not to those who have consciously rejected and refused to believe in the good news of Jesus Christ. It is also significant that the Catholic church considers whatever goodness or truth possessed by non-Christians to be a "preparation for the gospel." There is no implication here that the gospel need not be preached to non-Christians. In fact, the closing paragraph of this section from the Second Vatican Council warns that those who have not accepted the gospel often fail to attain eternal life because of the deception of Satan or through falling into despair:

> But rather often men, deceived by the Evil One, have become caught up in futile reasoning and have exchanged the truth of God for a lie, serving the creature rather than the Creator (cf. Rom 1:21, 25). Or some there are who, living and dying in a world without God, are subject to utter hopelessness. Consequently, to promote the glory of God and procure the salvation of all such men, and mindful of the command of the Lord, "Preach the gospel to every creature" (Mk 16:15), the church painstakingly fosters her missionary work. (LG, no. 16)

The presupposition of Catholics should be that unless a person has fully accepted the gospel of Jesus Christ, it is likely that the person will end up "serving the creature" or falling into despair, and not attain eternal life. To put it simply, we cannot assume that those who are not living as disciples of Jesus Christ will be saved. It is possible that they may receive the grace of Christ in an extraordinary way, but we cannot presume this. Our commission as disciples of Jesus Christ is clear. "Go therefore and make disciples of all nations, baptizing them in the name of the Father and of the Son and of the Holy Spirit" (Mt 28:19). We commend the destiny of those who have not heard or accepted the message of Jesus Christ to the plan and mercy of God, and continue to pray and work for their conversion to Jesus Christ, the one Savior of the world and only source of eternal life.

The Call to Discipleship

Jesus called everyone to follow him. All are called to be disciples of Jesus Christ. Although Jesus first called the Jews, "the lost sheep of the house of Israel" (Mt 15:24), he startled and scandalized his Jewish brethren by healing and delivering Gentiles, such as the Roman centurion's servant. Jesus praised the centurion for his faith in him, saying, "Truly I say to you, not even in Israel have I found such faith. I tell you, many will come from the east and the west and sit at table with Abraham, Isaac, and Jacob in the kingdom of heaven...." (Mt 8:10-11).

Jesus especially came "to preach good news to the poor" (Lk 4:18), but even the rich who were ready to renounce all for Jesus' sake could be saved, such as Zacchaeus in Luke 19.

Jesus' disciples included both men and women. Even though women had a limited social status in ancient society, Jesus personally invited a number of women to accept the good news of the reign of God. Many of Jesus' miracles were healings and exorcisms of women. He made no distinction on the basis of sex in his basic call to discipleship.

Jesus' call to follow him is universal. It extends to all races, nations, peoples, and cultures. The key to discipleship is faith in Jesus Christ—faith that expresses itself in love, commitment, and obedience. As St. Paul wrote to the Galatians:

> ... for in Christ Jesus you are all sons of God, through faith. For us many of you as were baptized into Christ have put on Christ. There is neither Jew nor Greek, there is neither slave nor free, there is neither male nor female; for you are all one in Christ Jesus. (Gal 3:26-28)

Catholics are called to "make disciples of all nations" by leading all people to salvation through faith in and discipleship to Jesus Christ. This is how we carry on Jesus' mission of proclaiming and establishing the reign of God in this world.

Discipleship and Jesus' Death

Discipleship can sound very exciting and oftentimes it is. Jesus' disciples rejoiced as they witnessed his mighty works and heard his teaching. They even saw a glimpse of his heavenly glory on the Mount of the Transfiguration. As those followers matured however, Jesus began to tell them of the suffering and painful death that awaited him and that also awaited many of them. Discipleship involves the cross. Jesus said, "If any man would come after me, let him deny himself and take up his cross and follow me. For whoever would save his life will lose it; and whoever loses his life for my sake and the gospel's will save it" (Mk 8:34, 35; also see Mt 16:24, 25; Lk 9: 23, 24). St. Paul prayed that he would never glory in anything but the cross of Christ, by which he was crucified to the world and its allurements (Gal 6:14). Scripture makes it clear that it is necessary to follow Jesus even when it means renouncing one's own preferences, opinions, comforts, and will—dying to oneself. Jesus did not live to please himself but to obey the will of his Father. The Father's will for the redemption of the human race was that his Son, Jesus, would suffer and die:

> And being found in human form he humbled himself and became obedient unto death, even death on a cross. (Phil 2:8)

Why did the Son of God have to die? Being God, he was not subject to death in his divine nature. He did not *need* to die. Rather, he *chose* to die (Mt 26:53-54). He chose to accept and conquer death for the sake of mankind (Heb 2:9-10; 7:27; 9:11-15; 1 Pt 3:18).

Jesus' death demonstrates the tremendous love that God has for us. As Jesus himself said, "Greater love has no man than this, that a man lay down his life for his friends" (Jn 15:13). Jesus laid down his life for the whole human race, to restore mankind to God's friendship—the friendship we had lost through the sin of Adam and our own personal sin. As St. Paul wrote:

> Why, one will hardly die for a righteous man—though perhaps for a good man one will dare even to die. But God shows his love for us in that while we were yet sinners Christ died for us. (Rom 5:7-8)

Jesus Christ died to prove God's love for us and to free us from the bondage of our sin. Jesus divested himself of the glory and majesty that was his as God in order to live among us and to die for us in order to save us from a second death.

How Jesus' Death Saves Us

The New Testament states repeatedly that Jesus died for all people (see 2 Cor 5:13-15; Rom 5:18; 1 Thes 5:10). Jesus himself told his disciples at the Last Supper: "This is my blood of the covenant, which is poured out for many" (Mk 14:24). But what does it mean that "Christ died for all people"? How could the death of one man, Jesus Christ, affect the whole human race?

This question opens a whole field of Christian theology, known as soteriology. It explores the question of how Jesus' death can be said to save (Greek: *soteria*) the human race. Many biblical scholars today conclude that it is impossible to determine exactly how Jesus' death saves us, but it is undeniable that it does. There are some approaches to understanding the saving value of Jesus' death that have arisen in Christian history:

1. Jesus' death as a ransom to redeem sinners. Jesus said of himself, "... the Son of Man also came not to be served but to serve, and to give his life as a ransom for many" (Mk 10:45).

Jesus himself is the "suffering servant" prophesied in Isaiah 52 and 53. Jesus' suffering and death may be looked at as a ransom, the price that Jesus paid to redeem, or free, the human race from its slavery to the devil. In other words, Jesus offered his own priceless life as a ransom given by God in exchange for the release of the human race from the bondage of Satan and sin. The effect of Jesus' death was to reconcile the human race with God (see 2 Cor 5:17-18).

2. Jesus' death as atonement or satisfaction for our sins. Mankind's sin is detestable and offensive to God. Jesus' death may be looked upon as a free *gift* offered to God to atone or make reparation for the sins of the human race. A later theology spoke about Jesus' death as satisfying the demand of justice that this infinite offense against God's love and honor be corrected. Jesus' death makes satisfaction; it satisfies God's just requirement that sin should be punished or repaired. One author says that, "Jesus made not only adequate but *superabundant* atonement and satisfaction because the measure of his love and obedience . . . surpassed human egoism. In Jesus a power of love and truth was operative (and shown in his death) which surpassed all the forces of evil and falsehood."[6]

3. Jesus as a "penal substitute" for us. Because of our sin, the human race deserved nothing but punishment and death. Jesus freely chose to accept, on behalf of the whole human race, the death penalty resulting from sin; he chose to substitute for each of us by accepting the penalty for sin in his suffering, abandonment, and terrible death on the cross. He represented, or substituted for, all of us as he carried the cross, was nailed to it, and died on it. "He himself bore our sins in his body on the tree, that we might die to sin and live to righteousness. By his wounds you have been healed" (1 Pt 2:24).

4. Jesus' death as a sacrifice to expiate our sins. The notion of offering sacrifice to make amends for sin is rooted in the Old Testament. The Letter to the Hebrews particularly stresses the sacrificial dimension of Jesus' death, though it is also found in the Gospels and elsewhere in the New Testament. In the Old

Covenant, the high priest would offer the flesh and blood of animals to God as a sacrifice to plead for the forgiveness of the people's sins. Hebrews portrays Jesus as the great High Priest who offers to God, once for all, his own body and blood for the forgiveness and redemption of the whole human race. A spotless lamb was the Jewish people's Passover sacrifice, and John the Baptist recognized Jesus himself as "the Lamb of God, who takes away the sin of the world" (Jn 1:29). The Book of Revelation also highlights the image of Jesus as the Lamb who was slain as a perfect sacrifice to expiate (remove) the sins of the human race.

Jesus himself acted as the great High Priest at the Last Supper when he offered his body and blood to the Father, anticipating and making present in a sacramental way the death he was to suffer less than a day later.

Jesus' Resurrection

The bodily resurrection of Jesus Christ from the dead is a central Christian belief, perhaps the central Christian belief. The heart of the earliest *kerygma* or proclamation of Christianity is simply this: Jesus the Nazorean, whom you crucified, God has raised from the dead (see Acts 2:22-24; 3:13-15; 4:10; 1 Cor 15:3-5).

St. Paul in 1 Corinthians 15:12-20 boldly summarizes:

> If Christ has not been raised, your faith is futile and you are still in your sins. Then those also who have fallen asleep [died] in Christ have perished. If for this life only we have hoped in Christ, we are of all men most to be pitied.
>
> But in fact, Christ has been raised from the dead, the first fruits of those who have fallen asleep. (1 Cor 15:17-20)

Later in the same Letter, Paul says: "If the dead are not raised, 'Let us eat and drink, for tomorrow we die'" (1 Cor 15:32).

The hope of Christians hinges on the reality of the resurrection of Jesus. The resurrection of Jesus is the act of God that reveals that death, sin, and Satan have been conquered. Jesus freely accepted death, but overcame death when he emerged from the tomb alive on the third day.

What Is the Resurrection?

What does it mean to say that Jesus was raised from the dead? No one actually witnessed the resurrection. Although there are variations among the four Gospel accounts of Easter Sunday morning, these all agree on two essential facts: (1) the tomb in which Jesus had been buried was found empty with the entrance stone rolled away; (2) Jesus appeared alive to his followers.

What was the risen Jesus like? The appearances of Jesus cannot be explained away as hallucinations, nor as the apostles' way of saying that even though Jesus was dead, he lived on in the hearts and minds of his followers. The earliest New Testament writing that speaks of Jesus' post-resurrection appearances is Paul's First Letter to the Corinthians, written in the early 50s A.D. Paul lists the witnesses who saw Jesus alive (including himself) and even mentions that on one occasion five hundred brothers saw Jesus "most of whom are still alive, though some have fallen asleep" (1 Cor 15:6). If anyone had any question about whether Jesus actually appeared alive after his resurrection, Paul provides a long list of eyewitnesses still alive twenty years after the event to confirm it. Is it possible that all these people (including the apostles) were victims of the same hallucination? It is far more likely that these people, many of whom gave their lives for their beliefs about Jesus, actually did see him risen from the dead.

What was Jesus' risen body like? There is an element of mystery in the Gospel accounts. Jesus could be touched and felt, but he could also appear, suddenly and unannounced, in locked rooms. According to some Gospel accounts, Jesus' own apostles and Mary Magdalene often did not immediately recognize him when he appeared (see Jn 20:14; 21:12; Mt 28:17; Lk 24:16, 37-39). The Gospel accounts imply that Jesus' risen body was in some ways the same as the body that was buried in the tomb, but it was also different. His risen body was not just a resuscitation of the corpse that was buried, but neither was it an entirely different body. We may best describe Jesus' body after the resurrection as a glorified body or a spiritual body, using St. Paul's terminology. Paul described the risen body of both Jesus, and each of us: "What is sown [buried] is perishable, what is raised is imperishable. It is sown in dishonor, it is raised in glory. It is sown in weakness, it is raised in power. It is sown a physical body, it is raised a spiritual body" (1 Cor 15:42-44).

What will our own risen bodies be like? Like the body of Jesus: "Just as we have borne the image of the man of dust [Adam], we shall also bear the image of the man of heaven [Jesus]" (1 Cor 15:49). And to the Philippians, Paul wrote that the Lord Jesus will "change our lowly body to be like his glorious body" (Phil 3:21).

This is the basis of Christian hope, to share in the resurrection of Jesus by having our own mortal bodies raised up, transformed, and glorified like the risen body of Jesus Christ (see 1 Cor 15:53-57).

Jesus' Ascension and Pentecost

The ascension of Jesus marks the conclusion of his appearances to his followers after his resurrection. "So then the Lord Jesus, after he had spoken to them, was taken up into heaven, and sat down at the right hand of God" (Mk 16:19). The ascension means that Jesus returned to his Father in heaven in his glorified body. Although he is the Second Person of God, Jesus forever retains this glorified human body.

The evangelist Luke, in both his Gospel and in the Acts of

the Apostles, places more emphasis than the other Gospels on the ascension, and specifies that it occurred forty days after the resurrection of Jesus (see Acts 1:1-11). Luke associates Jesus' ascension with his second coming in Acts 1:11: "'This Jesus, who was taken up from you into heaven, will come in the same way as you saw him go into heaven.'"

Although Jesus no longer dwells on earth bodily, nor appears in his glorified, risen body, Jesus is still present to us. He is present to us in the sacraments, especially the Eucharist. He is present in his followers, his church, which St. Paul called "the body of Christ" (see 1 Cor 12:27). But Jesus is also present to us through his greatest gift to his followers: the Holy Spirit. In one of his post-resurrection appearances, Jesus instructed his disciples:

> ... not to depart from Jerusalem, but wait for the promise of the Father which, he said, "you heard from me, for John baptized with water, but before many days you shall be baptized with the Holy Spirit." (Acts 1:4-5)

Jesus also spoke of this promise of the Father in John's Gospel:

> And I will pray the Father, and he will give you another Counselor, to be with you for ever, even the Spirit of truth. ... (Jn 14:16-17)

The Gospel of John reports that Jesus' apostles first received the Holy Spirit on Easter Day (Jn 20:19-23). Luke, in the Acts of the Apostles, recounts the first sending of the Holy Spirit as a gathering of Jesus' disciples in Jerusalem on the Jewish feast of Pentecost (Acts 2:1-5). The difference in time does not matter, since the Gospel writers were primarily interested in the meaning of the sending of the Holy Spirit rather than producing an accurate or consistent chronology of events. Luke's images of the coming of the Holy Spirit, including "a mighty wind" and "tongues as of fire" (Acts

2:2-3), are reminiscent of the fire and smoke of God's visitation to Moses on Mount Sinai, described in Exodus 19:16-19, when he delivered the Ten Commandments to Moses (Ex 20:1-17).

This similarity is not merely coincidental. On Mount Sinai, God delivered the law of the Old Covenant, the Ten Commandments, to Moses and the chosen people, Israel. At Pentecost, God sent his new people, the church of Jesus Christ, the law of the New Covenant, the Holy Spirit. The law of the Old Covenant was delivered to Moses on stone tablets, but the new law of the Spirit came as the prophet Jeremiah had announced concerning God's New Covenant: "I will put My law within them, and I will write it upon their hearts" (Jer 31:33; see also 2 Cor 3:3). St. Paul explained that the commandments or law of the Old Covenant was "good and holy" because it reveals God's will and points out our sinfulness, but it contains no power enabling us to overcome sin (see Rom 7:7-11). In the New Covenant, God has given us a new law, the Holy Spirit, who not only convicts us of sin but empowers us to overcome it. St. Paul wrote that:

> . . . we serve not under the old written code but in the new life of the Spirit . . . For the law of the Spirit of life in Christ Jesus has set me free from the law of sin and death. For God has done what the law, weakened by the flesh, could not do: sending his own Son in the likeness of sinful flesh and for sin, he condemned sin in the flesh, in order that the just requirement of the law might be fulfilled in us, who walk not according to the flesh but according to the Spirit. (Rom 7:6; 8:2-4)

Jesus said that he hadn't come to abolish the law of the Old Covenant, but to fulfill it (Mt 5:17-20). One aspect of this fulfillment is the sending of the Holy Spirit to empower Christians to fulfill the "just requirement of the law" and to live the radical new commandment of love and the beatitudes that Jesus taught. Thus, the sending of the Holy Spirit at Pentecost fulfills Jesus' promise and completes the establishment of the New Covenant.

Jesus and the New Covenant

At the Last Supper, Jesus told his disciples, "This cup which is poured out for you is the new covenant in my blood" (Lk 22:20). With these words, Jesus began the final chapter of his life, fulfilling Jeremiah's prophecy that God would establish a New Covenant with Israel (Jer 31:31-34). Under the Old Covenant, the shedding of the blood of sacrificial animals ratified a solemn covenant or agreement between God and man. Moses, in the Book of Exodus, ratified the covenant with God by pouring half of the sacrificial blood on the altar and the rest on the people with the words, "Behold the blood of the covenant which the Lord has made with you in accordance with all these words" (Ex 24:8). The Letter to the Hebrews in the New Testament focuses on the far superior effect of the sacrifice of the blood of Jesus:

> ... he entered once for all into the Holy Place, taking not the blood of goats and calves but his own blood, thus securing an eternal redemption.... Therefore he is the mediator of a new covenant.... he has appeared once for all at the end of the age to put away sin by the sacrifice of himself. (Heb 9:12, 15, 26)

There are numerous biblical images for Jesus that are related to his sealing of the covenant and removing our sins through the shedding of his blood. Hebrews also speaks of Jesus as the great High Priest who offered himself and his own blood as a perfect and eternal sacrifice for humanity's sins (Heb 2:17; 5:5-10; 7:3ff, 26-27).

The Lamb is another image of this type, originating from the Passover lamb that the Jewish people slaughtered before fleeing Egypt, sprinkling the blood of the lamb on the lintels of their doorposts to protect them from the angel of death. The prophet Isaiah said the suffering servant of YHWH was "like a lamb that is led to the slaughter, / . . . so he opened not his mouth" (Is 53:7).

Jesus is called "the Lamb of God, who takes away the sin of the world" (Jn 1:29) by John the Baptist, and the Book of Revelation also pictures Jesus as "a Lamb standing, as though it had been slain" (Rv 5:6). The Christian martyrs had "washed their robes and made them white in the blood of the Lamb" (Rv 7:14). Peter reminds us in his First Letter that "you were ransomed from the futile ways inherited from your fathers, not with perishable things such as silver or gold, but with the precious blood of Christ, like that of a lamb without blemish or spot. He was destined [for this] before the foundation of the world . . ." (1 Pt 1:18-20). Jesus is the spotless Lamb whose sacrifice of himself has cleansed the world of its sin and established a New Covenant, a new relationship between God and man. This New Covenant in his blood was announced by Jesus at the Last Supper, sealed by the shedding of his blood on the cross of Calvary, and completed in the revealing of the new way of life made possible for God's New Covenant people through the sending of the Holy Spirit on Pentecost.

Christ Will Come Again

The story of Jesus is not completed with his ascension to the Father or with the sending of the Holy Spirit at Pentecost. At his ascension, the angel told his disciples: "This Jesus, who was taken up from you into heaven, will come in the same way as you saw him go into heaven" (Acts 1:11). This is referring to the second coming of Christ or the *parousia*. Jesus came a first time as a spotless Lamb, sacrificed on the cross to take away the sins of the world; Jesus "will appear a second time, not to deal with sin but to save those who are eagerly waiting for him" (Heb 9:28).

During his ministry on earth, Jesus spoke of a Son of Man who would come to the earth in splendor and majesty to judge humanity. Jesus was certainly referring to the Son of Man described in the Book of Daniel who appeared before God to receive an eternal kingdom and who came on the clouds of heaven (Dn 7:13-14). Undoubtedly, this Son of Man is Jesus himself. Christians believe that Jesus will return in his glorified body and with all the unimaginable splendor of the king of the universe. Pilate, at his trial, asked Jesus if he were a king. Jesus replied that he was but that his kingdom was not of this world. When Jesus returns, the kingdom of God will be fully established on earth, and his glorious kingship will be revealed: "the kingdom of the world has become the kingdom of our Lord and of his Christ, and he shall reign for ever and ever" (Rv 11:15). But this is a glimpse of what will be appropriately discussed in a later chapter of this catechism. Now we live in the era between the first and the second comings of Jesus in which the reign of God has been established on earth by Jesus, but not yet brought to completion. This is the era of God's people of the New Covenant, the church.

FOUR

The Church—God's New Covenant People

The Meaning of Church

JESUS PROCLAIMED THE COMING of the kingdom or reign of God, but where was the reign of God to be found after his death, resurrection, and ascension? It was found in the community of Jesus' followers, who called themselves the church. Where did the term, "church" originate? What does it mean? Matthew's Gospel records that Jesus spoke of founding a church, "my church," which would prevail over the "powers of death" (Mt 16:18). The letters of the New Testament use the name "church" frequently for the group or body of believers committed to Jesus, and committed to one another in him (see Gal 1:13; Acts 8:1; Col 1:18).

The word "church" originated with the Jewish term, *qahal,* meaning an assembly or gathering. The *qahal* (or *kehal*) YHWH was a phrase often used in the Old Testament for the assembling, or assembly, of God's chosen people. The Greek term *ekklesia,* which we translate into English as church, also means to assemble or "call forth" a people. The church, then, is the assembly of those whom God has called forth to be his people and to do his will. They are the ones who believe that Jesus is truly the Messiah, the Son of God, and who have been formed by God into a people with a distinctive way of life. The church is commissioned and empowered to spread the good news of Jesus to the ends of the earth.

It should also be noted that the term *ekklesia* or church is used in two ways in the New Testament. It refers either to all of the believers in Jesus Christ, the universal church, or to the believers in a specific city or region, such as "the church in Galatia," or "the church in Corinth." These groups understood themselves to be local units or branches of the one universal church of Jesus Christ, not as independent churches. In the New Testament, the word church never referred to a building but always to a people—the believers in Jesus Christ. Actually, our English word, church, is derived from the German *kirche* which stems from a popular Greek word, *kyriake,* meaning "house of God." Thus, we may also think of the church as a building, the "house of God," remembering that its primary meaning is the "assembly of God's people."

The Birth of the Church

The church is such a tremendous reality that its meaning cannot be captured in a simple definition. The Bible uses numerous images to describe the church: the bride of Christ (2 Cor 11:2), the "body of Christ" (1 Cor 12ff), and "God's people" (1 Pt 2:10). Through faith, the Christian realizes that the church is more than just a human institution or organization. For the believer, the church is really, "a chosen race, a royal priesthood, a holy nation, God's own people. . . . Once you were no people but now you are God's people . . ." (1 Pt 2:9-10).

Let us now investigate the birth of this people of God. In Matthew's Gospel, Jesus told Simon, ". . . you are Peter ['Rock' in Aramaic], and on this rock I will build my church" (Mt 16:18). When did the Lord begin to fulfill this promise and to build his church on Peter? In John's Gospel, it appears to have begun at Jesus' post-resurrection appearance, in which Peter reversed his threefold denial of Christ, and Jesus commissioned him to feed and tend his sheep. Jesus shared his own responsibility of being the Good Shepherd (see Jn 21) with Peter. In Luke's Gospel, the church is born when Jesus fulfills his final promise (see Jn 16:7; Acts 1:4-5; Lk 24:49) by sending the Holy Spirit to his one hundred and twenty disciples on the Jewish Feast of Weeks, or Pentecost. The New Covenant is then fully established. The Holy Spirit empowers and impels this new people of God to do the Father's will and to spread the good news of Jesus Christ to the ends of the earth. In the Acts of the Apostles we see Jesus beginning to build his church upon Peter, as Peter bursts forth from the upper room as the first to proclaim the gospel in boldness and power. Peter tells his hearers what they must do to become followers of Jesus and members of his church: "Repent and be baptized every one of you in the name of Jesus Christ for the forgiveness of your sins; and you shall receive the gift of the Holy Spirit" (Acts 2:38). The account goes on to explain that faith and baptism were only the first step in becoming a Christian, an initiation into the life of the church. Being a Christian also required a commitment of the believer to a whole new way of life, the life of the church:

> And they devoted themselves to the apostles' teaching and fellowship, to the breaking of bread and the prayers.... All who believed were together and had all things in common; and they sold their possessions and goods and distributed them to all, as any had need. And day by day, attending the temple together and breaking bread in their homes, they partook of food with glad and generous hearts, praising God and having favor with all the people. (Acts 2:42-47)

Although the form of these elements of the first church in

Jerusalem were modified as time passed, all of them remain essential to the life of the church:

1. the apostles' teaching: the teaching of the apostles, as handed on in writing, by custom, or word of mouth, is the primary guide for the life and beliefs of the church;

2. fellowship or community (Greek, *koinonia*): Christians are to share their lives with each other by committing themselves to come together regularly for fellowship, that is, time spent together building their unity in the Lord;

3. the breaking of bread: this term refers to what Jesus did at the Last Supper when he "broke the bread and gave it to his disciples." Christians do this regularly in memory of Jesus, as he commanded. Catholics commonly call the breaking of bread the Eucharist, a word which means "thanksgiving";

4. the prayers: the church meets regularly to pray, now no longer in the Jewish temple but in church buildings or other places of gathering. "For where two or three are gathered in my name, there am I in the midst of them" (Mt 18:20);

5. sharing of possessions: although the church has expressed this part of its life in different ways, it has always been normal for Christians to be generous in sharing their material possessions with each other and especially with the poor.

From the very beginning of Christianity, it is clear that there were no solitary Christians. Becoming a follower of Jesus through faith and baptism meant becoming part of his body, the church. Life in the church is a shared life in which we receive our beliefs from the elders (the apostles' teaching); we receive spiritual nourishment from the Eucharist (the breaking of the bread) and prayer (both personal and communal); and we give and receive personal and material support (fellowship, or community, and sharing of possessions). These elements of the church's life have been evident and essential from its very beginning.

The Communion of Saints

Reflecting on this, someone might say that the church sounds like a family. It is. The church is God's family. This is not just a metaphor but the reality. Jesus revealed that God is our Father, and the members of the church are his adopted sons and daughters. We are brothers and sisters of the Son of God, Jesus Christ, who taught, "For whoever does the will of my Father in heaven is my brother, and sister, and mother" (Mt 12:50). This implies that all members of the church, whether living or dead, are related to each other as brothers and sisters in Jesus Christ and as sons and daughters of God, our Father.

Catholic theology calls this concept of the church as God's family "the communion of saints." As God's family, all members of the church, whom the apostle Paul called saints, are in communion or fellowship with one another. This is true regardless of whether we are in the church here on earth (the church militant, still fighting the good fight of faith); or fully united to God in heaven (the church triumphant, reigning in glory with Christ); or being cleansed from any remaining bondage of sin in purgatory (the church suffering, the souls in purgatory undergoing their final purification that they may enter worthily into God's holy presence). All are part of the church, God's family, united to one another in our Savior Jesus Christ and in the love of the Holy Spirit.

Catholics believe it is important to grasp this broader vision of the church. First, it is necessary to view the church as a united family of believers, committed to loving and serving one another because of our common recognition of God as our Father and our brotherhood in Jesus Christ and the Holy Spirit. The church should not be viewed primarily as just another human organization with functional goals. The ultimate goal of the church is to reflect the life of God by our faith and unity. Jesus said, " 'By this all men will know that you are my disciples, if you have love for one another' " (Jn 13:35).

Second, the membership of the church is not limited to those who are presently alive on earth. Jesus said, "Now he is not God of the dead, but of the living; for all live to him" (Lk 20:38). The Book of Revelation presents some marvelous images of the saints and martyrs who have passed from this life gathered around God's throne, praising him forever (see Rv 14:1-5; 19:1-8). Christians have believed since the time of the early church that it is possible for us here on earth to have fellowship or communion with these glorified saints through our prayer. In the same way that we ask fellow Christians on earth to pray for us and for our needs, we can ask the saints in heaven to pray and intercede for us before the throne of God. We are united to these saints in heaven as brothers and sisters in Jesus Christ in just as real a way as we are united to our fellow "saints" on earth. We do not worship the saints in heaven or pray to them as we pray to God, since worship (Latin, *latria*), or adoration, is due to God alone. But we may honor and venerate these saints as examples of Christian virtue; imitate their faith, love, and other qualities; and ask them to pray for us. The Bible nowhere prohibits such prayer, which has been practiced by Christians for centuries (see the writings of Saint Jerome and Saint Augustine). Note that the intercession of the saints and Mary on our behalf does not detract from the unique mediation of Jesus. All Christian prayer, whether of the saints, of Mary, or our own, is directed to the Father through Jesus Christ, who is the "one Mediator between God and men" (1 Tm 2:5).

There are some members of the church who have died and yet have not entered the glory of God's presence because of some unrepented sin or the effects of sin still remaining at the time of their death. Catholics have believed since the time of the early church that God, in his mercy, purifies these people and purges them of this sin and its effects so that they may worthily enter the presence of the all holy God before whom "nothing unclean shall enter" (Rv 21:27). This final act of God, freeing his people from any remaining bondage of sin, is called purgatory.[1] Just as the Lord purified the unclean lips of the prophet Isaiah with a burning coal (Is 6:5-7), so all those who have been basically faithful to God's call and grace in this life will be cleansed of their sin in purgatory. Catholics believe that the section of Paul's First Letter to the Corinthians (1 Cor 3:11-15) that refers to the testing of each person's work by fire is a reference to purgatory: "If any man's work is burned up, he will suffer loss, though he himself will be saved, but only as through fire" (1 Cor 3:15). Since this purgation by fire is painful, just as it is often painful when God breaks us from patterns of sin in this life, Christians have had a long tradition of praying for those who have died. We ask God's mercy on them, praying that any purification necessary for them to enter the full glory of heaven would soon be completed. Many leaders of the early church encouraged Christians to pray for the dead for this reason, and the Second Vatican Council taught:

> Very much aware of the bonds linking the whole Mystical Body of Jesus Christ, the pilgrim church from the very first ages of the Christian religion has cultivated with great piety the memory of the dead. Because it is "a holy and wholesome thought to pray for the dead that they may be loosed from sin" (2 Mc 12:46), she has also offered prayers for them. (LG, no. 50)

So it appears that the church, the communion of saints, is truly God's family with all the members having a mutual love and care for each other. Like an iceberg, only the tip of the church, those living in the church now on earth, is visible to us without the eyes of faith. With faith, we recognize those who now stand before God's throne in glory and all who are awaiting full entry into God's presence as he cleanses them of sin and its effects.

The concept of the communion of saints, the church as God's family, should be a great encouragement to us. We are not alone but part of a vast army of believers that spans the ages. As the Letter to the Hebrews exhorts us:

> Therefore, since we are surrounded by so great a cloud of

witnesses, let us also lay aside every weight, and sin which clings so closely, and let us run with perseverance the race that is set before us, looking to Jesus the pioneer and perfecter of our faith, who for the joy that was set before him endured the cross, despising the shame, and is seated at the right hand of the throne of God. (Heb 12:1-2)

Mary as Mother and Model of the Church

As we speak of the church as a family, we should call to mind that God has given this family a mother. From the cross, Jesus told John, "Behold, your mother," as he had told Mary, "Woman, behold, your son" (Jn 19:26-27). The early Christians understood this event as a powerful symbol: Jesus gave Mary to be the mother of all his disciples. Mary, in this sense, is the mother of the church.

It is because Mary was such an exemplary follower of Jesus that she is seen by Catholics as a model or type of the church. However, Mary is also a member of the church, redeemed by the grace of Jesus Christ, and called to imitate and follow him. Mary models or typifies all the virtues that should characterize the church. She was totally submitted to the will of God, as is seen in her response to Gabriel's announcement that she was to be the mother of God: "Behold I am the handmaid of the Lord; let it be to me according to your word" (Lk 1:38). She realized that any goodness or glory that she had came from God, as her Magnificat in Luke 1:46-55 illustrates. She acted in faith at all times, which led to Jesus' first miracle in John's Gospel, at the wedding feast at Cana (Jn 2:1-4). She served Jesus in humility even when she did not fully understand what his mission was (Lk 2:41-50). She followed him humbly throughout his public ministry, even up to his death on the cross when she remained with him when most of his disciples had fled. Finally, Mary was among the first disciples to receive the Holy Spirit, as she prayed with the disciples in the upper room at Pentecost, receiving once again the same Spirit that had overshadowed her to conceive Jesus in her womb (Acts 1:14; Mt 1:18). In her unmatched purity of heart and steadfast following of Jesus, Mary is a model of what the church is meant to be and to do. Mary is the woman of faith whom God has given to the church as its-mother and as a model for its life.

The final chapter of the Second Vatican Council's Dogmatic Constitution on the Church, entitled "The Role of the Blessed Virgin Mary, Mother of God, in the Mystery of Christ and the Church," gives a fuller description of Mary's relationship to the church as a member, mother, and model of the church. Chapter Ten more fully discusses devotion to Mary, and her role in God's plan of salvation.

Marks of the Church

Bishops at the first two ecumenical or worldwide councils of the Catholic church, held at Nicea in A.D. 325 and at Constantinople in A.D. 381, formulated a creed, a profession of faith, that we know today as the Nicene Creed. In this creed we profess belief in "one, holy, catholic and apostolic church." These characteristics of the church are important in understanding what the church is. They are also biblical characteristics of the church. For example, the Creed states that "the church is one." Jesus himself prayed to his Father, "that they [the believers in Jesus] may be one even as we are one . . . that they may become perfectly one, so that the world may know that thou hast sent me" (Jn 17:22-23). He taught that "There shall be one flock then, one shepherd" (Jn 10:16).

St. Paul also highly valued the unity of the church. He exhorted the Ephesians to:

> . . . maintain the unity of the Spirit in the bond of peace. There is one body and one Spirit, just as you were called to the one hope that belongs to your call, one Lord, one faith, one baptism, one God and Father of us all. . . . (Eph 4:3-6)

He begs the Philippian Christians, ". . . complete my joy by being of the same mind, having the same love, being in full accord and of one mind" (Phil 2:2).

Paul himself, as well as the other apostles, strove to maintain unity in the early church, realizing that there is only one body of Christ, which should not be divided. When crises emerged that threatened to divide the church of Jesus Christ, the apostles acted decisively to preserve unity. The Acts of the Apostles records two of these crises: the potential division between the Hebrew and Hellenist Jewish Christians in Acts 6:1-7 and the even more threatening dispute over the circumcision of Gentiles, which was resolved by the Council of Jerusalem (see Acts 15). This meeting, or council, of the apostles and elders affirmed that there is only one church of Jesus Christ and that one need not undergo the Jewish rites of initiation in order to become a Christian.

The Division of the Church and Ecumenism

It is a tragedy that in spite of the clear teaching of Jesus and the New Testament, the one church of Jesus Christ has been divided. Catholics recognize this as an objectively sinful situation, violating the will of God. The Decree on Ecumenism of the Second Vatican Council addresses this situation:

> Without doubt, this discord openly contradicts the will of Christ, provides a stumbling block to the world, and inflicts damage on the most holy cause of proclaiming the good news to every creature. (no. 1)

This decree also presents God's solution to this situation, the ecumenical movement:

> . . . there increases from day to day a movement, fostered by the grace of the Holy Spirit, for the restoration of unity among all Christians. Taking part in this movement, which

> is called ecumenical, are those who invoke the Triune God and confess Jesus as Lord and Savior. (UR, no. 1)

The Decree on Ecumenism presents clear guidance on how Catholics should look upon other Christians and how we are to pray and work for the reunification of the church of Jesus Christ. Note that the ecumenical movement, or ecumenism, is concerned with the restoration of unity among *Christians.* Jews, Moslems, Buddhists, and other non-Christians are not, properly speaking, the object of *ecumenical* activity or concern. The Second Vatican Council devotes another decree, the Declaration on the Relationship of the Church to Non-Christian Religions, to address the approach of the Catholic church to these non-Christians. (See the last section of this chapter, The Church and Salvation.)

How are Catholics to approach other Christians and promote the restoration of the unity of the church of Jesus Christ? A few guidelines, taken from the Decree on Ecumenism, will be summarized here:

1. Catholics bear a share of the blame for the division among Christians and ask forgiveness of God and of our fellow Christians for this sin. Catholics readily forgive our fellow Christians for their offenses against us and do not hold those born today into other Christian churches responsible for any sin of separation in the past (UR, no. 3).

2. The primary duty of Catholics in promoting ecumenism is to seek the renewal of the Catholic church so that its life may be a clearer witness to its teachings: "Let all Christ's faithful remember that the more purely they strive to live according to the gospel, the more they are fostering and even practicing Christian unity" (UR, no. 7).

3. Catholics consider that all those who are baptized and believe in the Trinity and in Jesus Christ as Lord and Savior "have a right to be honored by the title of Christian, and are properly regarded as brothers in the Lord by the sons of the Catholic church" (UR, no. 3). Thus, the Catholic church

considers other Christians as "separated brothers and sisters" in Christ, not as heretics or schismatics (UR, no. 3).

4. The Catholic church recognizes other bodies of Christians as churches or ecclesiastical communities that "the Spirit of Christ . . . has not refrained from using as means of salvation . . ." (UR, no. 3). In other words, Christians in other churches or ecclesiastical communities may be saved through the grace available in their churches, although "the fullness of grace and truth (is) entrusted to the Catholic church" (UR, no. 3).

5. Catholics can genuinely learn and receive support from other Christians. In fact, Catholics are encouraged both to study the beliefs and backgrounds of other Christian churches in order to understand them better and to meet individually or in groups to pray with other Christians. Catholics may attend the worship services of other Christians but normally may not participate in their communion services because of different understanding of the Eucharist (UR, no. 4; also see Chapter Six on the Sacraments).

6. In discussing our beliefs with other Christians, Catholics should state the teachings of the Catholic church clearly and non-defensively. As the Decree on Ecumenism instructs, Catholics should avoid a "false conciliatory approach" in presenting Catholic belief "which harms the purity of Catholic doctrine and obscures its assured genuine meaning." This decree also encourages Catholics to explain their beliefs "profoundly and precisely, in ways and in terminology which our separated brethren too can really understand" (UR, no. 11).

7. Finally, Catholics are encouraged to join with all Christians in professing to the whole world our "faith in God, one and three, in the incarnate Son of God, our Redeemer and Lord." The Decree reminds us that cooperation in matters of common social concern is essential (UR, no. 12). We must always bear in mind that what unites us as Christians, our common faith, hope, and mutual love, is far greater than what divides us. It is Satan who desires the continuance of divisions

among Christians. God desires our reconciliation, so that his church may be truly one, as we profess it to be in the Creed.

What will the unity that God desires for Christians look like? Exactly how will it come about? The Catholic church knows that this is ultimately in God's hands and that it will only come about as Christians constantly imitate and pray to our Savior, Jesus Christ, for it is in him that we will find our true unity. As the Decree on Ecumenism declares:

> This most sacred Synod urgently desires that the initiatives of the sons of the Catholic church, joined with those of the separated brethren, go forward without obstructing the ways of divine Providence and without prejudging the future inspiration of the Holy Spirit. Further, this Synod declares its realization that the holy task of reconciling all Christians in the unity of the one and only church of Christ transcends human energies and abilities. It therefore places its hope entirely in the prayer of Christ for the church, in the love of the Father for us, and in the power of the Holy Spirit. "And hope does not disappoint, because the charity of God is poured forth in our hearts by the Holy Spirit Who has been given to us" (Rom 5:5). (no. 24)

The Church Is Catholic

Catholic, as used in the Nicene Creed, means "universal" or "all-embracing." Jesus Christ intended his church to embrace all people, as he demonstrated in his own ministry to Greeks and Jews, rich and poor, woman and man, free person and slave alike. The early Christians shared this understanding that there were no limitations on who could enter the church.

The earliest recorded use of the term "catholic" in reference to the church was in a letter of Bishop Ignatius of Antioch, written around A.D. 110. For Ignatius, "catholic church" simply meant the whole church or the universal church. It was almost a century or more later that the term "Catholic church" was used to designate a particular body of Christians, distinguishing the original church of Jesus Christ from other groups that had broken away from it, such as the Montanists (second century) and the Arians (fourth century). Eventually, the faith of this Catholic church became the official religion of the Roman Empire. Still later, the name of the central city of the Catholic church was added to its name. This distinguished the Roman Catholic church from other churches that had emerged in the area encompassing the Eastern end of the Mediterranean Sea.

Today, it is necessary to distinguish between "catholic" as a mark or characteristic of the church of Jesus Christ, and Catholic as the name for the particular church or churches that developed out of the primitive church. As a mark of the church, catholic still means that the church of Jesus Christ is universal—not restricted to people of any particular nation, race, color, sex, or economic status. This reflects God's desire that all people become part of his body, the church, for God "desires all men to be saved and to come to the knowledge of the truth" (1 Tm 2:4).

Catholic as a formal name refers to those churches (Catholic churches) that have developed out of primitive Christianity and have basically preserved a common faith, though they may differ in certain aspects in what is known as rites. The Decree on Eastern Catholic Churches of the Second Vatican Council explains:

> Such individual churches, whether of the East or of the West, although they differ somewhat among themselves in what are called rites (that is, in liturgy, ecclesiastical discipline, and spiritual heritage) are, nevertheless, equally entrusted to the pastoral guidance of the Roman Pontiff.... They are consequently of equal dignity, so that none of them is superior to the other by reason of rite. They enjoy the same rights and are under the same obligations, even with respect to preaching the gospel to the whole world (cf. Mk 16:15) under the guidance of the Roman Pontiff. (no. 3)

This specific meaning of Catholic, then, refers to the different rites of the Catholic church which share the same basic faith, which are in submission to the pastoral guidance of the pope, and which maintain and foster some of their unique traditions in worship, discipline, and spiritual heritage. The existence of these different rites of the Catholic church demonstrates that the oneness or unity of the church does not imply total uniformity. A rich diversity of traditions can be maintained within the unity of the church, as long as the basic unity of faith and the Christian way of life is maintained. This diversity of tradition within the Catholic church expresses its catholicity or universality and adds to the church's beauty and richness.

A story from the Second Vatican Council that illustrates this was the celebration of the Mass in St. Peter's Basilica in the different rites of the Catholic church represented there. At one liturgy, some onlookers were stunned when an African bishop processed in wearing a large, colorful hat shaped something like a beehive, accompanied by the music of drums and other native African instruments. At the offertory, the gifts of bread and wine emerged from the hat! This experience accentuated, along with the presence of bishops and onlookers from all races, nations, colors and languages, the catholicity or universality of the church.

The Church Is Holy

What does it mean that the church is holy? Many people equate holiness with sinlessness and say that a holy church must be a perfect church, or at least a church well on the way to perfection.

The holiness of the church, however, does not refer primarily to the merits and virtues of its individual members. Something is holy because it is chosen or set apart by God for his purposes and service. God has chosen and set apart a people, the church, for his purposes and service, and has called it holy: "But you are a chosen race, a royal priesthood, a holy nation, God's own people. . . ." (1 Pt 2:9). The church is holy, not because of its own merits but because Jesus Christ died to win forgiveness for this people and to cleanse it of its sin:

> . . . Christ loved the church and gave himself up for her, that he might sanctify her, having cleansed her by the washing of water with the word, that he might present the church to himself in splendor, without spot or wrinkle or any such thing, that she might be holy and without blemish. (Eph 5:25-27)

The holiness of the church reflects the present status of the kingdom or reign of God in this world. The church is holy, because God has called it "a holy nation, God's own people" (1 Pt 2:9). Likewise, the church is the historic manifestation of God's reign or kingdom that Jesus established. But the church's holiness, like God's reign, is also something that God is bringing progressively to completion or fulfillment in history, until it is finally perfected when Jesus Christ comes again in glory.

Holiness, like the kingdom of God, is a free gift of God to his people, a share in his divine nature. To demonstrate that it is his gift, God has blessed, chosen, and set apart for his purposes a people who still struggle with sin. As St. Paul taught, "we have this treasure in earthen vessels, to show that the transcendent power belongs to God and not to us" (2 Cor 4:7). The church is holy because God has made it holy. Therefore, there is no contradiction when Catholics claim that the church is holy, and also a church of sinners. Holiness is God's gift to the church, its true nature. Sin is still part of the life of the church, since Jesus came to call sinners (Mt 9:13), and yet it is not the true nature of the church. Sin is overcome in the church as its members repent and incessantly turn to God for his mercy and forgiveness. In response, God sends the Holy Spirit to renew the church and sanctify its members, transforming them "into his likeness from one degree of glory to another" (2 Cor 3:18).

The Second Vatican Council summarizes this reality when it teaches in the Dogmatic Constitution on the Church: "while Christ, holy, innocent, undefiled (Heb 7:26) knew nothing of sin (2 Cor 5:21), but came to expiate only the sins of the people (cf. Heb 2:17), the church, embracing sinners in her bosom, is at the same time holy, and always in need of being purified and incessantly pursues the path of penance and renewal" (no. 8).

This understanding of the holiness of the church has many practical implications. For example, some people (past and present) have claimed that the Catholic church cannot be called holy because of the personal sinfulness of its members and leaders. Some individuals and groups have even broken away from the Catholic church because of this, desiring to found or join a truly holy sinless church. The irony of this is that those who condemn or leave the Catholic church because of its sinful members or leaders soon discover, if they are honest, that there is no sinless, perfect church or group of Christians. Sooner or later, every group of human beings reveals the fallen, sinful nature of man, and must cry out to God for mercy and forgiveness. The Catholic church claims to be holy because God has called it to be a people set apart for him and his purposes. The church trusts in him for pardon and the renewing grace of the Holy Spirit.

The Church Is Apostolic

The final characteristic of the church that Christians profess in the Nicene Creed is that the church is apostolic—"built upon the foundation of the apostles and prophets, Christ Jesus himself being the cornerstone" (Eph 2:20). How is the church founded or built on the apostles? First, the church announces and defends the true teaching of the apostles; Acts 2:42 states, "they devoted themselves to the apostles' teaching...." Second, the ministry or office of the apostles is continued in the church in unbroken succession to this day. As St. Paul wrote: "God has appointed in the church first apostles. . . ." (1 Cor 12:28, see also Eph 4:11).

When the original twelve apostles died, they were not replaced by a new set of apostles. Who then, continued the teaching and ministry of the apostles after they died? The Pastoral Epistles of the New Testament (1 and 2 Timothy, Titus), probably authored by the apostle Paul, clearly indicate that the bishops (Greek, *episcopoi*) assumed the ministry and office of the apostles in the early church. They were the primary teachers in the early churches: ". . . he [the bishop] must hold firm to the sure word [of the gospel] as taught so that he may be able to give instruction in sound doctrine and also to confute those who contradict it" (Ti 1:9; see also 1 Tm 3:2).

The bishops also were the primary shepherds and leaders of the local churches, representing the Chief Shepherd, Jesus Christ, in their care for the churches. Many early Christian writings exhorted the local Christian churches to honor and respect their bishop as they would Jesus Christ since they represented him just as the apostles had. The letters of Ignatius of Antioch, who was martyred for his faith in about A.D. 110, are particularly clear and powerful in presenting the importance of the bishops as the representatives of Jesus and successors of the apostles in their churches.

The bishops of the local churches also recognized their responsibility for the entire (catholic) church of Jesus Christ. Like the apostles they succeeded, the bishops viewed themselves as a body of men who were commissioned by the Lord to spread the gospel and lead the church in unity. The bishops of the early church expressed their unity by correspondence about important matters affecting the whole church, working together to develop creeds that expressed accurately the faith of Christians, and meeting together in regional or worldwide (ecumenical) councils or synods where they sought the Lord's guidance on important matters of Christian belief and practice.

The prototype of these councils of bishops was the Council of Jerusalem described in Acts 15. There, the apostles and elders reached a decision concerning Gentile circumcision and observance of the Jewish law that affected the whole church. In the letter they drafted as a result of the council, they stated, "For it has seemed good to the Holy Spirit and to us to lay upon you no greater burden than these necessary things . . ." (Acts 15:28). Later councils of bishops also believed that when they met as a body of elders representing the whole church, their decisions were assuredly guided by the Holy Spirit and thereby binding upon the whole church. The Catholic church recognizes the apostolic authority of twenty-one such worldwide, or ecumenical, councils of bishops that have been held from the time of the early church until today. Through these councils, Catholics believe that the Holy Spirit continues to guide the church through the apostolic authority of the bishops.

Bishops Today

Catholics believe that the bishops who govern and guide the Catholic church today are true successors to the apostles of Jesus. The principal duty of the bishop is to preach the gospel of Jesus Christ. This is most frequently done in the context of the Mass or other liturgies, which the bishop celebrates as one who possesses the fullness of the priesthood of Jesus Christ that is conferred upon him in his episcopal consecration. As the Dogmatic Constitution on the Church explains:

> . . . by means of the imposition of hands and the words of consecration, the grace of the Holy Spirit is so conferred, and the sacred character so impressed, that bishops in an eminent and visible way undertake Christ's own role as Teacher, Shepherd, and High Priest, and that they act in His person. (no. 21)

Also, the bishop has full apostolic authority within his local church to guide and govern its members in the name of Christ. Each bishop, at his consecration, is given a particular jurisdiction (usually a geographical area) in which he is empowered to shepherd and guide God's people with the same authority that Jesus conferred on his apostles.

Even though the bishops of the Catholic church have distinct ministries and jurisdictions, the Second Vatican Council emphasized that the bishops are to see themselves and to function as fellow members of a college or body of bishops. Just as the apostles were a body who worked together for the sake of Jesus and his kingdom, the bishops as a body are the successors of the apostles and are called to work together for the good of God's people, the church. Practically, this means that each bishop has a pastoral concern and care for the whole church as well as for his particular diocese or jurisdiction. This collegiality of the bishops is expressed most visibly when groups of bishops meet together for synods or councils, where they pray and confer about God's direction for the church. In fact, Catholics believe that when the bishops representing the entire world meet together for an ecumenical or worldwide council, the Holy Spirit is present in a special way. The solemn doctrinal definitions of ecumenical councils are believed by Catholics to be infallibly true, since we firmly believe that God would not allow Satan to deceive the whole body of bishops who have been called by God to teach and govern the church.[2] Jesus' promise to his apostles that he would send the Holy Spirit to guide the church into all truth (Jn 16:12-15) is certainly fulfilled when the bishops concur on a matter of faith or morals, even though an individual bishop may err. As the Dogmatic Constitution on the Church explains:

> Although the individual bishops do not enjoy the prerogative of infallibility, they can nevertheless proclaim Christ's doctrine infallibly. This is so, even when they are dispersed around the world, provided that while maintaining the bond of unity among themselves and with Peter's

> successor, and while teaching authentically on a matter of faith or morals, they concur in a single viewpoint as the one which must be held conclusively. This authority is even more clearly verified when, gathered together in an ecumenical council, they are teachers and judges of faith and morals for the universal Church. Their definitions must then be adhered to with the submission of faith. (no. 25)

Through the apostolic succession of the bishops, God has provided the Catholic church an unbroken ministry of teaching, governance, and sacramental life for almost two thousand years. We must be aware that other Christians do not share the Catholic belief in the apostolic succession of bishops. Many of them believe that the expression "the church is apostolic" means that the church faithfully preserves the teaching of the apostles, or simply that the church is missionary. They do not consider the unbroken historic succession of bishops from the apostles to be essential to the apostolic ministry but consider this ministry as a work of the Holy Spirit that could be conferred on any person at any time. Catholics observe that from New Testament times onward the apostles' role was assumed by the bishops, and that these bishops conferred this office on other men through prayer and the "laying on of hands." In precisely this way have bishops been recognized and consecrated for their ministry in the Catholic church from apostolic times to the present day.

Priests and Deacons

The bishop is assisted in his role of teaching, shepherding, and leading the church in worship by other ordained elders: priests and deacons. These three groups of ordained leaders together comprise the hierarchy of the church. The orders of priest and deacon originated in the early church. The Greek word *presbyteros,* meaning "elder," is often used in the New

Testament to designate one of the leaders of the local church. At first, there was apparently no sharp distinction (in at least some local churches) between the different types of elders—all were called presbyters. But by the time of the writing of the Pastoral Epistles (between A.D. 60 and 90) bishops and deacons are spoken of as distinct classes of elders.

Actually, the office of deacon (from the Greek *diakonos*, meaning servant) was one of the first distinct leadership roles in the church, tracing its origin back to the selection of the seven men in the Jerusalem church to oversee the distribution of food to the widows (see Acts 6). This service freed the apostles to devote themselves "to prayer and to the ministry of the word" (Acts 6:4). Deacons became the "right hands" of the bishops of the early church and continued to be a key office of the church into the Middle Ages. Although the office of deacon fell into disuse in the Catholic church, becoming a stage in preparation for priestly ordination, the Second Vatican Council has called for the restoration of the permanent diaconate according to the model of the early church. (The role of the permanent deacon will be discussed further in the chapter on the sacraments.)

The presbyter or elder gradually assumed a distinct role or office in the early church, subordinate to the bishop but carrying on many of the same tasks. The letters of Ignatius of Antioch in the beginning of the second century inform us that the churches to which he wrote all had a distinctive three-tiered leadership structure comprised of a single bishop, assisted by presbyters and deacons. This structure of ministry was universally accepted in the church by the middle of the second century and has been preserved in the Catholic church to this day in the ordained ministries of a single bishop presiding over each local church, assisted by priests and deacons.

Other Elders in the Catholic Church

Although the three-tiered hierarchy of bishop, priest, and deacon is the basic structure of leadership in the Catholic church, there are some special functions and roles that have developed in the church's long history. These include:

Cardinals. For many centuries, cardinals have been selected by the pope to assist him in the guidance and administration of the Catholic church. Before the eighth century, there were Cardinal-Priests, Cardinal-Deacons, and Cardinal-Bishops. Today, all of the cardinals are bishops, who are selected by the pope by virtue of their outstanding holiness and service to God's people. Their role is to assist the pope in the guidance and administration of the church. Many of them serve as heads of Roman Congregations, ecclesiastical commissions, and offices of the Curia, the governing organization of the Roman Catholic church located in Rome. A special task of the College of Cardinals is to elect a new pope, which they do gathered in conclave, meeting in a closed apartment in the Vatican where they stay until they elect a new pope, signaled to the waiting world by a column of white smoke.

Patriarch. This is a title used for the leader of an Eastern Catholic or Orthodox church.[3] It originated around the sixth century, when it was used to designate the bishops of the principal sees of Christendom: Rome, Alexandria, Antioch, Constantinople, and Jerusalem, who provided leadership for all Christians in their regions of the world. It is not currently used for any leader of the Roman Catholic church.

Metropolitan. This is the title of a bishop exercising some authority over a province, not only a diocese. Today, some regions of the Roman Catholic church are divided into provinces with a bishop assigned to serve as Metropolitan. The title is not commonly used in the Roman Catholic church.

Archbishop. An archbishop is the bishop of a large or important diocese or see. He has no more authority than a bishop, but the size or influence of his diocese makes his position one of special prominence. The local church that he pastors is called an archdiocese.

Ordinary. The bishop who has primary responsibility for pastoring a diocese is sometimes referred to as the ordinary. This distinguishes him from retired bishops or from auxiliary bishops who may be assigned to exercise pastoral leadership in a large diocese or archdiocese under the direction of the ordinary. Sometimes a coadjutor-bishop will be appointed to assist the diocesan bishop in his duties, as the designated successor to that bishop.

Monsignor. This is a title bestowed upon a priest, usually by the pope, to honor him for distinguished service. This title is not being conferred often in English-speaking countries today, although it is used in other countries (e.g., France) as a form of address for bishops and archbishops. There are a variety of other terms and titles used within the Catholic church, such as papal nuncio, acolyte, episcopal vicar, vicar general, and others, which designate specific roles of service within the church. The object of these is not to multiply titles but to clarify the different ministries and functions within the church. A good Catholic encyclopedia can be consulted to find the meaning of these and other titles and offices in the Catholic church.

The Role of the Pope

The chief representative, or vicar, of Jesus Christ and the spiritual head of the Roman Catholic church under Christ is the pope, the bishop of Rome. While Catholics understand the college or body of bishops to be the legitimate successors to the college of apostles, the pope is viewed as the successor to the specific apostle singled out by Jesus to be leader and shepherd of the whole church, St. Peter.

To understand and accept this statement involves a few stages. First, it is necessary to see that Jesus did single out Peter to have a special responsibility for the guidance and care of the whole church. The biblical evidence for this is convincing. Matthew's Gospel records Jesus saying:

> "And I tell you, you are Peter [Rock], and on this rock I will build my church, and the 'powers' of death shall not prevail

> against it. I will give you the keys of the kingdom of heaven, and whatever you bind on earth shall be bound in heaven, and whatever you loose on earth shall be loosed in heaven." (Mt 16:18-19)

Also, Luke's Gospel speaks of Peter "strengthening his brethren" after his repentance from denying Christ (Lk 22:31-32), and in John's Gospel, Jesus commissions Peter to "feed" and "tend" his sheep (Jn 21:15-17), assuming Jesus' own role as the Good Shepherd (Jn 10:14-18).

We might have reason to question or doubt these statements if Peter had not emerged as a leader of the church among the apostles. But the Acts of the Apostles and the other New Testament writings clearly indicate that Peter was the pre-eminent elder of the New Testament church, in spite of his human failings and weakness. Peter was the first to proclaim the good news of Jesus at Pentecost (Acts 2:14-40), the first to preach to and baptize Gentile converts (Acts 10:46-48), and is consistently portrayed as the spokesman or leader of the Twelve (Mk 8:29; Mt 18:21; Lk 9:20; 12:41; Acts 3:6-7, 12-16; 4:8-12; 5:3-9, 29-32; 8:20-23; 10:34-43; 11:4-18; 15:7-11). In fact, it would be unlikely that the Gospels of Matthew and John (written around A.D. 80 and 90-100 respectively) would have spoken so definitely about Peter's leadership if he had not actually served in the church as they indicate.

The second step in understanding the role of the pope is to determine whether Peter had a successor. There is no word of Jesus that indicates that either Peter or the apostles were to be succeeded by others in their positions of authority and leadership. However, Jesus intended the church he founded to endure until he returned at the end of time, and the early Christians recognized the importance of having a leader in each church. The bishops were comparable in authority to Jesus' apostles until Jesus returned. Likewise, the universal church gradually came to see the value and the necessity of recognizing the special authority of one of the bishops, just as Jesus gave Peter a special leadership role among the apostles. Who would that bishop be who would carry on the charism or role of Peter? Increasingly, the other bishops and Christians of the early church looked to the bishop of Rome to provide decisive guidance and direction for the church. This made sense, since the bishop of Rome was the bishop succeeding Peter and Paul, who both gave their lives witnessing to their faith in Rome. The great bishop of the early church, Irenaeus of Lyon, testified to this in his defense of the tradition of the Catholic church in his work *Against Heresies,* written in the late second century:

> . . . I can, by pointing out the tradition which that very great, oldest, and well-known Church, founded and established at Rome by those two most glorious apostles, Peter and Paul, received from the apostles, and its faith known among men, which comes down to us through the successions of bishops, put to shame all of those who. . . gather as they should not. For every church must be in harmony with this Church [the church in Rome] because of its outstanding pre-eminence, that is, the faithful from everywhere, since the apostolic tradition is presented in it by those from everywhere.[4]

Ireneaus goes on to trace the successors of Peter as bishop of Rome from the first, Linus, to the twelfth, Eleutherus, who was bishop of Rome at the time of his document's composition. His point is that the see of Rome and its bishops have special authority, pre-eminence as he says, because of their direct link to the apostles, Peter and Paul. By the middle of the fourth century, the bishop of Rome was first called pope, a title referring to his special care for the entire church as a "papa" or "father" to them. As a father of the church, the pope was often called upon to arbitrate disputes within the church, to be a final judge in matters of Christian doctrine, and even to defend the church against the incursions of secular rulers or invaders. Although the office of pope did not arise immediately in the early church, Catholic Christians recognize its emergence, and the recognition of the bishop of Rome as the successor of Peter, as a work of the Holy Spirit intended to strengthen the church and lead it into the fullness of truth, as Jesus promised (Jn 16:13).

The Gift of Infallibility

Jesus promised to be with the church until the end of time (Mt 28:20) and to send the Holy Spirit to guide it into the fullness of truth and reveal the things to come. This belief that the church cannot be led astray from the truth when it believes and defines a doctrine under the guidance of the Holy Spirit is called infallibility.

Catholics believe that infallibility in belief may be expressed in three ways. First, the church as a whole is infallible when it recognizes and agrees upon a truth in the sphere of faith and morals. As the Dogmatic Constitution on the Church of Vatican II pronounced:

> The body of the faithful as a whole, anointed as they are by the Holy One (cf. 1 Jn 2:20, 27), cannot err in matters of belief. Thanks to a supernatural sense of the faith ("sensus fidei") which characterizes the people as a whole, it manifests this unerring quality when "from the bishops down to the last member of the laity," it shows universal agreement in matters of faith and morals. (no. 12)

Of course, it is difficult to determine what all the faithful in the world believe. The Catholic church also teaches that Christian truth can be stated infallibly by the bishops of the church, in union with the pope. Their authority is comparable to a statement of faith by the apostles with Peter since the bishops and the pope are their genuine successors.

Finally, Catholics believe that the pope alone, in specific circumstances, can speak with the gift of infallibility that Jesus has given to his church. Since infallibility is a gift or charism of God, it is certainly possible for God to enable a single person to possess this gift at times. The apostle Peter sometimes spoke infallible, revealed truths, such as when he proclaimed at Caesarea Philippi that Jesus is the Messiah, and Jesus responded, "Blessed are you Simon Bar-Jona! For flesh and blood has not revealed this to you, but my Father who is in heaven" (Mt 16:17). Also, God revealed to Peter in a vision that Gentiles were not unclean and could be baptized (see Acts 10:9-48). Catholics believe that if Peter could receive divine guidance to speak with infallible truth, so can the successors of Peter. Although this doctrine of papal infallibility was not formally defined by the Catholic church until 1870 (in the decree *Pastor Aeternus* of the First Vatican Council), Catholics had long understood that the pope possessed this gift. The First Vatican Council defined more specifically when and how the pope was speaking with the charism of infallibility. The Second Vatican Council substantially repeated this statement in the Dogmatic Constitution on the Church:

> This is the infallibility which the Roman Pontiff (the Pope), the head of the college of bishops, enjoys in virtue of his office, when, as supreme shepherd and teacher of all the faithful, who confirms his brethren in their faith (cf. Lk 22:32), he proclaims by a definitive act some doctrine of faith or morals. Therefore his definitions, of themselves, and not from the consent of the church, are justly styled irreformable, for they are pronounced with the assistance of the Holy Spirit, an assistance promised to him in blessed Peter . . . For then the Roman Pontiff is not pronouncing judgment as a private person. Rather, as the supreme teacher of the universal Church, as one in whom the charism of the

infallibility of the church herself is individually present, he is expounding or defending a doctrine of Catholic faith. (no. 25)

The definition makes it clear that the pope is only speaking infallibly when he proclaims by a definitive act some doctrine concerning faith or morals. This clarifies that the pope is not speaking infallibly on every occasion. However, even when the pope is not speaking infallibly but teaching the church in some other way, his teaching is to be received by Catholics with "religious submission of will and of mind" (Dogmatic Constitution on the Church, no. 25). The seriousness with which Catholics should attend to papal teachings are often indicated by the nature of the document through which these teachings are promulgated. Official, infallible definitions of faith must be accepted and believed by all Catholics. The pope also addresses the church through (in order of importance) encyclical letters, apostolic exhortations, and then through a variety of other channels, such as letters from Vatican offices or congregations, speeches, and other letters to groups or individuals.

Only two recent statements have been presented by the popes as infallible. The first is the doctrine of the Immaculate Conception of Mary, defined in 1854, by Pope Pius IX; the second is the doctrine of Mary's bodily assumption into heaven, defined in 1950, by Pope Pius XII.[5] These doctrines were defined by the pope because there was unclarity both within and outside of the Catholic church concerning the Catholic belief about Mary on these points, even though these beliefs had been generally held by Catholics from very early in the church's history. There was no need for new infallible papal definitions of the many other areas of Catholic doctrine that had been previously defined by popes or ecumenical councils or which had been clearly taught in the Bible or universally held by Christians. The doctrine of papal infallibility of the

First Vatican Council in 1870 simply clarified the conditions under which a proclamation of the pope should be considered to be infallibly true.

Religious Life

So far we have introduced the special roles of ordained ministers in the Catholic church: bishops, priests, deacons, the pope, and others. There is also a special classification of men and women in the Catholic church who have dedicated themselves to God in a solemn and permanent way through their profession of vows of poverty, chastity (or celibacy), and obedience. Most of these men and women live these three evangelical counsels within religious orders of priests, brothers, or sisters. They commit themselves to a particular community of men or women guided by a rule of life, such as the Rule of St. Benedict, St. Francis, St. Ignatius of Loyola, or St. Augustine. Ordained religious, those who have received the sacrament of Holy Orders, form religious orders of priests. Whole orders of brothers and sisters (or nuns) have embraced the religious life and are not ordained. The Dogmatic Constitution on the Church explained:

> ...the religious state is not an intermediate one between the clerical and lay state. Rather, the faithful of Christ are called by God from both these latter states of life so that they may enjoy this particular gift in the life of the Church and thus each in his own way can forward the saving mission of the Church. (no. 43)

The religious life is a great resource and gift to the church. These men and women have responded decisively to Jesus' call to Christian perfection: "If you would be perfect, go, sell what you possess and give to the poor, and you will have treasure in heaven; and come, follow me" (Mt 19:21). Their response to this through living the evangelical counsels is a sign to the world and to the church of the reality and primacy of God's kingdom. "The religious state reveals in a unique way that the kingdom of God and its overmastering necessities are superior to all earthly considerations. Finally, to all men it shows wonderfully at work within the Church the surpassing greatness of the force of Christ the King and the boundless power of the Holy Spirit" (LG, no. 44). Besides a chapter on Religious in the Dogmatic Constitution on the Church, the Second Vatican Council also devoted an entire Conciliar decree to the Appropriate Renewal of Religious Life (*Perfectae Caritatis*). This decree has been the charter for the proper changes and renewal of religious life since the Second Vatican Council.

The Laity

When Catholics hear the phrase, "the church," what comes to mind? In the past, it was common for Catholics to think of the pope, bishops, clergy, or religious. Some even thought of the church building. Today, the Second Vatican Council emphasizes that the church is the whole people of God. Most members of this people are not ordained and have not devoted their lives to a religious state through special vows of poverty, chastity, and obedience. The church is mainly comprised of baptized believers who follow the call of Christ to live his gospel in the midst of the secular world, with occupations often not directly related to the church. The people who respond to this call, either in the married or single state of life, are the laity.[6]

A great breakthrough of Vatican II led Catholics to realize that to be a lay person was a genuine vocation—a call of the Lord to serve him in the church and the world in a unique way. As the Dogmatic Constitution on the Church states:

> . . . the laity, by their very vocation, seek the kingdom of God by engaging in temporal affairs, and by ordering them

> according to the plan of God... They are called there by God so that by exercising their proper function and being led by the spirit of the Gospel they can work for the sanctification of the world from within, in the manner of leaven. (no. 31)

This document proceeds to explain how lay people carry on the priestly, prophetic, and kingly ministry of Jesus Christ in a way that is different than clergy or religious but equally important in God's plan for the salvation of the world. While lay people certainly must use their talents and gifts within the church, they are also commissioned by Christ himself to represent him and bring the good news of salvation in the daily affairs and ordinary circumstances of human society: "Through their baptism and confirmation, all are commissioned to that apostolate by the Lord Himself" (LG, no. 33). While the clergy's ministry is specifically to the church, building up the body of Christ, the lay person's ministry is specifically to the world—to extend the body of Christ and bring the influence of the church and the gospel to bear upon the world's affairs.[7] There is no reason, then, for any lay Catholic to think of him or herself as "just a lay person." Not only have the laity been commissioned by Jesus himself to the apostolate of bringing the gospel to the world, they have been equipped for this apostolate by the gifts (charisms) of the Holy Spirit, which are given to each Christian for the upbuilding of the church and for the service and evangelization of the world. The Decree on the Apostolate of the Laity of the Second Vatican Council specifies that:

> ... from the reception of these charisms or gifts ... there arise for each believer the right and duty to use them in the Church and in the world for the good of mankind and for the upbuilding of the Church. In doing so, believers need to enjoy the freedom of the Holy Spirit who "breathes where He wills" (Jn 3:8). At the same time, they must act in communion with their pastors. The latter must make a

> judgment about the true nature and proper use of these gifts, not in order to extinguish the Spirit, but to test all things and hold fast to what is good (cf. 1 Thes 5:12, 19, 21). (AA, no. 3)

The Decree on the Apostolate of the Laity states repeatedly that lay people are called and equipped to be active in service and leadership in the church, working in willing cooperation with the church's ordained pastors. Any notion of competition—clergy versus laity—is excluded, since we are brothers and sisters working together as God's family for the cause of Christ and his kingdom.

One of the most significant statements of the Second Vatican Council expressing the importance and equality of all members of the church—regardless of their vocation or state of life—was the chapter of the Dogmatic Constitution on the Church entitled, "The Call of the Whole Church to Holiness." Regardless of whether one is a priest, married person, religious, single man or woman, or the pope—*all* are equally called by God to holiness or Christian perfection. The Dogmatic Constitution on the Church, states:

> The Lord Jesus, the divine Teacher and Model of all perfection, preached holiness of life to each and every one of His disciples, regardless of their situation: "You therefore are to be perfect, as your heavenly Father is perfect" (Mt 5:48) . . . Thus it is evident to everyone that all the faithful of Christ of whatever rank or status are called to the fullness of the Christian life and to the perfection of charity.

Of course, Christians must pursue holiness and perfection in Christ according to their state in life and particular calling from the Lord. A married woman with small children, for example, will seek holiness in a different way from a cloistered contemplative nun. But both are equally called to holiness and equally able to attain it, though in different ways (see AA, no.

4). Therefore, there is no vocation or state within the church that is inherently better than another. The best way to holiness is for each individual Christian to discern and follow the Lord's personal call to him or her, whether to priesthood, religious life, the married state, or to single life. But the individual's total and willing response to God is indispensable. As the Decree on the Apostolate of the Laity affirms:

> Since Christ in His mission from the Father is the fountain and source of the whole apostolate of the Church, the success of the lay apostolate depends on the laity's living union with Christ. For the Lord has said, "He who abides in Me, and I in him, he bears much fruit, for without Me you can do nothing" (Jn 15:5). This life of intimate union with Christ in the Church is nourished by spiritual aids which are common to all the faithful, especially active participation in the sacred liturgy. . . . (no. 4)

The Church and Salvation

Who will be saved and attain eternal life with God? Many questions arise concerning the relationship of the church to salvation: Must a person belong to a church to be saved? Catholics sometimes ask if only Catholics are saved. Some of our Protestant brothers and sisters ask if Catholics can be saved. What does the church have to do with conferring salvation and the merits of Christ upon individuals?

Eternal life, or salvation in the sense we will use this term here, is a free gift of God. Catholics believe that God can confer this gift of eternal life upon anyone, even those who do not belong to a Christian church. However, the Catholic church teaches that membership in the church is the normal or ordinary way to salvation. In fact, the Dogmatic Constitution on the Church of the Second Vatican Council states that the church is "necessary for salvation" because Jesus himself "affirmed the necessity of faith and baptism (cf. Mk 16:16; Jn 3:5) and thereby also affirmed the necessity of the Church" (no. 14). For Catholics, the church is necessary because Jesus established it (Mt 16:18), and it is through this church of Jesus Christ that his life and grace come into the world.

In primitive and early Christianity, it was unheard of for a believer in Christ to live apart from the church that Jesus founded. Why? Simple logic. Salvation comes from Jesus Christ, and it is within the church that a person comes into a living relationship with Jesus, his Father, and the Holy Spirit. One comes to know and relate to God in the church through the Bible (the book of the church), through the preaching and teaching of God's word, through the Eucharist (the Body of Christ) and the other sacraments, and through fellowship and worship with other believers. Official Catholic documents often refer to these specific ways of coming into contact with God in the church as "means of salvation."

As we have seen, Jesus taught that there is only one church, and therefore he only established and founded one church. Where is this one church of Jesus Christ to be found today? Catholics believe that one place the church of Christ truly exists (or subsists) is in the Catholic church. The Dogmatic Constitution on the Church states that: "This Church [the unique Church of Christ which in the Creed we avow as one, holy, catholic, and apostolic] subsists in the Catholic Church, which is governed by the successor of Peter and by the bishops in union with that successor. . ." (no. 8). The Vatican's Congregation for the Doctrine of the Faith explained that, "Catholics are bound to profess that . . . they belong to that Church which Christ founded and which is governed by the successors of Peter. . . ."[8] For this reason, it is correct for Catholics to say that they belong to the authentic church of Jesus Christ which is governed by the successors of Peter and the other apostles.

The positive teaching stated here is that the Catholic church is a genuine expression of the church of Christ. Never does the Second Vatican Council or any papal teaching say that the church of Jesus Christ and the grace of salvation, is limited to the Catholic church. To the contrary, immediately after the Dogmatic Constitution on the Church states that the church of Christ subsists in the Catholic church, it adds that "many elements of sanctification and truth can be found outside of her [the Catholic church's] visible structure" (no. 8). The Decree on Ecumenism is even more explicit and detailed on this topic:

> Moreover some, even very many, of the most significant elements or endowments which together go to build up and give life to the Church (of Christ) herself can exist outside the visible boundaries of the Catholic Church: the written word of God; the life of grace; faith, hope, and charity, along with other interior gifts of the Holy Spirit and visible elements. All of these, which come from Christ and lead back to Him, belong by right to the one Church of Christ...
>
> It follows that these separated Churches and Communities [Christian bodies separated from the Catholic church]... have by no means been deprived on significance and importance in the mystery of salvation. For the Spirit of Christ has not refrained from using them as means of salvation which derive their efficacy from the very fullness of grace and truth entrusted to the Catholic Church. (no. 3)

The teaching of the Catholic church is that although the Catholic church possesses and preserves the fullness (or fullest measure) of Christian truth and the means of salvation, other Christian churches and communities also possess some measure of truth and grace that can genuinely lead their members to salvation. The Decree on Ecumenism also states that the worship and liturgical actions of those Christian bodies "can truly engender a life of grace and can be rightly described as capable of providing access to the community of salvation" (no. 3).

These teachings are intended to break down the simple and incorrect dichotomy of one church being the "true church," and all others being "false" churches. Catholics believe that the Catholic church is unique not because it is the *only* true church or body of Christians but because it possesses the *fullness* of Christian truth and the means of salvation. As the Second Vatican Council taught in the Decree on Ecumenism, ". . . it is through Christ's Catholic Church alone, which is the all-embracing means of salvation, that the fullness of the means of salvation can be obtained" (no. 3). The Dogmatic Constitution on the Church made a similar statement:

> They are fully incorporated into the society of the Church who, possessing the Spirit of Christ, accept her entire system and all the means of salvation given to her, and through her visible structure are joined to Christ, Who rules her through the Supreme Pontiff and bishops. This joining is effected by the bonds of professed faith, of the sacraments, of ecclesiastical government, and of communion [fellowship]. (no. 14)

Thus, Catholics do not look upon themselves as the only Christians but as those who are "fully incorporated" into the church of Jesus Christ because the Catholic church possesses "the fullness of the means of salvation." The Dogmatic Constitution on the Church also states that the church of Jesus Christ "subsists in the Catholic Church, which is governed by the successor of Peter and by the bishops in union with that successor, although many elements of sanctification and of truth can be found outside of her visible structure" (no. 8). The Decree on Ecumenism sheds light on the meaning of the word "subsists" by stating that "the Spirit of Christ has not refrained from using them (other Christian Churches and Communities) as means of salvation which derive their efficacy from the very fullness of grace and truth entrusted to the Catholic Church" (no. 3). This implies that it is incorrect to equate the church of Jesus Christ with the Catholic church.

Although Catholics believe that their church possesses the fullness of grace, truth, and the means of salvation, many genuine elements of the church of Jesus Christ exist in other Christian churches and communities and can lead their members to salvation. In fact, as recently as 1949, the Roman Catholic church vigorously rejected the opinion supposedly expressed by an Irish Catholic priest, Fr. Leonard Feeney, in Boston, that only Catholics could be saved.[9] Thus, even before the Second Vatican Council, the Catholic church acknowledged that it did not have a monopoly on the means of salvation.

The above discussion might appear rather "triumphalistic" to Protestant and Orthodox Christians, and even to some Catholics. Is the Catholic church being proud or narrow-minded in claiming that it alone possesses the fullness of Christian truth and the means of salvation? Consider these points. First, this claim is based on an historical argument: that the Catholic church has preserved and faithfully handed on Christian truth and practice down through the centuries in spite of the personal sinfulness of its members and its corporate weaknesses and failings. Second, the same documents that make these statements readily admit that the Catholic church is not perfect but is a pilgrim people always needing to repent and to receive God's mercy and grace. Whatever goodness or truth there is residing in the Catholic church is due to God. In fact, the Dogmatic Constitution on the Church sounds a severe warning to nominal Catholics who think they will be saved simply because of their church membership. It also corrects those Catholics who boast of their church as if its merits came from its members:

> He is not saved, however, who though he is part of the body of the Church, does not persevere in charity. He remains indeed in the bosom of the Church, but, as it were, only in a "bodily" manner and not in his heart. All the sons of the [Catholic] Church should remember that their exalted

> status is to be attributed not to their own merits but to the special grace of Christ. If they fail moreover to respond to this grace in thought, word, and deed, not only will they not be saved but they will be more severely judged. (no. 14)

Protestant Christians will be encouraged to note that Catholics, too, believe that salvation is totally based on the grace of Jesus Christ. This grace must be responded to "in thought, word, and deed," through both faith (the faith that we come to know and embrace through the church) and also through love, or charity. In other words, the salvation won for us through Jesus Christ comes to us through the church because it is through the church's preaching and teaching that we receive and believe the good news of salvation. It is within the church that we learn how to love each other, as Jesus himself taught and commanded. This is why the Second Vatican Council calls the church "the all-embracing means of salvation."

A third point should be added here. Out of ecumenical sensitivity, Catholics should be aware that other Christian churches believe themselves to possess the fullness of Christian life and doctrine, such as the Orthodox churches, Full Gospel churches, and many others. Catholics believe that nothing genuinely Christian is foreign to the Catholic church, and so we should be ready to appreciate and learn from the genuinely Christian heritage and aspects of other Christian churches.

We must remember, though, that ultimately the church doesn't save us. God saves us in the person of Jesus Christ. The Catholic church provides all of the means (including the Bible) through which we can encounter Jesus and enter into his life. It is up to each person to take advantage of these means of coming to know, love, and follow Jesus. It is because the Catholic church possesses an abundant fullness of these means of salvation that those Catholics who fail to take advantage of them will be judged more severely and forfeit the eternal life that God is offering to them through their church. ". . . to whom much is given, of him will much be required. . . ." (Lk 12:48). In fact, the Second Vatican Council teaches that "whosoever, . . . knowing that the Catholic church was made necessary by God through Jesus Christ would refuse to enter her or to remain in her could not be saved" (LG, no. 14). God holds all people responsible for what they know of his truth. Those who know that God has established the Catholic church as the fullest way to eternal life must act according to that knowledge or accept the consequences of eternal death. Likewise, Catholics cannot judge or condemn those who do not recognize the Catholic church as having been established by God for their salvation. God will judge them according to how they have responded to the grace offered them and to the degree of knowledge of his truth that they have received.

FIVE

How God Reveals Himself

HOW CAN CHRISTIANS claim to know with certainty things about God and his will for the human race? Many people even question whether God exists, although the Bible and Christian tradition affirms that God's existence should be evident from observing the beauty and order of the universe—God's creation (see Ps 19:1; Rom 1:19-20). Catholic theology claims that nature or the universe reveals God's existence; we call this natural revelation.

However, natural revelation does not tell us all that we would like to know, or should know, about God. Christians believe that God offers the human race a more accurate and complete knowledge of himself and his will through what theology calls supernatural revelation. The Second Vatican Council explained this concept in the Dogmatic Constitution on Divine Revelation:

> In His goodness, God chose to reveal Himself, and to make known to us the hidden purpose of His will... Through this revelation, ... the invisible God out of the abundance of His love speaks to men as friends and lives among them, so that He may invite them and take them into fellowship with Himself. (no. 2)

This statement emphasizes that God reveals, not primarily a

set of rules or commandments, but himself and his infinite love for us. Through supernatural revelation God invites each of us into a living and personal relationship of love with our Father and creator, in order to discover the true meaning and joy of life. Not only this, but God has even demonstrated his love and shown his plan for our lives in action by coming to live among us as a man—Jesus Christ. Thus, God's revelation is personal because it comes to us through the person of Jesus. Jesus invites each person to come to know God as our Father and to live in fellowship with him. Revelation leads to life: true, abundant life in this world (Jn 10:10) and eternal life with God in the age to come.

What comprises supernatural revelation? The Second Vatican Council's Dogmatic Constitution on Divine Revelation explains that through supernatural revelation God reveals himself through both *words* and *deeds*. The faith of Christians and Jews is based on the belief that God acts in unique and specific ways in human history and that he also speaks to humanity in various ways. The Old Testament for example, recounts God's mighty act of delivering the Hebrew people from captivity in Egypt. It also testifies that God spoke to Abraham, Moses, the prophets, and other men and women of the Old Covenant through dreams, visions, voices, angelic messengers, and other means. The New Testament tells of Jesus' mighty works of healing, expelling demons, and finally redeeming the human race through his death on the cross. Christians understand these works of Jesus of Nazareth as the greatest intervention of God in human history. Further, the New Testament proclaims that God spoke to the human race in a unique and unsurpassable way through Jesus. His words and teaching present to us God's pure, perfect revelation, for "in him all the fulness of God was pleased to dwell. . . ." (Col 1:19).

The Holy Spirit Reveals God's Truth

God entered our history as a man, Jesus of Nazareth, yet, it is impossible to recognize who Jesus is without the enlightenment of the Spirit of Truth, the Holy Spirit. St. Paul, for example, wrote that "... no one can say 'Jesus is Lord' except by the Holy Spirit" (1 Cor 12:3). In St. John's Last Supper discourse, Jesus tells his apostles that it is to their advantage that he is leaving them because when he departs he will be able to send them the Holy Spirit.

> "I have yet many things to say to you, but you cannot bear them now. When the Spirit of truth comes, he will guide you into all the truth. . . ." (Jn 16:12-13)

Jesus promised to send the Holy Spirit to guide his people into all truth. In this light, we can speak of the Holy Spirit as the revealer, the faithful source of God's revelation in the church. The Gospel of John affirms that the Holy Spirit will call to mind the words and teachings of Jesus (Jn 14:26). He will "teach you in all things" (Jn 14:26) and "declare to you the things that are to come" (Jn 16:13).

The Catholic church has always emphasized that the ultimate source of revelation in the church is not a book (the Bible), nor a thing (tradition), nor even a human group or person (the magisterium or the pope), but is God himself, particularly in the person of the Holy Spirit. The Holy Spirit certainly reveals God's truth through the channels just mentioned, but it is the Spirit who guides the church through these channels into the fullness of truth.

Public Revelation: the Foundation of Christian Truth

How does the Holy Spirit reveal the truth to God's people? A primary work of the Spirit is to testify to Jesus Christ, who is the climax of God's revelation of himself to mankind. Jesus is "the way, and the truth, and the life" (Jn 14:6); the fullness of human life in this age, and eternal life in the age to come, is received only through Jesus. The Catholic church recognizes that the lifetime of Jesus and of his apostles was a privileged time of God's foundational revelation, which is sometimes called the period of public revelation. God has revealed himself in an unsurpassed way in Jesus and through the teaching of his apostles. Hence, the Second Vatican Council proclaims in the Dogmatic Constitution on Divine Revelation that "we now await no further new public revelation before the glorious manifestation of our Lord, Jesus Christ (cf. 1 Tm 6:14 and Ti 2:13)" (no. 4). This means that God will send no new savior to mankind, nor will there be any further revelation of God bearing the same authority or significance as his revelation in and through Jesus Christ.[1] As St. Paul warned, "But even if we, or an angel from heaven, should preach to you a gospel contrary to that which we preached to you, let him be accursed" (Gal 1:8). No other revelation is valid if it contradicts the good news received through the apostles and in the traditions that they have passed on. St. Paul exhorted the Thessalonians, "stand firm and hold to the traditions which you were taught by us, either by word of mouth or by letter" (2 Thes 2:15).

God's Word in Sacred Tradition

The Catholic church teaches that the normative revelation of God, for all times and situations, comes to us from the Holy Spirit through two channels: sacred Scripture and sacred tradition. The Second Vatican Council's Dogmatic Constitution on Divine Revelation explains that "Sacred tradition and sacred Scripture form one sacred deposit of the word of God, which is committed to the church" (no. 10). The phrase "the word of God" is used by many Christians to refer only to the Bible, but Catholics understand that both the Bible and sacred tradition are God's revealed word:

> . . . For both of them, flowing from the same divine wellspring, in a certain way merge into a unity and tend toward the same end. For sacred Scripture is the word of God inasmuch as it is consigned to writing under the

> inspiration of the divine Spirit. To the successors of the apostles, sacred tradition hands on in its full purity of God's word which was entrusted to the apostles by Christ the Lord and the Holy Spirit. . . ." (DV, no. 9)

It is simpler to think of the entirety of God's word as a neatly bound book—the Bible. However many aspects of Christian life, worship, and belief coming from the time of the apostles were not written in the Bible. They were handed on (which is the literal meaning of "tradition") by the apostles and their successors as essential parts of the life of God's New Covenant people, the church. As the Second Vatican Council states:

> . . . the apostles, handing on what they themselves had received, warn the faithful to hold fast to the traditions which they have learned either by word or mouth or by letter (cf. 2 Thes 2:15), and to fight in defense of the faith handed on once and for all (cf. Jude 3). Now what was handed on by the apostles includes everything which contributes to the holiness of life, and the increase in faith of the People of God; and so the Church, in her teaching, life, and worship, perpetuates and hands on to all generations all that she herself is, and all that she believes. (DV, no. 8)

For the sake of clarity, the Second Vatican Council distinguishes sacred tradition from the Bible or sacred Scripture, even though the New Testament itself is a compilation of primitive Christian tradition about Jesus, and his teaching. Sacred tradition, sometimes called apostolic tradition or the Tradition, includes every aspect of God's revelation outside of the Bible that God intends to be believed and followed by the whole church in every age: "all that she herself is, and all that she believes." Some aspects of sacred tradition pass on to us the fullest way to worship God in the church, or the proper way to honor the angels and the saints, including Mary, the Mother of God. Other aspects of sacred tradition present God's will about how we are to live (the moral life), which is not always explicitly or fully spelled out in the Bible. Part of the role of sacred tradition is to safeguard the true meaning of the sacred Scripture by presenting the church's authoritative interpretation of certain passages of the Bible.

Some Christians mistakenly think that Catholics are diminishing the importance of the Bible by also following sacred tradition. To the contrary, Catholics express their great respect for the Bible by acknowledging that we often must rely on sacred tradition to preserve the true meaning of the Bible. No element of sacred tradition can contradict the teaching of the Bible since both are expressions of the one truth of God. However, sacred tradition sometimes enables us to interpret certain passages of the Bible correctly (especially those which may appear contradictory). The Holy Spirit also uses sacred tradition to present the church with a fuller and deeper understanding of sacred Scripture. Certain themes which are only mentioned or implied in the Bible often are presented in greater fullness and depth through sacred tradition. An example of this is the Catholic beliefs about Mary's Immaculate Conception and Assumption into heaven, which are not explicitly stated in the Bible but which flow out of and deepen the biblical teaching about Mary. Nowhere does the Bible teach that the Scripture *alone* is inspired by God. Concerning sacred tradition and its place in the church, the Second Vatican Council teaches in the Dogmatic Constitution on Divine Revelation:

> This tradition which comes from the apostles develops in the Church with the help of the Holy Spirit. For there is a growth in the understanding of the realities and the words which have been handed down. This happens through the contemplation and study made by believers, who treasure these things in their hearts (cf. Lk 2:19, 51), through the intimate understanding of spiritual things they experience, and through the preaching of those who have received

> through episcopal succession the sure gift of truth. For, as the centuries succeed one another, the Church constantly moves forward toward the fullness of divine truth until the words of God reach their complete fulfillment in her. (no. 8)

Even though the church received its foundational "public revelation" during the lifetime of Jesus and his apostles, the Holy Spirit is active in the church, as Jesus promised, to provide us with an even fuller and more complete understanding of God's truth. It is through sacred tradition that God accomplishes this. It is important to note that not every tradition that develops within the church is part of the divine revelation that Catholics refer to as sacred tradition or Tradition. There are many human traditions that are part of the church's life that are subject to change. Such traditions may either be merely human customs, or they may be part of God's will and intention for the church for a particular situation or period of time in the life of God's people, but not for all time and every situation. It is important to distinguish between the two. It is the bishops of the church (the *magisterium,* or leading office, of the church) who have the responsibility and gift (charism) to discern the difference between authentic sacred tradition and other traditions, and to faithfully preserve, interpret, and proclaim God's revelation as it comes to us from the Holy Spirit through both sacred Scripture and tradition.

A final question often asked is where the sacred tradition of the church may be found. There is no single volume that contains all of what the Catholic church considers sacred tradition, since this tradition includes much of the life of God's people, such as ways of worship, devotion, moral teaching and wisdom, and the interpretation and practical application of the Bible. There are books that summarize the official teachings of ecumenical councils and popes of the Catholic church. These represent a large portion of sacred tradition, where formal definitions of Catholic belief and practice have been made by the magisterium (teaching office) of the Catholic church over many centuries. However, sacred tradition also includes many things that have been consistently taught by the Fathers, Doctors, and saints of the church which have never been formally defined by the magisterium, such as by an ecumenical council or a papal decree. Many Catholic beliefs in the area of Christian living and morality fall into this category, such as the rejection of homosexual practice, abortion, euthanasia, and infanticide (see GS, no. 27). Catholics should be eager to grow in their understanding of the revelation of God to the church through sacred tradition, which along with the sacred Scripture is the primary way that God's truth comes to us to guide and encourage us in our Christian lives. Let us now examine more fully how God addresses us through his written word, the Bible.

God's Revelation in Scripture

Each Christian should at times ask the questions, "Where do my beliefs come from?" and "How did I receive them?" Many of the essential teachings and traditions about Jesus in the primitive church were eventually written down. The basic written compilation of Christian belief is the record of God's works and teachings found in the Bible, the sacred Scripture of Christianity. The Bible includes both the record of God's revelation to the Hebrew people under the Old Covenant, known as the Hebrew Scripture or the Old Testament, and also the record of revelation under the New Covenant established by Jesus Christ, known as the New Testament. The Second Vatican Council strongly affirmed that the Bible is rightly called the word of God because its composition is inspired by the Holy Spirit, the Third Person of God: "For sacred Scripture is the word of God inasmuch as it is consigned to writing under the inspiration of the divine Spirit" (DV, no. 9). The Council explained that ". . . the sacred Scriptures contain the word of God and, since they are inspired, really are the word of God" (DV, no. 24). Even the Bible itself attests to its divine origin. St. Paul wrote to Timothy concerning the Bible of his day, the Hebrew Scriptures: "All scripture is inspired by God [literally "God-breathed"] and profitable for teaching, for reproof, for correction, and for training in righteousness, that the man of God may be complete, equipped for every good work" (2 Tm 3:16, 17).

The Value of the Old Testament

As we saw in Chapter Two, Christians accept the Hebrew Scriptures, or Old Testament, as inspired by God and thus important for instruction and guidance. However, there is a potential misunderstanding (held, for example, by Marcion in the second century A.D.) which sees the Old Testament as unimportant or dispensable because it has been surpassed by the New Testament, God's revelation of himself in Jesus Christ.

The Catholic church has always valued and urged the study of the Old Testament, even though some elements of it (such as dietary laws and other ritual observances) have been surpassed or rendered unnecessary, based on Jesus' teaching and example. The Second Vatican Council affirms St. Augustine's saying that the New Testament is hidden in the Old, and the Old is made manifest in the New (DV, no. 16). Father Avery Dulles, S.J., warned against the danger of considering the Old Testament to be valuable *only* as a foreshadowing of the New Testament, instead of having value in itself. Father Dulles writes:

> It would be wrong to imagine that the Old Testament has a merely provisional value, and that everything in the Old Testament is better, more clearly, and more completely stated in the New. If that were the case, the Church could altogether dispense with the Old Testament, but of course it cannot. The *Constitution on Divine Revelation* affirms the abiding value of the Old Testament, and quite rightly, for on many points it remains unsurpassed, for example, in the sublime instructions of the prophets about God and in the

> models of human prayer afforded by the Psalms (cf. *Dei Verbum*, no. 15). As article 16 of the *Constitution on Revelation* points out, the two Testaments shed light upon each other. In Christian eyes the Old Testament, no doubt, needs completion by the New, but the New Testament cannot be correctly interpreted except in the light of the Old. We cannot rightly understand Jesus unless we meditate on Old Testament categories such as Son of Man and Son of God, nor can we rightly understand the God of Jesus Christ unless we recognize Him as the God of Abraham, Isaac, and Jacob. Many things which lie hidden in the New Testament become evident only when we ponder the Hebrew Bible.[2]

It is important, then, for Catholics to study the Hebrew Scripture in order to fully and properly understand the New Testament, and to receive the Old Testament's own unique and valuable divine teaching.

An unfortunate result of the rift between Catholics and Protestants is the disagreement over the canon (official list of inspired writings) of the Old Testament. Catholics recognize as divinely inspired the writings included in the ancient Greek version of the Hebrew Scriptures that was used in the early church, known as the Septuagint. Protestants accept only the writings found in an early Hebrew version of the Bible, which did not include the books of Tobit, Judith, Wisdom, Ecclesiasticus, Baruch, 1 and 2 Maccabees. Protestants usually call these books the Apocrypha. Many Protestants read and respect these writings, although they do not consider them divinely inspired. Catholics often refer to these books as deutero-canonical (a second canon) because they have been disputed. Even so, Catholics accept them as divinely inspired works that are fully part of the canon of the Old Testament.

The Origins of the New Testament

The forty-six writings that Catholics recognize as the Old Testament were written, edited, and handed down over a period of many centuries. The twenty-seven writings that both Catholics and Protestants accept as the canon[3] of the New Testament took relatively less time to advance from their initial form to their general recognition by the church as a set of inspired writings—only about three hundred years!

How did the New Testament, our primary witness to Jesus and his message, come into being? For the first two or three centuries of Christianity, Christians had no New Testament that they could open and read with the confidence that everything written there was divinely inspired truth. Instead, letters from the apostles and other followers of Jesus were circulated among the local churches, and various traditions (literally "things passed on") about Jesus were either retold as stories or in preaching, or were eventually written down in bits and pieces. Beginning twenty or thirty years after Jesus' death and resurrection, some men, including the four evangelists, began to compile these traditions about Jesus and to write unified accounts of Jesus' life and ministry, known as the Gospels. One of these evangelists, St. Luke, describes his task in the introduction to his Gospel:

> Inasmuch as many have undertaken to compile a narrative of the things which have been accomplished among us, just as they were delivered to us by those who from the beginning were eyewitnesses and ministers of the word, it seemed good to me also, having followed all things closely for some time past, to write an orderly account for you, most excellent Theophilus, that you may know the truth concerning the things of which you have been informed. (Lk 1:1-4)

However, besides the four Gospels that Christians recognize today, there were a number of other gospels (accounts of Jesus' life and ministry) circulating among the early Christian churches. Not all of these gospels were in agreement on certain points, and some accounts (such as the Gospel of Thomas and others) appeared to many Christians to be evidently unreliable or untrue. Also, Christians wondered whether the various letters of the apostles and other writings being passed around were all to be considered as totally true and genuinely inspired by God. There was no New Testament to refer to as a measure of truth—only the traditions about Jesus and his teaching that were being circulated by word of mouth or by letter.[4]

The question that the early Christians faced was, *Who* is to decide which teachings and writings about Jesus, which traditions, are true and to be believed without doubt? The answer they found, based on Jesus' promise, was that the Holy Spirit would guide the church to recognize the teachings and writings that he had inspired. The Holy Spirit did this particularly through the chief elders of the church, the bishops. In caring for the flock of Christ, one of the bishops' tasks was to insure that correct doctrine was taught. Along with the rest of the church, the bishops needed to discern which writings and teachings that were being widely distributed were truly God's word for the whole church and which were not.[5]

By the fifth century, the bishops of the church reached a general agreement about which letters and gospels were truly inspired by God, even though the status of some writings were still disputed after this time. Thus was the New Testament "born," substantially the same as we know it today.[6] This is why Catholics regard the Bible as the book of the church—because it came into being as a product of the tradition of the church and through the judgment and discernment of the church, led by the church's bishops. Catholics believe that the bishops continue their role of authentically proclaiming and interpreting the Bible through the guidance of the Holy Spirit.[7] As different letters and gospels that claimed to have apostolic origins were read within the early Christian churches, the bishops of these churches prayerfully discerned their authenticity, and oftentimes discussed this subject with other bishops in the region. Over time, the bishops increasingly agreed upon which letters and gospels were truly in harmony with the traditions they had received from the apostles.

The Meaning of Inspiration

What does it mean that the Bible, or a particular book of the Bible, is inspired by God? To say that a writing is inspired means that God is, in some way, its author. The Dogmatic Constitution on Divine Revelation of Vatican II affirms this when it states:

> ... the books of the Old and New Testament, whole and entire, with all their parts (were) written under the inspiration of the Holy Spirit, and as such they have God as their author and have been handed on to the Church itself. (no. 11)

To say that the Bible has God as its author emphasizes that it is the word of God and that it is a gift to the church, God's people. As one Catholic theologian described this:

> Although the writers of the Old and New Testament belonged to a believing community of faith, and gave expression to the faith of their community, they did so by a special grace or charism, known as inspiration. In some cases the inspiration of the biblical writer coincided with the gift of prophecy [Isaiah, the seer of the Apocalypse], in some cases with apostleship [Paul], in some cases with gifts of wisdom [the sapiential literature] or poetic creation [Psalms]. In other instances inspiration took the form of an impulse and endowment for composing sacred history [Kings and Luke]. Biblical inspiration, therefore, is a term that covers a variety of charisms, the common characteristic of which is the efficacious divine assistance to express in its purity the faith of the people of God in their formative

> period, in such a way as to serve as a norm for the church in later ages.[8]

The Catholic understanding of inspiration also has another dimension, however. The human persons who wrote the sacred Scriptures were not just passive recipients of God's word who merely served as secretaries for what God was dictating. Rather, the Dogmatic Constitution on Divine Revelation says that God "made use of their powers and abilities" and calls them "true authors," even though they "consigned to writing everything and only those things which He wanted" (no. 11). Thus, the author of the Bible is both God and man.

This Catholic view of inspiration has far-reaching implications. One of the most important implications is that in the interpretation of the Bible, the human dimension of the text needs to be taken into account if it is to be correctly understood. The Dogmatic Constitution on Divine Revelation says:

> Seeing that, in sacred Scripture, God speaks through men in human fashion, it follows that the interpreter of sacred Scriptures, if he is to ascertain what God has wished to communicate to us, should carefully search out the meaning which the sacred writers had in mind, that meaning that God had thought well to manifest through the medium of their words . . . rightly to understand what the sacred author wanted to affirm in his work, due attention must be paid both to the customary and characteristic patterns of perception, speech and narrative which prevailed at the age of the sacred writer, and to the conventions which the people of his time followed in their dealings with one another . . . Indeed the words of God, expressed in the words of men, are in every way like human language, just as the Word of the eternal Father, when He took on Himself the flesh of human weakness, became like men. (nos. 12, 13)

The sacred Scripture may rightly be called "the word of God in the words of men," just as Jesus was the divine Word of God who nonetheless possessed the form and nature of a normal human person.

A recent result of this insight is that beginning with the encyclical letter of Pope Pius XII in 1943 (*Divino Afflante Spiritu*), the Catholic church has given positive encouragement to biblical scholars to employ modern methods of biblical criticism in order to understand more fully the human dimension of the Bible and its composition. Paragraph 12 of the Dogmatic Constitution on Divine Revelation (echoing paragraph 23 of *Divino Afflante Spiritu*) strongly urges biblical scholars to seek out what the authors of Scripture really meant and intended when they wrote. Scholars determine what literary forms they used, their customary and characteristic styles of perception, speech and narrative, and the conventions that prevailed in the biblical authors' world. The importance of this is that the meaning of the word of God sometimes can be understood fully or correctly only when the historical situation and the literary style of the human author of Scripture is understood properly.

On the other hand, this section in the Constitution on Divine Revelation is immediately followed by an implicit warning that the findings of biblical scholars, using the so-called historico-critical method or any other modern scientific approach to Scripture, is not enough in itself to determine the authentic meaning of God's word. The Constitution also insists that the ". . . Holy Scripture must be read and interpreted according to the same Spirit by whom it was written" (DV, no. 12). The Bible must be approached with faith and prayer if it is to be correctly understood. Also, the meaning of the sacred text, and consequently the meaning of an individual section of Scripture, must be seen in light of "the content and unity of the whole of Scripture" (DV, no. 12). Individual passages cannot be isolated from the overall message of Scripture if they are to be interpreted correctly. Likewise "the living tradition of the whole Church must be taken into account along with the harmony which exists between elements of the faith" (DV, no. 12).

To insure that the tradition of the Catholic church would be taken into account in interpreting the Bible, Pope Pius XII strongly urged Scripture scholars to study assiduously the Fathers and Doctors of the church and renowned interpreters of past ages.[9] The 1985 Extraordinary Synod of Catholic Bishops affirmed that "the exegesis of the original meaning of Sacred Scripture, most highly recommended by the Council (cf. *Dei Verbum*, no. 12) cannot be separated from the living tradition of the Church (*Dei Verbum*, no. 10)."[10] All this is simply to recognize that modern approaches to biblical study, as valuable as their findings may be, are not adequate by themselves to elucidate the full meaning of the Bible. In order that these newer approaches to biblical study fulfill their constructive role of illuminating the true meaning of the sacred Scripture and of building up the faith and life of God's people, they must be carried out in the context of faith, prayer, appreciation of the biblical interpretation of the great Catholic scholars and saints of the past, and, finally, obedience to the teaching office of the church "which carries out the divine commission and ministry of guarding and interpreting the word of God" (DV, no. 12).

The Inerrancy of Scripture

Biblical inspiration means that God has spoken his word to humanity through the medium of human authors. Even though fallible human authors are involved in the composition of the Bible, the Catholic church has continually insisted that there is a sense in which the sacred Scripture is without error.[11] The Second Vatican Council states that, "the books of Scripture must be acknowledged as teaching firmly, faithfully, and without error that truth which God wanted put into the sacred writings for the sake of our salvation" (DV, no. 11).

What does it mean to say that the Bible is inerrant or without error? There are different understandings of the inerrancy of the Bible among Christians. Some Christians generally believe that everything stated by the Bible is literally true and that this truth is usually readily understandable to the modern reader without the use of modern methods of biblical scholarship. On the whole, this literalist approach finds little in sacred Scripture that is obscure if sufficient reflection, prayer, and careful study of the entire Bible is undertaken by the reader. In general, the Bible is thought to mean what it says.

The Catholic understanding of the inerrancy of the Bible has developed in the past one hundred years, with the growing recognition of the value of modern methods of biblical study and their results. Specifically, the Catholic church has recognized that we cannot define how the Bible is inerrant without first determining what truth the biblical authors and editors wished to convey. In doing this, we may discern the truth that God wished to convey through these authors and their writings. For example, if the authors of the Gospels had no particular interest in conveying a perfectly accurate chronology of the events of Jesus' life, then we should not be surprised if the four Gospels present different (and sometimes conflicting) reports of when and where things happened in Jesus' public ministry and after his resurrection. The Gospel authors may have had little interest in absolute accuracy in historical details or in their recording of the order and location of particular events in Jesus' life.[12]

The same questions may be asked of the Old Testament. What truth did the authors and editors of the various Old Testament writings wish to convey? What did God wish to communicate to us? When the Book of Genesis says, in one account, that the world was created by God in seven days and in a particular way, is this account to be read primarily as an historical and scientific report of creation? Or did God (and the biblical author) wish to convey more important truths to us, on a different plane entirely, using symbols and language meaningful to those living at the time of the book's composition? The Old Testament itself indicates that historical accuracy was not the highest priority. Occasionally, conflicting reports of the same event are both included in the Old Testament (often in the same writing), such as the order of creation in Genesis 1:1-31 and 2:5, and the way God parted the Red Sea in Exodus 14:21-27. Sometimes the Old Testament places two historically conflicting accounts side-by-side, which should indicate to the reader that the historical facts involved really are not the most important thing that God is saying through the accounts.

The Catholic Understanding of Biblical Inerrancy

The challenge, then, is to define more clearly in what respect the Bible is without error. With the emergence of modern methods of biblical scholarship, especially over the past hundred years, the Catholic church has made a number of formal statements on this subject.[13] At present, the development of official Catholic teaching on this subject is best summarized in the Dogmatic Constitution on Divine Revelation which states "that the books of Scripture must be acknowledged as teaching firmly, faithfully, and without error that truth which God wanted put into the sacred writings for the sake of our salvation" (no. 11). The phrase, "for the sake of our salvation," is essential to understand this correctly. The official footnote to this passage in the Vatican II document refers to a statement of St. Thomas Aquinas:

> Any knowledge which is profitable to salvation may be the object of prophetic inspiration. But things which cannot affect our salvation do not belong to inspiration. ("On Truth," Q 12, A2, C)

As an example of this principle, St. Augustine "says that although the sacred writers may have known astronomy,

> nevertheless the Holy Spirit did not intend to utter through them any truth apart from that which is profitable to salvation. He adds that this may concern either teachings to be believed or morals to be practiced."[14]

In commenting on this, Fr. R.A.F. Mackenzie says,

> The Bible was not written in order to teach the natural sciences, nor to give information on merely political history. It treats of these [and all other subjects] only insofar as they are involved in matters concerning salvation. It is only in this respect that the veracity of God and the inerrancy of the inspired writers are engaged.[15]

The Catholic church has learned this principle from long reflection and experience. At the time of the emergence of modern astronomy, for example, the Catholic church mistakenly condemned the scientific teaching of Galileo Galilei that the sun, not the earth, was the center of the solar system. Galileo's theory appeared to contradict the Bible's teaching on this point. Since then, modern science has blossomed with the encouragement and support of the Catholic church, and a clearer understanding of the inter-relationship of science, history, and Christian faith has developed. Recognizing the legitimate autonomy of the human sciences, the Catholic church today holds that the inerrancy of the Bible (and the teaching authority of the church) applies to science or history only where matters pertaining to salvation, faith in God, or morality are involved. God has inspired the sacred Scriptures primarily to reveal himself, and his plan for all his creation in relationship to himself. The Bible infallibly reveals how we are to relate to God and to each other in this world in order to fulfill God's plan and attain eternal salvation. The Bible is absolutely without error when it speaks of these things. There may be other truths contained in the Bible, but the Catholic church believes that only these are without error as a result of God's inspiration of the sacred Scripture.

Interpretation of the Bible

Even in matters regarding salvation, faith, and morality, it is true that the meaning of very few passages of the Bible have been officially defined by the Catholic church. This leaves room for the contributions of saints, biblical scholars, and others who prayerfully reflect on the meaning of the Scriptures. Pope Pius XII taught in his encyclical letter *Divino Afflante Spiritu* in 1943, that

> . . . in questions of doctrine regarding faith and morals, and . . . in the immense matter contained in the Sacred Books—legislative, historical, sapiential and prophetical—there are but few texts whose sense have been defined by the authority of the Church, nor are those more numerous about which the teaching of the Holy Fathers is unanimous. There remains, therefore, many things, and of the greatest importance, in the discussion and exposition of which the skill and genius of Catholic commentators may and ought to be freely exercised, so that each may contribute his part to the advantage of all, to the continued progress of the sacred doctrine and to the defense and honor of the Church. (no. 47)

While the Catholic church has encouraged those who seek out the true meaning of God's word in the sacred Scripture, it has also issued some necessary warnings and cautions. Pius XII's encyclical letter *Humani Generis* (1950) warned against relying on human reason alone in interpreting the Bible and stressed that we need to consider "the analogy of faith and the Tradition of the Church."[16] The destructive effect of rationalism in interpreting the Bible cannot be underestimated. The Instruction of the Pontifical Biblical Commission of April 21, 1964, warned that some biblical scholars,

> . . . motivated by rationalistic prejudices, refuse to recognize the existence of a supernatural order. They deny the

> intervention of a personal God in the world by means of Revelation in the strict sense, and reject the possibility or actual occurrence of miracles and prophecies. Some start out with an erroneous concept of faith, regarding faith as indifferent to, or even incompatible with, historical truth. Some deny, *a priori* as it were, the historical nature and historical value of the documents of Revelation. And finally, some minimize the authority of the Apostles as witnesses to Christ. Belittling their office and their influence in the primitive community, these people exaggerate the creative power of the community itself. . . .
>
> All these opinions are not only contrary to Catholic doctrine, but also devoid of scholarly foundation and inconsistent with the sound principles of the historical method.[17]

This same Commission, in 1950, said that in determining the meaning of a particular text of Scripture, the scholar "ought to search out accurately what sacred Scripture teaches in other similar passages, and what the explanation of the text is in the Holy Fathers and in the Catholic tradition and finally, if the case warrants it, what the teaching authority of the Church has decided about the text in question."[18] The Instruction of April 21, 1964, agrees:

> The Catholic exegete, under the guidance of the Church, should take advantage of all the contributions made by earlier commentators, by the Fathers and Doctors of the Church, and carry on their work. (I, General Guidelines for the Exegete).

The Catholic who wishes to learn more about the meaning of the Bible should seek out books and authors that utilize the best in modern biblical scholarship along with the Fathers and Doctors of the church, in the framework of loyalty to the

Catholic church's teaching office in case of any disputed interpretation (see DV, no. 12).

Safeguarding Authentic Biblical Interpretation

The Catholic church teaches that God guides the bishops of the church in discerning the true meaning of the Scriptures and that they cannot teach error whenever they meet together in an ecumenical or worldwide council and officially interpret a disputed passage of Scripture; or when they universally agree, even without formally meeting, on the meaning of a particular biblical text or condemn an erroneous interpretation. Catholics also believe that the pope, by virtue of his office of chief teacher in the church, possesses a special gift of God enabling him to proclaim and interpret the Scripture correctly. While only his formal definitions on matters of faith and morals are considered by Catholics to be infallibly true, even the pope's ordinary magisterium, or teaching, on the Bible is to be respected and followed by Catholics, on the assumption that it, too, is true and helpful in living the Christian life more fully and faithfully.

The Bible, Tradition, and the Church's Teaching Office

Catholic Christians today believe that their understanding of the relationship between the Bible, tradition, and church authority is the same as that which developed in the early church. This teaching is expressed fully and clearly in the Dogmatic Constitution on Divine Revelation of the Second Vatican Council, especially in chapter two of that document, "The Transmission on Divine Revelation." The following is the conclusion of chapter two of this Dogmatic Constitution:

> Sacred scripture is the word of God as it is put down in writing under the inspiration of the Holy Spirit. And tradition transmits in its entirety the word of God which has

been entrusted to the apostles by Christ the Lord and the Holy Spirit. It transmits it to the successors of the apostles so that they may faithfully preserve this word of God, explain it, and make it more widely known. . . .

The task of authentically interpreting the word of God, whether in its written form or in the form of tradition, has been entrusted exclusively to the living teaching office of the church, whose authority is exercised in the name of Jesus Christ. This teaching office is not above the word of God, but serves it, teaching only what has been handed on; listening to it devoutly, guarding it scrupulously, and explaining it faithfully by divine commission and with the help of the Holy Spirit: it draws from this deposit of faith everything which it presents for belief as divinely revealed.

It is clear, therefore, that sacred tradition, sacred scripture, and the teaching authority of the church, in accord with God's most wise design, are so linked and joined together that one cannot stand without others, and that all together and each in its own way under the action of the Holy Spirit contribute effectively to the salvation of souls. (nos. 9, 10)

I envision sacred Scripture, tradition, and the teaching authority of the church as three legs of a tripod. They are mutually dependent and support each other. If one leg of the tripod falls, the whole structure collapses. Remove sacred Scripture, and the tradition and the church's teaching office have no firm basis. Remove tradition, and the way Scripture has been understood and interpreted over the centuries by the church disappears and is lost leaving us to interpret Scripture according to societal or personal biases. Remove the church's teaching authority, and there is no united way that either sacred Scripture or Christian tradition can be authoritatively interpreted and applied to practical situations in the present.

Confusion and disunity is the result. But God, in his goodness, has provided not only the revelation of himself and his plan in the Bible but also the means by which revelation is to be faithfully preserved and passed on, fully understood and authentically interpreted from the time of Christ down to the present day. Catholics are not only grateful to God for the Bible but also for sacred tradition and the church's teaching authority by which the fullness of God's truth is safeguarded and brought forth in the unity of the Catholic church.

Private Revelation and its Forms

Earlier in the chapter we noted that there is "no new public revelation" after the time of Jesus and his apostles. However, this does not mean that God has ceased speaking or revealing himself to the human race. The Holy Spirit provides ongoing revelation and guidance to God's people through various means, building upon the foundational revelation that God has given in Jesus.

One form of the Holy Spirit's ongoing activity in the church is termed private revelation. There are certain truths that God reveals through the Holy Spirit that either are not intended for the entire church or are not intended to be truths relevant for all times in the church's life. These are truths either directed toward a particular individual or group within the church or intended for a particular time or period in human history.

Private revelation includes such things as words spoken through the gift of prophecy; messages from God spoken to an individual or a group through angels, saints, or Mary, the Mother of God; visions, dreams, or voices that present a word from God to a person or persons; or even a word or appearance of God himself. The Catholic church insists that such private revelations must be discerned or tested carefully to insure that they are truly from God, lest some people be deceived. One important test is that no private revelation can contradict or disagree with public revelation, what God has revealed through the Bible or authentic Christian tradition. Genuine private revelation always complements and supports God's public revelation to his people. Even when the church, after discernment, finds no objection to a private revelation, the Catholic church does not require any of its members to believe in it or its message since it is not part of the foundational public revelation of God. However, God often has an important purpose in presenting a special private revelation, such as to awaken the church to a part of public revelation that he desires his people to pray and act upon or to call attention to his work and plan during a particular time in human history.

A good example of the Catholic church's painstaking discernment of private revelation is its approach to the many reported appearances of Mary, the Mother of God. Some reported apparitions of Mary investigated by the Catholic church have been judged to be false. Others, such as appearances of Mary at Guadalupe (Mexico), Lourdes (France), and Fatima (Portugal) have received widespread approval in the Catholic world, and some popes even have made pilgrimages to these sites. Nonetheless, no Catholic is required to believe that Mary has appeared and spoken a word from God because these apparitions still remain in the realm of private revelation. However, if it is possible that God is speaking prophetically or sending messengers, such as Christ's Mother, to speak special words from him for our time, it would be wise for Catholics to be attentive and to consider them prayerfully. Authentic private revelation, like public revelation, is a gift of God and should be received with thanksgiving.

God not only continues to speak to his people but also continues to reveal himself and his presence by performing mighty acts among his people. Miracles, healings, exorcisms, and other mighty works are done in the name of Jesus and by his power. This should not surprise us, for Jesus told his followers that they would perform even greater works than his (see Jn 14:12). Christians should rejoice and be grateful that God has not chosen to remain hidden but that he has made himself known to us in both his words and deeds, in the past and today.

Immersing Ourselves in God's Revelation

God has shown an incredible love by revealing himself to us in the Bible, in the authentic Christian tradition, through the teaching authority of the church, and even in special private revelation. One way that we can respond to God's love is to desire to know God through his revelation—to become immersed in it.

In an audience on April 8, 1986, Pope John Paul II emphasized the importance of "a reverential love for the word of God, for the Incarnate Word, our Lord Jesus Christ, and for the inspired word contained in the Sacred Scriptures." He went on to urge that

> ... priests, deacons, catechists and other lay people—should be *immersed in the Scriptures* through constant reading and diligent study, accompanied by prayer. As far as possible, they should be acquainted with the insights of modern biblical scholarship. Attention must be given to the literary forms of the various biblical books in order to determine the intention of the sacred writers. And it is most helpful, at times, crucial, to be aware of the personal situation of the biblical writer, to the circumstances of culture, time, language and so forth which influenced the way the message was presented.
>
> At the same time, an adequate formation for the biblical apostolate directs attention to the unity of all the books of the Bible and takes into account the *living Tradition of the Church.* In this way, it is possible to avoid a narrow fundamentalism which distorts the whole truth, and also possible to resist the temptation to place one's personal interpretation above or even in opposition to the authentic

> interpretation of God's word which belongs exclusively to the bishops of the Church in union with the Pope.[19]

How can Catholics better come to know God and his revealed truth?

1. Reading and studying the Bible. The primary way that Catholics should come to know God's revealed truth is through reading the Bible daily. Even though the Bible is not the *only* source of God's revelation, it is a *primary* source that is normally accessible to every believer (2 Tm 3:16, 17).

Some Catholics (and other Christians) may ask whether the Catholic church has ever prohibited its members from reading the Bible. Because the meaning of the Bible was being disputed, and misinterpreted by some, at the time of the Protestant Reformation, Pope Pius IV declared in 1564, that lay Catholics had to obtain permission from their bishop to read the Bible in their native language—the vernacular. Reading the official Catholic Bible of the time, the Latin Vulgate, was never prohibited. Later, Catholics had to obtain permission from the Sacred Congregation of the Index in Rome, or from the pope himself, in order to read the Bible in the vernacular. This was done to protect Catholics from inaccurate translations and from misinterpreting the Bible. Catholics still heard the Scriptures proclaimed and explained at Mass and in other contexts by the clergy, as they always had.

In the nineteenth century, the Catholic hierarchy lifted all restrictions on reading the Bible in the vernacular as long as a Catholic edition was used. In 1896, Pope Leo XIII encouraged Bible reading among Catholics by granting a plenary indulgence to all Catholics who read Scripture fifteen minutes a day.[20]

Today, the Second Vatican Council has taught:

> Easy access to Sacred Scripture should be provided for all the Christian faithful. . . . This sacred Synod earnestly and specifically urges all the Christian faithful . . . to learn by

> frequent reading of the divine Scriptures of the "excelling knowledge of Jesus Christ" [Phil 3:8]. "For ignorance of the Scriptures is ignorance of Christ" [St. Jerome]. Therefore, they should gladly put themselves in touch with the sacred text itself, whether it be through the liturgy . . . through devotional reading, or through instructions suitable for the purpose and other aids . . . And let them remember that prayer should accompany the reading of Sacred Scripture, so that God and man may talk together; for "we speak to Him when we pray; we hear Him when we read the divine sayings" [St. Ambrose]. (DV, nos. 22, 25)

2. *Studying teachings of past councils and popes.* God's revelation of himself also includes his truth passed on in the authentic tradition of the Catholic church. This tradition may be found in the decisions and declarations of the ecumenical councils of the church, and in the teachings of past popes. All Catholics today should become familiar with the teachings of the Second Vatican Council by reading the sixteen documents of the Council since this council presents the tradition of the Catholic church and God's revelation of himself directed specifically to us who live at this era of history. Through reading and studying the documents of councils of the church and past popes, we become familiar with the rich tradition and life of the Catholic church.

3. *Hearing the teaching of our present pope and bishops.* Finally, we encounter God's revelation of himself and his will through keeping in touch with the teachings and statements of the living magisterium or teaching office of the church—our present pope and bishops. We can do this by reading publications containing their official teachings, including the publications of national Catholic publication offices and magazines and newspapers containing current teachings of the popes and bishops. Nevertheless, it should be noted that there are different levels of authority among the teachings of the pope and bishops of which the reader should be aware. Some

teaching contains specific directives in the area of faith and morals that are binding on the conscience of Catholics. Other teachings, such as general political or economic reflections, do not have the same authority but are to be respectfully received and considered by Catholics. The reading of these teachings of whatever level of authority will enable Catholics to be informed about God's current direction and guidance of the Catholic church through those who have been set apart to carry on the apostles' task of faithfully preaching and teaching the word of God.

SIX

The Sacraments

HOW DO CATHOLICS APPROACH God in worship? Do Catholics view God as the mighty, transcendent, wholly other God who is so majestic that he is unapproachable? Or is God, for Catholics, like an intimate friend, who is familiar, close to us?

The prayers of Catholics should provide a clue to answering this question. Are Catholics' prayers to God formal and dignified, reverent even in style? Or are they informal, spontaneous, and from the heart?

A study of Catholic worship would reveal that both of these contrasting approaches are part of how Catholics view God, and speak to him. This is because they reflect two basic truths about God himself.

God is mighty, transcendent, and awesome. "For as the heavens are higher than the earth, / so are my ways higher than your ways / and my thoughts than your thoughts" (Is 55:9). God holds the entire universe in existence at each moment, and he knows each detail of it. Human language utterly fails in expressing the power and grandeur of God. Holy, which means "set apart," is the best word we can use to summarize who God is. God is set apart from all he has created, for he is not a creature, but the Creator of all. The prophet Isaiah had a vision of the seraphim singing before the mighty throne of God, "Holy, holy, holy is the Lord of hosts; / the whole earth is full of his glory" (Is 6:3). How should creatures worship this holy God? The Letter to the Hebrews says, "let us offer to God acceptable worship, with reverence and awe; for our God is a consuming fire" (Heb 12:28-29). The Old Testament frequently speaks of the fear of the Lord being the beginning of wisdom and virtue. This does not mean being afraid of God, but having a proper awe and humility before God, who is the fullness of truth, might, and justice. If we know who God is, our response should be to fall on our faces before him, as the twenty-four elders do in the Book of Revelation (see Rv 4:10).

Yet, at the heart of Christian revelation is the surprising disclosure that this same mighty, all-holy God, has not distanced himself from the human race. Rather, out of his great and pure love for us fragile creatures, it has pleased God to come and walk among us as an ordinary man, like us in all things except sin (Heb 4:15)—Jesus Christ.

God could have continued to speak to humanity, as in the Old Covenant, through messengers, prophets, voices, and burning bushes. Instead, mankind has seen God and his glory revealed fully in Jesus Christ. As Paul exclaims in 2 Cor 3:18, "... we all, with unveiled face ..." behold "... the glory of God in the face of Christ" (2 Cor 4:6).

If God has come to the human race as a man, Jesus Christ, it is only sensible to ask how Jesus instructed his followers to approach and worship God. Jesus taught his followers to address God as "Abba," or dear Father, which means coming to God with great affection and intimacy, as well as awe and respect. Jesus invited his followers, including us, to enter into the same intimate and loving relationship with the almighty Father that he himself had. Jesus often told his apostles that they should confidently approach God their Father with their needs, especially their need for the Holy Spirit and their desire for the kingdom of God to come. It should be noted that the loving intimate relationship Jesus had with God never detracted from the respect and reverence that Jesus showed to his heavenly Father, nor diverted him from the desire to do the Father's will perfectly as the guiding principle of his life.

When the Holy Spirit revealed to the apostles and early Christians that Jesus himself is God incarnate, they approached Jesus in the same way as he had taught them to approach God the Father: with reverence, respect, and awe, but also with great love and confidence. Jesus had taught them, "You are my friends if you do what I command you. No longer do I call you servants, for the servant does not know what his master is doing; but I have called you friends, for all that I have heard from my Father I have made known to you" (Jn 15:14, 15). Those who obey Jesus, who live a life of discipleship, have been drawn into God's friendship. Jesus Christ is God who has become our brother—"the first-born among many brethren" (Rom 8:29).

Therefore, Catholic worship seeks to maintain this carefully balanced perspective. We come with awe and reverence before the mystery of the God who is our mighty King and Creator. At the same time, we know the personal love and friendship of the God who has drawn close to us in Jesus Christ, walking among us as a man, laying down his life for us on the cross, and now dwelling in our hearts through the gift of the Holy Spirit.

Catholic Worship: The Sacramental Dimension

Catholics approach God, as Jesus did, both in personal prayer and in communal worship. The center of Catholic communal worship is our sacramental life, especially the Eucharist. Why do Catholics value the sacraments so highly? Why not just have personal or nonliturgical prayer? The major reason is that Catholics believe that God himself has given sacraments to the church to be privileged channels of his grace, his life, and his power.

Where do the sacraments come from? How has God given them to the church? Catholics believe that all of the sacraments flow from the life and ministry of Jesus himself as recorded in the New Testament. All of the sacraments are based on some important aspect of Jesus' life, teaching, or ministry, even those which he did not institute through an explicit word or command. The sacraments are Jesus continuing his ministry among his people after his resurrection and ascension. Jesus promised to remain with his people "to the close of the age" (Mt 28:20). One way that Jesus fulfills this promise is through the sacraments; through them he continues to walk among us and minister to us.

The sacraments are a continuation or an extension of the incarnation of the Word of God. In Jesus, God became man so that he could approach us, and we approach him, in a way that is perfectly suited to our bodily human nature. We are not pure spirits, like the angels. God created us as bodily as well as spiritual beings who relate to reality through our five senses. Should it surprise us, then, that God would choose to relate to us and reveal himself to us through our senses? This is basically what a sacrament is: a visible, tangible sign through which God approaches us, enters into our lives, and draws us to himself through his grace.

Given this definition of sacrament, the greatest sacramental expression of God's love for us is Jesus Christ himself. Jesus, being the incarnate Son of God, is the ultimate visible sign of God's presence among us. He is the unsurpassable means by which the fullness of God's grace and love came into the world to restore the human race to right relationship with him. The First Letter of John begins:

> That which was from the beginning, which we have heard, which we have seen with our eyes, which we have looked upon and touched with our hands, concerning the word of life—the life was made manifest, and we saw it, and testify to it, and proclaim to you the eternal life which was with the Father and was made manifest to us. . . . (1 Jn 1:1-2)

This Word of life is, of course, Jesus Christ. Through the ultimate sacrament of God, Jesus Christ, we are brought into fellowship or communion with God the Father.

There is also a sense in which the whole church of Christ may be called a sacrament. When Jesus departed the earth at his ascension, he left behind not just his spiritual presence, but a visible body of faithful believers, his church. Through this church, subsequent generations of people could come into contact with Jesus Christ and believe in him through its preaching and example. As the Catholic bishops at the Second Vatican Council declared in the Dogmatic Constitution on the Church: "By her relationship with Christ, the church is a kind of *sacrament* of intimate union with God, and of the unity of all mankind, that is, she is a *sign* and *instrument* of such union and unity. . ." (no. 1).

The church of Jesus Christ is the universal sacrament. It is a sign, spread throughout the world, of the presence of God through Jesus Christ.The constitution also states:

> Christ . . . through his Spirit, has established His body, the Church, as the universal sacrament of salvation. Sitting at the right hand of the Father, He is continually active in the world, leading men to the Church, and through her joining them more closely to Himself. (LG, no. 48)

It is this visible church that carries on the work of Jesus Christ and makes him present through its preaching, its actions, and through the particular saving sacraments that Jesus himself established and left for us within the church.

Origin of the Sacraments

Where do the seven sacraments of the Catholic church originate? The word "sacrament" itself comes from a Latin translation of the Greek "mysterion" or "mystery" (see Eph 1:9

ff), which refers to the mystery of God's salvation coming to us in visible form. As we have just discussed, this mystery is first seen in the incarnation. The mystery unfolds through God's continuing presence among us in the body of Christ, the church. It is further seen in the visible signs of God's presence among us in the church—the sacraments. "Mystery" or "sacrament" is a fitting word to describe this incomprehensible miracle of God coming to mankind in visible form, whether in Jesus, in his church, or in the individual sacraments of Christ and the church.

Sacraments have a twofold nature. First, they are signs that point to the presence of God among his people; second, they are also efficacious signs, that is, they bring about or effect what they signify. Catholics believe that God wills to make himself present and to confer his grace upon us in a particular way whenever a sacrament is properly enacted within the church.

To obtain the full benefits and grace that God wishes to confer through the sacraments, it is important that we come to them with the proper dispositions (SC, no. 11). The suitable attitudes that Catholics should have in approaching any sacrament are first, *faith* (believing in God and in the particular way that he has chosen to come to us and bless us through the sacrament), and second, *reverence* before the mystery of God and his presence in the sacrament.

Any interpretation of the sacraments as magic—conjuring up God or controlling God—are false. It is God who chooses to be present and to grant his graces and blessings through the sacraments, out of his infinite love and mercy. God is to be embraced there by the faith and love of his people.

A Theology of the Sacraments

What makes up a sacrament? A more theological description of a sacrament of Christ and the church would include a number of points. First, there is an outward, visible sign or action, such as water, bread, wine, oil, the laying on of hands, or other visible, public acts. Second, the sacrament involves the proclamation of God's word, announcing what God is doing in the particular sacrament. Third, the sacrament must be carried out by the appropriate minister of the church, since God has entrusted these sacraments to the life and care of his New Covenant people. Concerning that third point, since the sacraments are based on words and actions of Jesus himself, most sacraments are administered by those in the church who have been set apart to represent Christ and to carry on his ministry in the church in a special way. These are the bishops and priests, and sometimes the deacon.[1]

From an historical perspective, the term "sacrament" was used more loosely in the early church than it is today. The church Fathers of the first six centuries used *sacramentum* (Latin) or *mysterion* (Greek) to refer to many aspects of church life. Gradually, in the Middle Ages, sacrament came to have a more precise meaning, and it became necessary to determine which of the church's ancient practices fit the more precise definition. In the twelfth and thirteenth centuries, Catholic theologians and bishops began to reach an agreement on the precise meaning of sacrament and came to recognize seven sacraments. The Council of Trent in the sixteenth century officially confirmed that there were seven, and only seven, sacraments of the church. Although it took time for the church's formal understanding and enumeration of sacraments to emerge, the important fact is that the actual practice of these seven sacraments was a vital part of Christian life and worship from the first century onwards.

The Sacraments as the Extension of Jesus' Ministry

After defining the sacraments in a more precise and theological way, it is always important to return to the basic truth that the seven sacraments recognized by the Catholic church are vital because they embody nearly every aspect of Jesus' ministry while he was on earth.

Catholics do not glorify the material things used in the sacraments, such as water, bread, wine, and oil, nor do we divinize the ministers of the sacraments, nor exalt merely human rituals. Again, Catholics use these material things, and respect the authority of the ministers of the church, only because Jesus himself used such things, and commanded his apostles to carry on his ministry with his authority.

The seven sacraments are not ends in themselves; they possess no power in themselves. They are simply channels of God's grace and mercy coming to the human race. The Fathers of the church described them as flowing from the pierced side of Christ on the cross. The grace and life of God, won for us through the cross of Christ, flows down to us within the church, century after century, through these channels (SC, nos. 10, 61).

Finally, our recognition and acceptance of the sacraments as channels of God's grace is based on faith. Faith is the foundation of a mature Christian's relationship with God. Some Christians reject the sacraments because they claim that they don't experience anything or feel any different when receiving them. However, grace, God's life, is not something that can be accurately detected or measured by human experience or feelings. Catholics recognize the sacraments because we believe that they have been instituted by Jesus Christ, through his word or example, as a primary means of receiving his life and grace, not because we necessarily feel different when we receive them.

On the other hand, it is true that a Catholic's experience or perception of God's presence in the sacraments can grow, especially over the course of time. For example, in receiving the sacrament of reconciliation regularly, Catholics should begin to see the power of God at work in their lives, liberating them from sin. Catholics who often receive the Eucharist frequently should expect to see the fruit of this in their lives over the course of weeks or years. The sacraments cannot be evaluated simply on the basis of experience, but they do have power.[2] Catholics should grow in expectant faith that God desires to strengthen, restore, and refresh us when we receive the sacraments in faith.

Baptism: New Life in Christ

In the sacrament of baptism, Jesus breaks the bondage of sin—especially original sin, the root sin binding the whole human race—and shares with us his own divine life, the very life of God! In baptism, Jesus sends the Holy Spirit to dwell within us, making us "temples of the Holy Spirit" (see 1 Cor 6:19). He also makes us a part of his body, the church (Acts 2:41, 47). Christians are delivered through baptism from sin and darkness and made God's sons and daughters, members of his holy people.

Baptism flows directly from the ministry of Jesus. In Matthew 28:19, Jesus commands his followers:

> "Go, therefore and make disciples of all nations, baptizing them in the name of the Father and of the Son and of the Holy Spirit. . . ."

The Gospel of Mark reports Jesus as saying:

> "Go into all the world and preach the gospel to the whole creation. He who believes and is baptized will be saved; but he who does not believe will be condemned. (Mk 16:15, 16)

In John's Gospel, Jesus declares that "unless one is born of water and the Spirit, he cannot enter the kingdom of God" (Jn 3:5).

These passages indicate that God's life and eternal salvation are not something humans are born with naturally or receive automatically. Our relationship with God and his life in us is a sheer gift. It is God's gift of a new birth, being born anew or born again, as Jesus explained to Nicodemus (Jn 3). St. Paul said that Christians must consider themselves "dead to sin and alive to God in Christ Jesus" (Rom 6:11). It is through baptism that we first die to sin and become "alive for God" (Rom 6:3, 4). Through baptism we receive what Catholic theology calls "sanctifying grace"—the grace that makes us holy, like God. We are "born again" into a living relationship with God.

The New Testament indicates that Jesus had taught his disciples to baptize (see Jn 4:2). At the first public preaching of the good news at Pentecost, Peter exhorted the crowd to "repent, and be baptized every one of you in the name of Jesus Christ for the forgiveness of your sins; and you shall receive the gift of the Holy Spirit" (Acts 2:38). Throughout the Acts of the Apostles, baptism accompanied by faith is described as the first step in becoming a Christian (see Acts 2:38; 8:12-13, 37-38; 9:18; 10:47; 16:15; 19:5).

St. Paul was the first of Jesus' followers to develop a thorough theology of baptism. He described it as dying to sin and rising to new life in Christ. He wrote:

> Do you not know that all of us who were baptized into Christ Jesus were baptized into his death? We were buried therefore with him by baptism into death, so that as Christ was raised from the dead by the glory of the Father, we too might walk in newness of life. . . . The death he died he died to sin, once for all, but the life he lives he lives to God. So you also must consider yourselves dead to sin and alive to God in Christ Jesus. (Rom 6:3-5, 10-11)
>
> . . . and you were buried with him in baptism, in which you were also raised with him through faith in the working of God, who raised him from the dead. (Col 2:12)

Paul's imagery of being buried with Christ came from the early baptismal ceremony itself, in which those being baptized were fully immersed (buried) in water three times, signifying Jesus' three days in the tomb. Later, baptism could be administered through pouring or sprinkling water over the candidate's head, but the spiritual reality of dying and rising with Christ in the sacrament remains the same.[3]

Paul also spoke of baptism as "putting on Christ" (Gal 3:27), with the result that the baptized person has an entirely new life "in Christ." "Therefore, if any one is in Christ, he is a new creation; the old has passed away, behold, the new has come" (2 Cor 5:17). As "new creations," Paul believed that those who are baptized into Jesus Christ are freed from the power of sin and the condemnation that flows from it. In Romans, chapter 7, Paul vividly describes the law of sin that oppresses and binds those who have not been freed by Jesus Christ. In Romans 8, Paul contrasts this with the freedom that comes from entering into the life of Christ through baptism. The chapter begins: "There is therefore now no condemnation for those who are in Christ Jesus. For the law of the Spirit of life in Christ Jesus has set me free from the law of sin and death" (Rom 8:1-2).

The Catholic church recognizes other major spiritual effects of baptism. Two effects that Peter mentioned in his Pentecost sermon are the forgiveness of sins and reception of the Holy Spirit (see Acts 2:38). Also, the baptized person enters into the fellowship of the church, as well as becoming a son or daughter of God. "For by one Spirit we were all baptized into one body . . . and all were made to drink of one Spirit" (1 Cor 12:13).

In the early church, the newly baptized persons (called neophytes) were clothed in white robes, symbolizing their rebirth as new creations in Jesus Christ. Baptism normally occurred at the Easter Vigil, when they tasted the power of Christ's resurrection for the first time. After being baptized and confirmed, they were led into the assembly of the believers where they celebrated and received the Eucharist for the first time with the local church. Upon receiving these three sacraments, they became new, full-fledged adult members of the church. They experienced the first-fruits of their salvation through the Holy Spirit entering their lives through baptism (see Rom 8:23).

The basic form, or rite, of baptism is to pour water over a person's head three times (or immerse the person in water three times), while saying: "(Name), I baptize you in the name of the Father, and of the Son, and of the Holy Spirit." Although the clergy (bishops, priests, or deacons) are the normal ministers of baptism, any Catholic (or even a non-Christian who has the intention of baptizing according to the belief of the Catholic church) may baptize, and should be prepared to baptize in case of an emergency.[4]

Infant Baptism

Although in the primitive church it appears that mainly adult converts were baptized, there is some evidence in the New Testament that children or infants were baptized as well. In Acts 2, Peter explains that the promise of salvation is "to you and to your children" (Acts 2:39), and the New Testament speaks of the baptism of "whole households" (1 Cor 1:16; Acts 11:13b, 14; 10:48a; 16:15, 33; 18:8), which in the normal Greek usage would include children. Paul drew a parallel between baptism and circumcision, which was normally administered to children (Col 2:11-12). Jesus himself urged that little children be allowed to come to him for his blessing, "for to such belongs the kingdom of God" (Mk 10:14).

Although the Bible does not explicitly command that infants and children be baptized, it does not forbid this practice. The early church decided that infant baptism was legitimate.

Considerable evidence of this practice is found beginning in the third century A.D., and by the fifth century, baptism of infants was universally accepted throughout the church. St. Augustine explained the importance of baptizing infants for the remission (forgiveness) of original sin. Christian parents baptized their children because they desired their salvation, which came through sharing in the new life in Christ conferred in this sacrament.

A common question about infant baptism today is how an infant or child can be baptized, or saved, without a personal and mature faith in God. Is faith no longer the foundation of a genuine relationship with God?

The first factor to consider in answering this question is God's desire to save and share his life with people of all ages. Jesus never refused to bless or heal anyone on account of their age. He even spoke of little children as those who would inherit the kingdom of God on account of their utter dependence on God and simple trust in him. This underscores that salvation is a free gift of God. When someone baptizes, it is Christ who baptizes (SC, no. 7). He is the one who saves us all, out of his sheer love and mercy. Infant baptism reminds us that we cannot "earn" or "merit" salvation, even through our faith. Faith only enables us to receive or accept God's free gift of life in Jesus Christ.

Secondly, even in infant baptism, there is someone capable of believing in God and thus receiving his gift of divine life. The parents or godparents, as well as the witnessing church community, believe in God and accept his gift of new life on behalf of the child when he or she is baptized. This faith of the church is present and sufficient when an infant or child is baptized. Consider how, in the gospels, Jesus healed children, exorcised them, and even raised them from the dead when their parents approached Jesus in faith and asked for those things. How much more would Jesus desire to free an infant or child from the bondage of sin and eternal death when the parents and the Christian community present the child to be baptized!

In presenting a child to be baptized, it is necessary that the parents or godparents truly believe that God desires to give the child new life in baptism. The Catholic church teaches that presenting a child to be baptized requires a commitment on the part of the parent or guardian to raise the child in an environment where he or she can grow in the Catholic faith. This will prepare the child to make a personal faith commitment to Jesus Christ upon reaching maturity. This personal faith commitment is absolutely necessary for the mature Christian.

Renewal of Baptism, or Rebaptism?

One way that the Catholic church stresses the necessity of personal faith and commitment to the Lord is by calling upon each person to renew their baptismal vows or covenant each year at the Easter Liturgy. Baptized Catholics who have fallen away from their faith have no need to be rebaptized if they are reconciled with God and the church through the sacrament of reconciliation and return to active church participation. Rebaptism implies that God's work of salvation in the sacrament of baptism was ineffective the first time. The Catholic church believes that baptism imparts a permanent mark or character that sets the person apart, in God's eyes, as being one of his people, even if the person sins seriously or stops practicing the faith. Like the prodigal son in Jesus' parable, any baptized Catholic who desires to return to full participation in the church after falling away should simply repent and seek forgiveness in the sacrament of reconciliation in order to renew and refresh the grace first received at baptism. In the Catholic church's view, the person who goes astray remains a member of God's family. He or she need only turn away from sin and return to the church to be joyfully welcomed back with full family status, as the father in Jesus' parable of the prodigal son rejoiced at his son's return (Lk 15:11-32).

The Continuing Work of the Holy Spirit: Confirmation

Chapter 16 of the Gospel of John and the first chapter of the Acts of the Apostles focus on Jesus' promise to his apostles that he would send them the Holy Spirit. The Holy Spirit would bring them the power to witness to the ends of the earth (Acts 1:8) and lead them into all truth (Jn 16:13). This is an exciting promise.

The Catholic church understands that the Holy Spirit normally first enters a person's life through the sacrament of baptism. Baptism initiates one into the life of Christ and the church. In early Christianity, this initiation was completed by a prayer and anointing for a fuller empowerment of the baptized person by the Holy Spirit. This is the origin of the sacrament of confirmation.

The Bible does not use the term confirmation, but it does speak about certain sendings of the Holy Spirit distinct from baptism (Jn 20:22; Acts 2). The Acts of the Apostles records two instances in which baptized persons were not aware of the presence or power of the Holy Spirit in their lives (see Acts 8:15-17; 19:6). On both occasions, the apostles laid their hands on and prayed over these people, and they received the Holy Spirit in a way clearly evidenced by gifts of the Spirit. This had first occurred on a larger scale at Pentecost when the disciples of Jesus and others received the Holy Spirit with power and spiritual gifts that equipped them to live as Christians and proclaim the good news of Jesus Christ with new boldness.

The sacrament of confirmation is intended by God to play the same role in the lives of Christians today. Based upon Jesus' own promise to send the Holy Spirit (Jn 16; Lk 24:49; Acts 1:4-8), the bishops of the church from early times have prayed with baptized Christians using the laying on of hands and anointing with oil (to symbolize strengthening), asking God to send the Holy Spirit in fullness upon them. We know with assurance that this prayer of the church will be answered, for Jesus himself taught:

> For every one who asks receives, and he who seeks finds, and to him who knocks it will be opened.... If you then, who are evil, know how to give good gifts to your children, how much more will the heavenly Father give the Holy Spirit to those who ask him! (Lk 11:10, 13)

Regardless of whether there are any outward signs or manifestations of the Spirit's coming, Catholics rely on Jesus' promise and know in faith that God grants through confirmation the gift of the Spirit that he so desires to give.

One might ask, why do Catholics need a second prayer and anointing for the Holy Spirit to come into their lives after baptism? Isn't baptism sufficient? Baptism does fully initiate a person into the life of Christ and the church, but there is always need for more grace and power, as the apostles themselves discovered on the day of Pentecost. Although they had already believed in Jesus and in his resurrection, and had received his commission to preach the gospel to the ends of the earth, they still lacked the power to do so . . . until the Holy Spirit descended upon them in a new way. Through this sacrament, God offers each person a fuller participation in the gifts and fruits of the Holy Spirit, as described in Isaiah 11:2-3; 1 Corinthians 12; Ephesians 4; and Galatians 5.

Confirmation is another sacrament that changes a person in so profound a way that it can be received only once. In confirmation, God confers a new character, marks a person as his witness in a way that can never be effaced. To show the significance of the event, each person to be confirmed chooses a sponsor, often a godparent, as a support in this new dimension of his or her Christian life, and also a new name, the name of a saint who will support the person in prayer.

As in all the sacraments, the full benefits of the sacrament of confirmation are realized only when it is approached with a clear understanding of its meaning, and with expectant faith in what God wishes to do through the sacrament. Today, many Catholics are discovering how much God wishes to confer his power and the gifts of the Holy Spirit through this sacrament, and are preparing people for confirmation with this in mind. There are different views in the Catholic church about the optimal age for confirmation. In the early church, confirmation was part of the rite of initiation into Christ and the church, accompanying baptism and immediately preceding the first reception of the Eucharist. When baptism of infants later became common, the Eastern church continued to administer the sacrament of confirmation at the time of baptism, as they do today. The Western church entrusted baptism to the priests, but reserved confirmation to bishops, who conferred this sacrament when they made pastoral visits to the churches under their care. Today the Roman Catholic church administers confirmation to older children, adolescents, and adults.

The Eucharistic Presence of Christ

The Second Vatican Council reminds us of the many ways that Jesus Christ is present to his people. In the Mass, Christ is present in the minister (priest) who represents him, in the sacrament of the Eucharist and the other sacraments enacted in this liturgical context, in his word proclaimed from the sacred Scripture, and in the congregation, the people of God who are gathered in Jesus' name to worship God. Catholics recognize the presence of the Lord in all of those dimensions of their life and worship (see SC, no. 7).

Here we will look particularly at the presence of the Lord in the sacrament of the Eucharist. Catholics believe that when Jesus told his apostles at the Last Supper to "do this in remembrance of me" (1 Cor 11:24; Lk 22:19), he was commissioning them to re-enact Jesus' action of blessing and distributing the bread and wine with the words, "Take; this is my body" (Mk 14:22); "This is my blood . . ." (Mk 14:24).

How are these words of Jesus to be understood? Since the Reformation, Protestant Christians have proposed different explanations of what happens at the Lord's Supper or Eucharist. Some hold that Jesus was speaking symbolically, that the bread and wine of the Lord's Supper represent the body and blood of Jesus Christ, but certainly there is no real change in these elements. Others emphasize that Christians do receive the body and blood of Christ at Holy Communion through our faith or through the action of the Holy Spirit but teach that the actual elements involved in the sacrament remain bread and wine.

Catholic Christians understand Jesus' words concerning the Eucharist in light of the commentary on them given in the Gospel of John and Paul's letters, and in light of the testimony of the early Christians. Chapter 6 of John's Gospel, probably the last Gospel written, indicates the insistence of the early Christians that the eucharistic bread and wine were truly the body and blood of Jesus. This belief had apparently become a source of scandal to the Jews and others who were considering becoming Christians. John emphasizes that Jesus really meant that he expected his followers to eat his flesh and drink his blood (Jn 6:51-57) and that he predicted that many people would be scandalized and fall away from following him because of this teaching (Jn 6:60-66). When Jesus said, "unless you eat the flesh of the Son of man and drink his blood, you have no life in you" (Jn 6:53), he was speaking about them receiving his body and blood in the bread and wine of the Lord's Supper or Eucharist. This was no symbolic reception, according to John, but was actually eating the body of Christ and drinking his blood even if this body and blood still appears to our senses as bread and wine. This teaching is as much of a challenge to the faith of Christians today as it was to the readers of John's Gospel. Catholic Christians accept this challenging teaching at its face value, and believe that when they receive the bread and wine of the Eucharist, they are actually partaking in the body and blood of Jesus Christ.

This understanding is also affirmed by the apostle Paul, who wrote in his First Letter to the Corinthians: "The cup of blessing which we bless, is it not a participation in the blood of Christ? The bread which we break, is it not a participation in the body of Christ? Because there is one bread, we who are many are one body, for we all partake of the one bread" (1 Cor 10:16-17). Further on in this letter, after restating Jesus' words of institution, Paul concludes: "Whoever, therefore, eats the bread or drinks the cup of the Lord in an unworthy manner will be guilty of profaning the body and blood of the Lord. Let a man examine himself, and so eat of the bread and drink of the cup. For any one who eats and drinks without discerning the body eats and drinks judgment upon himself" (1 Cor 11:27-29).

The most straightforward interpretation of these passages is that Paul considered the eucharistic bread and wine to be literally the body and blood of Christ.

How did the early Christians understand the Bible's teaching about the bread and wine of the Lord's Supper? To summarize a vast amount of literature, nearly every notable writing of the early church that mentions the Eucharist either implies or directly states that the bread and wine of the Lord's Supper is truly the body and blood of Jesus Christ. These include the writings of Ignatius of Antioch (c. A.D. 110, *Letter to the Smyrneans,* 7:1),

> They hold aloof from the Eucharist and from services of prayer because they refuse to admit that the Eucharist is the flesh of our Savior, Jesus Christ. . . ;[5]

Justin Martyr (c. A.D. 150, *First Apology,* Ch. 66),

> For we do not receive these things as common bread or common drink; but as Jesus Christ our Savior being

> incarnate by God's Word took flesh and blood for our salvation, so also we have been taught that the food consecrated by the word of prayer that comes from Him . . . is the flesh and blood of that incarnate Jesus. . . ;[6]

Irenaeus of Lyon (c. A.D. 185, *Against Heresies,* Book V, Ch. 2),

> . . . He [Jesus] declares that the cup, [taken] from the creation is His own blood . . . and He has firmly assured us that the bread, [taken] from the creation, is His own body . . . For when the mixed cup and the bread that has been prepared receive the Word of God, and become the Eucharist, the body and blood of Christ, . . . by these our flesh grows and is confirmed. . . ;[7]

Cyril of Jerusalem (c. A.D. 250, *Mystagogical Catechesis,* "Fourth Address: On the Body and Blood of Christ"); Saint Augustine (c. A.D. 400, Sermon 272); and many others. It appears that every reliable early Christian writer who wrote on the subject believed that the bread and wine of the Eucharist is the body and blood of Christ. The Catholic understanding of the Eucharist as truly the body and blood of Christ appears to be supported by both the New Testament and the early Christian church.

Thus, Catholics speak of the "real presence" of Jesus Christ in the bread and wine of the Eucharist. This presence of Jesus can only be accepted in faith, since the outward appearance of the bread and wine does not change. Medieval Catholic theologians used the term "transubstantiation" to describe the mystery that the inner reality, or essence, of the bread and wine is transformed into the body and blood of Jesus, while the outward appearance, or accidents, remains the same. (Today we would say that there is no change in the molecular structure of the bread and wine of the Eucharist.) This doctrine is not intended to explain how this happens, as if to reduce this mystery of faith to something totally comprehensible to the human mind. It simply affirms, in faith, that Jesus' words are literally true: the bread and wine offered to God in the Eucharist become his body and blood. This explains why Catholic Christians have great reverence for the eucharistic bread and wine, since they believe that the Word of God is present there just as fully as he was present in the physical body of Jesus. Catholics do not worship a piece of bread or a cup of wine, but worship Jesus Christ whom they discern by faith to be present "body and blood, soul and divinity" under the appearance of bread and wine.

The Eucharist or the Lord's Supper

For Catholics, the heart of the Mass and the center of Christian worship is the Eucharist. "Eucharist" means "thanksgiving." In the ancient Jewish tradition, the term eucharist refers to the thanksgiving to God that the head of the household pronounces before the Passover meal or other Jewish festive meals over the third cup of wine, the cup of blessing (cf. 1 Cor 10:16), for all the benefits God had given them. Therefore, in the Christian tradition, we give thanks for the great gift and sacrifice of God's Son, Jesus, who at his Last Supper diverged from the Jewish customs by passing around the one bread and his own cup, saying "Take, eat; this is my body . . ." (Mt 26:26); "Drink of it, all of you; for this is my blood of the covenant, which is poured out for many for the forgiveness of sins" (Mt 26:27-28). By the beginning of the second century, Christians were using the word "eucharist" to designate their coming together to commemorate and reenact this great event, the Lord's Last Supper.

What does the Eucharist mean? This cannot be expressed in just a few words, because it is, in a sacramental way, the realization and summation of the entire Christian mystery of salvation.[8] The meaning of the Eucharist is multi-dimensional like a priceless diamond. A major error of some past theology has been to artificially separate the various dimensions of the

Eucharist, or even to deny the validity of some aspects. Let us briefly examine some of the dimensions of the Eucharist.

1. The Eucharist as covenant. The Hebrew people understand their entire relationship with God to be based on a covenant with Him—a solemn agreement involving mutual commitment. Moses sealed the first covenant with God with the shed blood of sacrificial animals. The blood that sealed the new and final covenant of God with man is the blood of Jesus, the Son of God. Jesus declared at the Last Supper: "This cup which is poured out for you is the new covenant in my blood" (Lk 22:20). The Letter to the Hebrews (9:11-28; 10:19-31) proclaims the surpassing power of the blood of Christ in purifying and liberating God's people of the New Covenant.

2. The Eucharist is a memorial in which Jesus is continually made present. After Jesus offered his apostles the bread of his body and the cup of his blood, he commissioned them to: "Do this in remembrance of me" (Lk 22:19; 1 Cor 11:24, 25). The Eucharist is also an *anamnesis,* a remembrance or memorial, of what Jesus did at the Last Supper, and of his whole life and ministry. The semitic, biblical concept of memorial meant more than merely remembering something mentally, or commemorating it symbolically. It meant making something from the *past* actually *present* once more. Thus, Catholic Christians have always understood the Eucharist as memorial to mean that the reality of Jesus' body and blood is truly made present in the sacrament, under the appearances of bread and wine. As described earlier, Catholics speak of the real presence of Jesus Christ in the Eucharist, which ultimately results from Jesus' commission to his apostles to reenact the first Eucharist "in remembrance of Me" (Lk 22:19).

3. The Eucharist as thanksgiving and sacrifice. At the Last Supper, Jesus led the traditional Jewish table prayers that focused on praise and thanksgiving (*berakhah*) to God (see Lk 22:17-20). The early Christians called their celebration of the

Last Supper "the Eucharist," the thanksgiving to God for his greatest gift, his Son, Jesus Christ.

The Old Testament often speaks of a sacrifice of thanksgiving, or praise (Psalms 50:14, 23; 116:17; 119:108). The concepts of thanksgiving and sacrifice, seen in the Jewish sacrificial meal of the Passover, are closely connected. The sacrifice most pleasing to God is the offering of our entire being to him in thanksgiving and praise (Ps 40). Jesus himself offered the most perfect thanksgiving to God by offering his life as a sacrifice, according to his Father's will (see Heb 10:10, 12, 14), to atone for the sins of humanity.

Some Christians object that it is blasphemous to call the Mass a sacrifice, because Jesus offered the perfect sacrifice of thanksgiving once for all when he died on Calvary (Heb 9:11, 25-28). They think Catholics believe that Jesus is sacrificed again every time that the Eucharist is celebrated. Catholics actually believe that in the Mass Christ's one sacrifice on Calvary is re-presented (made present once again) or perpetuated (see SC, no. 47). Christ's death on the cross is both an historical and a transhistorical event. It is as real and powerful today as it first was nearly two thousand years ago. Catholics believe that God, in his love and mercy, desires to make the one, eternal sacrifice of Christ present to his people in the sacrament of the Eucharist, so that we may enter ever more deeply into its saving power (see SC, no. 6).

4. The Eucharist as communion. The Eucharist is a sacrament of unity, or communion. First, it establishes a New Covenant between God and his people. "This cup which is poured out for you is the new covenant in my blood" (Lk 22:20; cf. 1 Cor 11:25). In the Eucharist, we reaffirm our covenant relationship with God, sealed by the blood of Jesus. If any Catholic has broken this covenant with God through serious sin, he must seek forgiveness and be reconciled with God through the sacrament of reconciliation before receiving the Lord's Body and Blood.

Second, through the Eucharist we also reaffirm our covenant with one another in the church. "The bread which we break, is it not a participation in the body of Christ? Because there is one bread, we who are many are one body, for we all partake of the one bread" (1 Cor 10:16-17). Participation in the Eucharist expresses our unity. If there is anything serious dividing Christians, it should be settled before approaching the altar (see Mt 5:23-24). The kiss of peace at the Mass is not just a ritual, but a visible sign of our unity in Christ.

For this reason, the Catholic church does not allow intercommunion, Christians of different denominations and traditions indiscriminately receiving Holy Communion together. For Catholics, the Eucharist is the highest, most primary sign of the reality of our communion with God and our unity with one another. If there is a serious disagreement among Christians that results in division into different denominations or churches, the Catholic church believes that reconciliation must first occur before we can approach the altar of the Lord together for Communion, for the unity of the altar is the goal of ecumenism and not a means of ecumenical endeavor.

Fortunately, some significant steps toward Christian unity have been made through the ecumenical movement. We must continue to pray and work for the day when the church's unity is fully restored and all Christians will be able to approach the table of the Lord together in full communion of mind and heart.

5. The Eucharist as nourishment. The Eucharist is spiritual nourishment for our lives. In the Gospel of John, Jesus calls himself the "true bread from heaven" (Jn 6:32) and tells his followers: "I am the bread of life; he who comes to me shall not hunger, and he who believes in me shall never thirst.... he who eats my flesh and drinks my blood has eternal life, and I will raise him up at the last day. For my flesh is food indeed, and my blood is drink indeed" (Jn 6:35, 54, 55).

We receive this nourishment and life when we approach the Eucharist in faith, truly discerning that this is the Body and Blood of the Lord (1 Cor 11:27-29); for we are nourished by Jesus himself who becomes our spiritual food.

6. The Eucharist as a work of the Holy Spirit, anticipating the age to come. Just as the Holy Spirit guided Jesus throughout his life and led him to his final sacrifice on the cross, the Holy Spirit leads Christians to the Eucharist and enables them to recognize Jesus Christ truly present there. The eucharistic prayer in the liturgy begins with the *epiclesis,* the invocation or calling down of the Holy Spirit. The Spirit is asked to bless the bread and wine, preparing it to become the body and blood of Christ, and to bless the community gathered, that by receiving the Body of the Lord, they themselves might become more profoundly the body of the Lord, lifting up their hearts and minds to God in praise and thanksgiving.

The Holy Spirit also points toward the future, when the sacramental presence of Christ will be replaced by seeing him face-to-face. As St. Paul taught, "For as often as you eat this bread and drink the cup, you proclaim the Lord's death until he comes" (1 Cor 11:26). The Holy Spirit stirs up in the hearts of believers the reality of the eucharistic response: "Christ has died! Christ has risen! Christ will come again!" Indeed "The Spirit and the Bride [the church] say, 'Come!'" (Rv 22:17). "Amen. Come, Lord Jesus!" (Rv 22:20).

It is in the Eucharist that Jesus manifests himself and gives himself to his church most fully. Likewise, the church is an eucharistic community, a community which exists to give thanks and praise to God. This happens most perfectly when the church unites its prayers and offerings with the perfect offering of Jesus himself on Calvary.

Ongoing Conversion: the Sacrament of Reconciliation

Through baptism, Christians are freed from the bondage of sin and rebellion against God that inevitably leads to death. However, since God has gifted humanity with free will, the baptized Christian can fall back into sin. God, in his mercy, offers forgiveness of sins to those baptized into Christ through the sacrament of reconciliation.

The origin of this sacrament is Jesus himself, whose entire ministry focused on reconciling mankind to God and to one another. He told the paralytic, "Your sins are forgiven," leading some to ask, "Why does this man speak thus? It is blasphemy! Who can forgive sins but God alone?" (Mk 2:7; Lk 7:49). Jesus also forgave the woman caught in the act of adultery (Jn 8:1-11), Mary Magdalene the prostitute (Lk 8:2), Peter, who denied Christ three times (Jn 21:15-19), and even those who crucified him (Lk 23:34). Jesus' ministry was clearly one of reconciliation and forgiveness.

Reconciliation and forgiveness did not end with Jesus; it has become the ministry of the church. "... Christ reconciled us to himself and gave us the ministry of reconciliation; ... So we are ambassadors for Christ, God making his appeal through us. We beseech you on behalf of Christ, be reconciled to God" (2 Cor 5:18-20).

Jesus Christ conferred special authority to forgive sins in God's name upon the apostles. Certainly all Christians are expected to forgive those who sin against us as we pray in the Lord's prayer (Mt 6:14; 18:21-23; Lk 17:3-4). However, Jesus shared with his apostles the unique authority that he possessed to forgive the sins of all persons, even those guilty of grave offenses against God and man. To Peter he said, "whatever you bind on earth shall be bound in heaven, and whatever you loose on earth shall be loosed in heaven" (Mt 16:18, 19). Later he told the other apostles the same thing (Mt 18:18). Even more directly, in John's Gospel, Jesus appeared to the apostles on Easter and said, "Receive the Holy Spirit. If you forgive the sins of any, they are forgiven; if you retain the sins of any, they are retained" (Jn 20:22-23).

In the early church, the apostles and their successors, the bishops, exercised this authority given them by Christ. The church's official act of forgiveness, sometimes called absolution, was reserved for those who had committed very serious sin, such as murder, adultery, or apostasy (denying one's faith), and it was accompanied by a long period of severe public penance. A person could normally receive absolution for these sins only once in a lifetime. The early Christians took seriously the teaching of Paul about becoming a new creation when baptized. It was expected that a baptized person had the grace to avoid serious sin.

Because the formal forgiveness of serious sin in the church was restricted and involved severe penances, many converts to Christianity began to delay being baptized until late in their lives. They feared falling into serious sin after baptism and the rigors of public penance. A change in the understanding of this sacrament took place in the sixth and seventh centuries. Irish monks, probably in the context of spiritual direction, developed the practice of forgiving sins in Jesus' name as part of a more frequent private confession that included less serious sins. This eventually became the standard form of the sacrament.

Common Questions about the Sacrament of Reconciliation

Some questions about the sacrament of reconciliation frequently arise. Why is this sacrament necessary? Why not confess your sins directly to God, instead of to another human being?

Catholics believe that it is appropriate and even essential to repent directly before God for one's sins. When Catholics participate in this sacrament they are primarily expressing their repentance and sorrow for sin to God, and seeking to be reconciled to him. However, Catholics believe that Jesus had a purpose in granting particular persons the authority to forgive sins in God's name. In this sacrament, as in all the others, the priest acts *in persona Christi,* "in the person of Christ." That is, the priest acts as a special representative of Christ by virtue of his ordination, and exercises the authority of Jesus Christ in his sacramental ministry. In the sacrament of reconciliation, it is not the priest who grants forgiveness of sins, but God who uses the priest as an instrument and sign of his mercy. When our sins are forgiven by one who has been set apart by the church to represent Jesus Christ in a special way, we can experience the mercy of Jesus himself through that person and his ministry.

Second, confessing sins to a person reminds one of the social dimension of sin. When someone sins, he not only offends God; his sin also has an effect, either direct or indirect, on other people. The priest who grants God's forgiveness not only represents Jesus Christ, but also the whole Christian community, the church. Hence, the priest has the authority to reconcile a sinner to the body of Christ, the church.

Third, the priest or minister is often able to counsel and encourage the penitent, or even pray with the penitent for healing of some area of sin or brokenness in the person's life. Jesus often uses his representative, the priest, to minister to the needs of people in remarkable ways through the sacrament of reconciliation.

The Anointing of the Sick

Like the sacrament of reconciliation, the anointing of the sick is another healing sacrament of the church, carrying on Jesus' own ministry of healing. While the sacrament of reconciliation focuses on healing sin and the effects of sin, this sacrament calls on God's healing for those physically or psychologically ill.

The scriptural roots of the sacrament of anointing of the sick are clear. Jesus healed the sick and commanded and empowered his disciples to do the same. "And they cast out many demons, and anointed with oil many that were sick and healed them" (Mk 6:13). The elders or priests in the early church continued this practice: "Is any among you sick? Let him call for the elders [priests] of the church, and let them pray over him, anointing him with oil in the name of the Lord; and the prayer of faith will save the sick man, and the Lord will raise him up; and if he has committed sins, he will be forgiven" (Jas 5:14-15). The Bible explicitly teaches that the "presbyters" of the church should be called to pray over the sick and anoint them with oil for healing and forgiveness. The sacramental signs are the laying on of hands and the anointing with oil, and the presbyter, either bishop, priest, or deacon, is the biblically appointed minister of the sacrament.

This sacrament has been practiced since the earliest days of the church, but its focus has shifted at times. Until recently, the emphasis was on preparation for death, but the Second Vatican Council restored an emphasis on prayer for physical and spiritual healing for all seriously ill persons. This sacrament does not preclude the practice of individual Christians praying for the sick or even anointing them with blessed oil. It simply acknowledges Jesus' command to his apostles to anoint and heal the sick and recognizes the power that has always been at work through their ministry and through that of the elders who succeeded them.

This sacrament does not guarantee that every sick person will be healed in a particular way. God's ways are above our ways, and often God will allow sickness or suffering to continue, yet will work on a deeper level in the person. Many texts in the New Testament exhort Christians to rejoice in their sufferings, and to consider them a sharing in the suffering of Christ (Rom 8:16, 17; Col 1:24; 2 Tm 1:11-12; 1 Pt 4:13; 2 Cor 4:16-18). Yet, our God is a healing God, and he often responds to the prayer of Christians and works through the sacrament of the anointing of the sick to restore to health those who are suffering. Catholics will see the power of God manifest as they pray for the sick with expectant faith and call upon his healing power through this sacrament.

Special Sacraments of Christian Vocation

God invites each person into relationship and union with him by calling the person to a particular state of life or vocation, which means "calling." It is through or by means of this vocation that the person will attain the Christian perfection or holiness that is required of all followers of Jesus Christ.[9] It is important that each Christian pray fervently and seek counsel to discern the vocation that would best enable the person to know, love, and serve God fully.

God has a plan for the life of each of us. Respecting the freedom that he has given us, God allows us to choose freely the path we are to follow. However, we can believe with assurance that if we seek the guidance of the Holy Spirit in choosing our vocation and do our best to obey what God appears to be speaking, we will find the state in life which will enable us to mature as Christians, grow in holiness, and advance the kingdom of God.

Married Life—The Sacrament of Marriage

Two Christian vocations are consecrated to God in a special way through sacraments of the church: ordination to the ministerial priesthood and marriage. Since these states of life are sealed by Jesus Christ through a sacrament, when legitimately entered into and carried out, they are both considered by the Catholic church to be indissoluble in God's eyes in this life. Jesus himself taught about marriage, "What therefore God has joined together, let not man put asunder" (Mt 19:6), and of priesthood, the Old Testament says, "You are a priest forever / after the order of Melchizedek" (Ps 110:4).[10]

God calls most Christians to marriage because, as the Book of Genesis tells us, God made man and woman to come together and "become one flesh" (Gn 2:24), bringing forth children and mutually supporting each other on the road to holiness. The Catholic church today continues to recognize procreation and conjugal love (that is, faithful mutual love and support within the marriage covenant) as the two greatest benefits of marriage.

Marriage existed long before Christianity because of the natural laws of human attraction and the natural recognition of the importance of fidelity and stability within human families. It was Jesus Christ who raised marriage to a new level, basing its existence and conduct clearly on the law of God (see Mt 19:3-9). The Letter to the Ephesians recognizes marriage as a sacrament when it describes the love of husband and wife as a visible sign of the love of Christ for his church (Eph 5:21-33). With this understanding, marriage cannot be viewed merely as a human agreement or even as only a civil or religious contract. The relationship of a married couple is a *covenant,* a solemn promise involving the man, the woman, and God himself at the center. This covenant is modeled upon the New Covenant between Jesus Christ and the church, sealed by the blood of Christ.

> ". . . For this reason a man shall leave his father and mother and be joined to his wife, and the two shall become one." This mystery is a profound one, and I am saying that it refers to Christ and the church. . . . (Eph 5:31-32).

The man and the woman who make this covenant receive special graces to remain faithful to the covenant and to carry out the duties of this state of life with the spirit of Christ (GS, no. 48). Besides the duty of faithful, mutual love and support of each other, the couple may also receive the blessing of children whom they have the duty to raise in the faith of the church and for the service of God.

As part of their marriage covenant, Catholic couples vow to receive children lovingly from God. Thus, a new social unit, the family, is the normal and precious fruit of Christian marriage, unless the couple is unable to conceive children. In the face of much confusion in society today, Catholics must be clear that the call to marriage is a call to accept the responsibility and joy of children and family life. The Catholic church has always highly valued the family and has done everything in its power to protect it and preserve its integrity. The Pastoral Constitution on the Church in the Modern World calls the family "the foundation of society" (no. 52), and teaches about the vital responsibilities of both the husband and the wife, working together, in making this foundation strong:

> The family is a kind of school of deeper humanity. But if it is to achieve the full flowering of its life and mission, it needs the kindly communion of minds and the joint deliberation of spouses, as well as the painstaking cooperation of parents in the education of their children. The active presence of the father is highly beneficial to their formation. The children, especially the younger among them, need the care of their mother at home. This domestic role of hers must be safely preserved, though the legitimate social progress of women should not be underrated on that account. (no. 54)

The call to be married in Christ is a high one, and today one that challenges Catholic married couples and families to be the "salt of the earth" (Mt 5:13) and the "light of the world" (Mt 5:14) in the midst of an increasingly insipid and dark society. Catholic married couples are to proclaim the value and gift of life, against the swelling tide of artificial contraception, abortion, and infanticide; the value and gift of fidelity, where infidelity, separation, and divorce are rampant; and the value and gift of Christian family life, against the inroads and attacks of radical feminism, materialism, selfish individualism, pornography, the anti-Christian values proclaimed in music and in the media, and a host of others (GS, no. 52). Christians can advance in hope and confidence, knowing that God's grace offered in the sacrament of marriage is sufficient to overcome any obstacle to Christian marriage and family life, if we only turn to him continually in faith and ask for that grace: ". . . for he who is in you is greater than he who is in the world" (1 Jn 4:4).

Catholic married couples and families can also support one another in their marriages and family lives, promoting and instilling Christian values and a Christian way of life. Christian communities and other associations are ways that Christian families can come together to support each other. Only through such means of unity and mutual support can Catholic families today hope to build a truly Christian culture in the midst of secular society. Those in other states of life and vocations—priests, religious, and single people—can also strengthen and support Catholic marriages and family life in diverse ways.

Holy Orders—the Call to Christ's Ministerial Priesthood

All Catholics are members of the royal priesthood (1 Pt 2:9) of Jesus Christ, and share in his threefold ministry of priest, prophet, and king. However, Jesus selected certain men from among his followers to share in his ministry in a particular way. He chose twelve men, his apostles, and set them apart to lead his people after his death, resurrection, and ascension. The synoptic Gospels record that on the night before he died, Jesus shared the bread, his body, and the cup of wine, his blood, with them and commissioned them to, "Do this in remembrance of me" (Lk 22:19). John's Gospel recounts that when he appeared to these same men three days later, after his resurrection, he said: "'Peace be with you. As the Father has sent me, even so I send you.' And when he had said this, he breathed on them, and said to them, 'Receive the Holy Spirit. If you forgive the sins of any, they are forgiven; if you retain the sins of any, they are retained'" (Jn 20:21-23).

The apostles were empowered by Jesus Christ to lead and

teach his followers, celebrate the Eucharist, and forgive sins. The bishops later carried on the mission of the apostles. Bishops in early Christianity normally were set apart for this through a ceremony of the laying on of hands, an anointing with blessed oil, and prayer by other bishops (cf. 1 Tm 4:14; 2 Tm 1:6-7). This later became known as episcopal consecration. The consecration of a bishop, or *episcopos,* which was recognized by the Catholic church as the fullness of the sacrament of Holy Orders (see LG, no. 26). Now this is simply called ordination of bishops, to link it to the ordination of priests and deacons. In the early church, presbyters, or priests, and deacons received through their ordination a share in Christ's authority to teach, govern, and make holy God's people in a particular region in union with and under the authority of the bishop of that territory. This is summarized well by the Dogmatic Constitution on the Church of the Second Vatican Council:

> Christ, whom the Father sanctified and sent into the world (Jn 10:36) has, through His apostles, made their successors, the bishops, partakers of His consecration and His mission. These in their turn have legitimately handed on to different individuals in the Church various degrees of participation in this ministry.
>
> Thus the divinely established ecclesiastical ministry is exercised on different levels by those who from antiquity have been called bishops, priests, and deacons. Although priests do not possess the highest degree of priesthood, and although they are dependent on the bishops in the exercise of their power, they are nevertheless united with the bishops in sacerdotal dignity. By the power of the sacrament of orders, and in the image of Christ the eternal High Priest (Heb 5:1-10; 7:24; 9:11-28), they are consecrated to preach the gospel, shepherd the faithful, and celebrate divine worship as true priests of the New Testament. (no. 28)

Just as Jesus called and set apart the apostles to lead and minister to God's people, God continues to call men today to serve his people in the ordained priesthood of Jesus Christ.[11] The mission of the priest or bishop continues to be: (1) to proclaim, teach, and guard the word of God found in Scripture and authentic Catholic tradition, with the authority of Christ; (2) to carry on the priestly ministry of Jesus by presiding over the Eucharist or Lord's Supper while acting in the person of Christ, and serving as the normal ministers of the other sacraments; (3) to shepherd and govern God's people according to the example of Jesus, the Good Shepherd (Jn 10), and according to his word and teaching. Those ordained "have taken up the service of the (Church) Community, presiding in the place of God over the flock whose shepherds they are, as teachers of doctrine, priests of sacred worship, and officers of good order. . ." (LG, no. 20).

As with lay people, the ordained ministers of the church "grow in love for God and neighbor through the daily exercise of their duty" (LG, no. 41). Like Christian marriage, the sacrament of Holy Orders also provides a special grace to enable the priest to carry out his vocation faithfully and successfully. The Second Vatican Council's Decree on the Ministry and Life of Priests affirms that

> . . . since every priest in his own way represents the person of Christ Himself, he is also enriched with special grace . . . consecrated by the anointing of the Holy Spirit and sent by Christ, priests mortify in themselves the deeds of the flesh and devote themselves entirely to the service of men. Thus, they can grow in the sanctity with which they are endowed in Christ, to the point of perfect manhood. (no. 15)

In the Roman Catholic church the discipline of celibacy is required for ordination and priesthood. Jesus taught that there would be those who renounced sexual relationships "for the sake of the kingdom of heaven. He who is able to receive this, let him receive it" (Mt 19:12). The apostle Paul extols the benefit of celibacy "to promote good order and to secure your undivided devotion to the Lord" (1 Cor 7:35). For nearly two thousand years, many Christian men and women have heard this call to renounce the good of marriage for the sake of the kingdom of God. Although celibacy is not a doctrinal requirement for priesthood, as married priests in Eastern Catholic churches testify, it is a discipline of the Roman Catholic church that has clear biblical precedent and has borne much good fruit over the centuries in the evident holiness and freedom for service of so many Roman Catholic priests, bishops, and deacons. Again, if God calls a man to this vocation, he will provide the grace and strength for it to be faithfully carried out.

The call to union with God through the sacrament of Holy Orders is one that must be discerned by both the person and the church. The decline in number of vocations to the priesthood is a cause for the concern of many Catholics. God may have other ways of making up for this lack, but it is certain that the mission of the ordained ministers of the church, the clergy, is vitally important to the church and cannot be replaced. Once again, Catholics are called to faith and hope in God, that he will issue resoundingly the call to priesthood to many men, and that they would heed this call in faith and trust. Like married life today, the priesthood needs support from priests banding together to love and encourage each other, and from lay people and religious continuing to pray for priests and to support them in their vital ministry.

SEVEN

Catholic Prayer, Devotion, and the Work of the Holy Spirit

HAVING DISCUSSED THE SACRAMENTS of Christ and his church, it is necessary to speak about other aspects of the new life of the baptized Christian, beginning with the life of prayer. A Christian cannot grow in his or her relationship with God without regular, personal encounter with God in prayer.

Personal Prayer

No relationship can continue or grow without communication. Prayer is communication with God. It is two-way communication: we speak with God, and God speaks to us. Just as married persons should normally speak with their spouses every day, hopefully in a significant and mutual way, so Christians should set aside a time every day to speak with God. After all, he is the one we are called to know, love, and serve with our whole heart, mind, soul, and strength (Dt 6:5).

How should we pray? The New Testament reports that Jesus often went off before dawn to pray, or even spent whole nights in prayer when making important decisions (see Lk 5:16; 6:12; 9:28; 22:32, 41 ff). Jesus always approached God in a personal way, addressing him as *Abba,* "Father" (see Mk 14:36; Rom 8:15; Gal 4:6), and he instructed his followers to pray in the same manner (Lk 11:2). The one formal prayer that Jesus taught his followers is personally addressed to "our Father," speaking to him simply and directly. That is how Christians are to approach God in personal prayer: simply, directly, humbly, and unpretentiously.

When and how often should Christians pray? Jesus told a parable about the need to pray continually (Lk 18:1). St. Paul urged the Thessalonians to "pray constantly" (1 Thes 5:17) and told the Ephesians to "Pray at all times in the Spirit . . ." (Eph 6:18). There have been many methods and interpretations of this in Christian history, but basically those Christians who "pray always" are vitally aware that they live their whole lives in God's presence, knowing that they have the privilege of constantly turning to God. They turn to him with their joys, problems, hopes, fears and plans. They turn to him during work, recreation, meals, or any other activity. Jesus and Paul taught their followers to foster an attitude of prayer. The method may vary—ejaculations ("Jesus, I love you"), the "Jesus Prayer,"[1] formal prayers, praying in tongues, visible reminders of God's presence, and others. Yet the goal is always the same: to be aware of God's presence and be constantly turning our thoughts and attention to him and to the accomplishment of his will.

It is also important to devote a particular time each day to focus our attention fully on God. Christians need a time each day when they can speak to God, and listen to him, with a minimum of distractions. Most people find it best to select a regular time and place for this prayer alone with God, a time when the body, mind, and heart are awake and attentive, and distractions are kept to a minimum.

How does a Christian spend this time with God? Again,

methods vary, but the basic elements remain consistent:

1. Adoration—We worship and praise God simply for who he is. Songs or hymns, recitation of psalms, or spontaneous praise often express this;
2. Thanksgiving—We thank God for his many blessings, past and present, both to us personally, and to all of God's people;
3. Repentance—We examine our consciences to see how we have rebelled against God and have violated his laws, both individually and as a people. We sincerely ask God's forgiveness and resolve to avoid sin in the future, asking God for his grace to do this;
4. Petition—We ask God for what we need—both our own needs and the needs of others—and entrust these things to his will and loving care;
5. Listening—Too often Christians spend all their time in prayer talking to God and no time listening to Him. A few minutes of quiet, perhaps reflecting on God's word in a Scripture reading, or just being quiet in his presence gives God an opportunity to speak to us.

God usually doesn't speak in an audible way, but rather through the thoughts and gentle urgings that the Holy Spirit stirs up in our minds and hearts. One important way that God speaks to us is through his word in Scripture, and through the writings of saints or of holy men and women. Reading and reflecting on these sources may be done along with the daily prayer time, or at a different time during the day. Christians should have *at least* a brief (5 to 10 minutes) exposure to God's revealed word in the Bible every day, and to other Christian literature, as well, when possible.

In order to love God, we must come to know him, and we come to know him most simply and directly by reading what he has revealed about himself in the sacred Scriptures. As the Second Vatican Council exhorted:

> This sacred Synod earnestly and specifically urges all the Christian faithful, too, especially religious, to learn by frequent reading of the divine Scriptures the "excelling knowledge of Jesus Christ" [Phil 3:8]. "For ignorance of the Scriptures is ignorance of Christ" [St. Jerome]. (DV, no. 25)

Methods of Personal Prayer

There are many forms of personal prayer in the Catholic tradition—either fixed prayers like the Lord's Prayer or prayers taught us by saints, the church, or other Christians; prayers expressed in our own words; or prayer in words given us by the Holy Spirit, known as *glossolalia* or "speaking in tongues" (1 Cor 12:10; Rom 8:26).

Christians can also pray without words, which is generally called mental prayer. Mental prayer may be done either during a specific time devoted to prayer, or it may be done informally or spontaneously at other times during the day. Mental prayer is the mind's reflection on God and on our relationship with him. Methods of mental prayer have been developed by great saints, such as St. Ignatius of Loyola (*The Spiritual Exercises*), St. Francis de Sales (*Introduction to the Devout Life*), and many others. Those methods all are simply meant to help Christians to raise their hearts and minds to God, and to converse with God interiorly.

There are different types of mental prayer. Meditation or pondering involves an active, conscious reflection on God or on some revealed truth(s) about God. Meditation, for the Christian, is not introspection but pondering or reflecting on God's word and his truth. In other forms of mental prayer, God's initiative and activity increases, and the person's role is more to rest in God and cooperate with what he is doing. However, in all forms of prayer, God is active, even in stirring up in a person the desire to pray.

As Christians grow closer to the Lord through prayer, the character of their prayer is likely to change. When two persons come to know each other fairly well, sometimes they can communicate their love without words or activities. Just being together is enough. God can draw a person into a relationship in which it is not always necessary for the person to speak to God or actively meditate on him but simply to be present to God and allow him to speak and act as he wills. The Catholic mystical tradition, which includes such great saints as Teresa of Avila and John of the Cross, teaches about this gift of prayer and describes different types or stages of this prayer. As a general category, the most mature stage of mental prayer is called contemplation. In this type of prayer a person experiences God as fully as is possible in this life. This may involve unity with Christ in his cross and suffering through the experience of "dark nights," as described by St. John of the Cross, or it may take the form of the unspeakable joy and peace of knowing God's presence, like a "mystical marriage" with Christ.

The Catholic church has always cautioned against seeking spiritual experiences for their own sake. Christian prayer is not selfish, primarily concerned with what we can get out of it or with what stage of perfection we can attain. True prayer is selfless, seeking to love, worship, and serve God simply because he is worthy of all love, praise, and adoration. The best measure of the success of personal prayer is not how we feel while we pray or what consolations we receive, but how faithful we are to prayer, regardless of how we feel. The true test of prayer is how fully we seek to worship God and give over our lives entirely to him and his will, whatever his will may be for us. God wants each Christian to draw near to him through prayer. St. James wrote, "Resist the devil and he will flee from you. Draw near to God and he will draw near to you" (Jas 4:7, 8). Jesus said, "Behold, I stand at the door and knock; if anyone hears my voice and opens the door, I will come in to him and eat with him, and he with me" (Rv 3:20).

Communal Prayer: Prayer With Others

Personal prayer is the Christian's life-line to God, but it also is a preparation for prayer with the community of God's people, the church. Catholics understand that God relates to us and saves us not as isolated individuals, but as members of a people, the body of Christ (LG, no. 7). A Christian who does not have a personal relationship with God and a regular individual time of prayer will probably find that communal prayer (prayer with other Christians or with the church) is not very meaningful or rewarding and has little impact on his or her life. Personal prayer is the foundation of meaningful communal prayer, while communal prayer can enrich personal prayer. As the Second Vatican Council taught in the Constitution on Sacred Liturgy:

> The spiritual life, however, is not confined to participation in the liturgy. The Christian is assuredly called to pray with his brethren, but he must also enter into his chamber and pray to the Father in secret [cf. Mt 6:6]; indeed, according to the teaching of the Apostle Paul, he should pray without ceasing [cf. 1 Thes 5:17]. (SC, no.12)

The goal of our individual prayer and personal relationship with God is to draw us more fully into our identity and life as God's people. God has created human beings to be social, and the most important society that he calls all men to belong is to the church of Jesus Christ. As the Dogmatic Constitution on the Church of the Second Vatican Council stated,

> All men are called to belong to the new People of God. It was for this reason that God sent His Son, whom He

> appointed heir of all things, (cf. Heb 1:2), that He might be Teacher, King and Priest of all, the Head of the new and universal people of the sons of God." (no. 13)

And what is this people of God created to do? Its highest calling is to worship God. After all, this is the eternal, eschatological destiny of the church—to be united to God forever in praise and worship (LG, no. 51). That eternal destiny begins even now, as Jesus taught us to pray to the Father "... Thy will be done, / on earth as it is in heaven" (Mt 6:10). In communal prayer, we come together as God's people to fulfill our most exalted task—to worship and praise our Creator. All of our individual works, activities, intentions, and needs are gathered together and brought to God when his people join to worship as a united body.

Forms of Communal Prayer

As with personal prayer, there are different forms of communal prayer. There are informal gatherings of Christians who join in various forms of shared prayer. These include prayer meetings, fellowship groups, prayer breakfasts, rosaries and novenas prayed together, and others. Among Catholics, these gatherings may be led by someone other than an ordained Catholic minister, and they are viewed as a supplement to the official, liturgical worship of the Catholic church. These gatherings sometimes may be ecumenical or interdenominational in nature, and may involve the exercise of some of the gifts of the Holy Spirit mentioned by St. Paul (see 1 Cor 12; Eph 4). The Decree on Ecumenism of the Second Vatican Council teaches that—

> ... it is allowable, indeed desirable, that Catholics should join in prayer with their separated brethren. Such prayers in common are certainly a very effective means for petitioning for the grace of unity, and they are a genuine expression of the ties which even now bind Catholics to their separated

> brethren. "For where two or three are gathered together for My sake, there am I in the midst of them" (Mt 18:20). (no. 8)

The Decree distinguishes this type of common prayer from joining in formal, liturgical worship with other Christians (*communicatio in sacris*), which is strictly regulated, particularly with regard to intercommunion.

The Second Vatican Council and recent popes (Paul VI, John Paul II) have also approved and encouraged Catholics to exercise the charismatic gifts in personal and communal prayer, while reaffirming some of St. Paul's advice about the need for spiritual discernment of these gifts, and the need to avoid pride and ostentation in their exercise (see 1 Cor 12; 14; 1 Thes 5:12, 19-21).

Liturgical Prayer

Liturgy is the official communal prayer of the whole church. The word "liturgy" literally means the "work" or "service" of the people, reminding us that the primary work or service of God's people is to worship together as a body, the body of Christ. The Constitution on the Sacred Liturgy taught that—

> . . . the liturgy is the summit toward which the activity of the Church is directed; at the same time it is the foundation from which all her power flows. For the goal of apostolic works is that all who are made sons of God by faith and baptism should come together to praise God in the midst of His Church, to take part in her sacrifice, and to eat the Lord's supper. (no. 10)

The Lord's Supper, more commonly called the Eucharist or the Mass by Catholics, is the highest form of liturgical prayer. At Mass, Catholics bring to God all the cares and joys of the past day or week and offer them to God as a sacrifice, uniting them with perfect sacrifice of Jesus Christ on the cross. The unity of the church, including our unity with God and with one another, finds its fullest expression in the celebration of the death and resurrection of Christ in the Eucharist.

Liturgical prayer also includes many other forms of communal worship established and overseen by the Catholic church. These include the "Liturgy of the Hours" (the official daily prayer of the church, focusing on scriptural and spiritual readings and recitation of the psalms); Benediction (communal prayer focusing on worship of the Lord present in the Blessed Sacrament, the reserved Eucharistic Host); and the communal celebration of all the sacraments, with their accompanying prayers and ritual actions.

Although liturgy is a work of the people, it is first God's work. God comes among his people to bless us and share his grace. The Constitution on the Sacred Liturgy further notes:

> But in order that the sacred liturgy may produce its full effect, it is necessary that the faithful come to it with proper dispositions, that their thoughts match their words, and that they cooperate with divine grace lest they receive it in vain (cf. 2 Cor 6:1). (no. 11)

There are some necessary prerequisites for fruitful common worship. Common worship requires faith and active participation. "Before men can come to the liturgy they must be called to faith and to conversion . . ." Liturgy also requires the "full, conscious, and active participation" of "all the faithful," which is the major reason for many of the changes in liturgy called for by the Second Vatican Council (see SC, nos. 9, 14, 34).

Liturgical prayer is at the heart of the Catholic life, the life of a people united with God in worship and praise. Liturgy always incorporates the sacred Scripture, which the Constitution says is "of paramount importance" (no. 24), and often includes music, art, and other supportive elements. However, the indispensable aspect of liturgical prayer is the presence and active participation of the people of God, joined to worship God "in spirit and truth" (Jn 4:23-24), according to the rites and forms determined by the church.

Some people object that liturgical prayer is too formal because most of its prayers are determined. However, one aspect of the beauty of the liturgy is its universality, that it is the common prayer of Catholics throughout the world. That is why no one, not even an ordained minister, is free to change it to suit his own taste or theology (SC, no. 22). Yet, Catholic liturgy can never be totally uniform or rigid, because within the liturgy there is room for legitimate variation, for the unique insights and styles of different preachers and celebrants, and for appropriate cultural adaptation. Liturgical worship is rich, because it is the worship of God's people that has developed in the church for nearly two thousand years, and is brought to life again each day through the faith of a living community and the enlivening presence of the Holy Spirit, God himself, in our midst. If liturgical prayer is ever deadening, it is not because *it* is dead, but because *we* have not fully come alive to God or to what we are doing when we worship together as his people. Even spontaneous prayer repeated again and again often becomes very unspontaneous and rigid. Christians must always ask the Holy Spirit to enliven our prayer, whether personal or communal, so that it might strengthen us and be truly pleasing to God who is the object of our love and worship. As the Constitution on the Sacred Liturgy reiterates, the liturgy can manifest the body of Christ to others:

> For it is through the liturgy, especially the divine Eucharistic Sacrifice, that 'the work of our redemption is exercised.' The liturgy is thus the outstanding means by which the faithful can express in their lives, and manifest to others, the mystery of Christ and the real nature of the true Church. (no. 2)

The Mass

The Mass is the center of Catholic liturgical prayer, because it recalls and re-enacts the greatest event of history and of Christian faith: the paschal mystery—the passion, death, resurrection and ascension of our Lord and Savior Jesus Christ. The Mass re-presents, makes present again in the midst of God's people, the one eternal sacrifice of Jesus Christ, who gave up his human life on the cross of Calvary so that all might be saved from sin and eternal death. As we have seen earlier, this sacrifice of Christ is foreshadowed in many places in the Old Testament, especially in the sacrifice of the spotless lamb at the Israelite's exodus from Egypt. The blood of that lamb, sprinkled on the doorposts of the Hebrew people, signaled the angel of death to "pass over" their houses and kill only the first-born of the Egyptians. This final plague convinced Pharaoh to allow the Israelites to "pass over" from slavery in Egypt to freedom. The New Testament, especially the Letter to the Hebrews, explains how the Christian people are saved from destruction and eternal death by the blood of the spotless Lamb of God, Jesus Christ. Jesus enables us by his sacrifice on Calvary to "pass over" from the slavery of sin and Satan into the freedom of the sons and daughters of God. The central feast of Judaism, the Passover, is replaced in Christianity by the "Christian Passover," or paschal mystery—the death, resurrection, and ascension of Jesus, which is made present to us in the sacrament every time Catholics celebrate the Mass.

Even though the form of the Mass has developed over the course of centuries, it has always been the center of communal Christian prayer. The Acts of the Apostles notes that those who were converted at Pentecost "devoted themselves . . . to the breaking of bread and the prayers" (Acts 2:42). The apostle Paul admonished the church in Corinth, instructing them to purify the way they were conducting the Lord's Supper (1 Cor 11:17-35), which he recognizes as a central part of their community life. Some of the earliest Christian writings such as the *Didache,* or the "Teaching of the Twelve Apostles," chapters 9-10 (late first and early second century), and the *First Apology* of Justin Martyr, chapters 65-67 (about A.D. 155), describe the primitive form of the Mass and its prayers in a way that bears striking resemblance to the basic format of the Mass today. In fact, the main elements of St. Justin's description of the Mass are almost identical to the form Catholics now employ. This should not surprise us because the Catholic church has sought to preserve in the Mass the basic form of the communal worship of primitive Christianity, adding or adapting prayers only after careful discernment. The Constitution on the Sacred Liturgy of the Second Vatican Council called for restoration of the Catholic liturgy, distinguishing between the "unchangeable elements divinely instituted, and elements subject to change" (no. 21). The goal of this restoration is that "both texts and rites be drawn up so that they express more clearly the holy things which they signify. Christian people, as far as possible, should be able to understand them with ease and to take part in them fully, actively, and as befits a community" (no. 21). A better translation of the phrase "active participation," which is so often found in the liturgy document, is "actual" or "real" participation. The emphasis is not primarily on how much we sing or respond, but on the depth and quality of our prayer and participation in the liturgy.

Besides active or real participation in the Mass and receiving the Lord in Holy Communion, Catholics also express the eucharistic focus of their worship by adoration of the Lord in the Blessed Sacrament. The consecrated eucharistic bread, the body of Christ, is kept in the tabernacle of every Catholic church, usually marked by a vigil candle, and Catholics believe that there the Lord is present in a special way.

The Structure of the Mass

In its structure, the Mass has always included two basic parts: readings from the sacred Scriptures, now called the

Liturgy of the Word, and the breaking of the bread and the offering and sharing of the cup of the Lord, comprising the Liturgy of the Eucharist. It is through both God's word proclaimed and Jesus Christ, the Bread of Life, received in the sacrament of the Eucharist, that God's people are fed or nourished spiritually.

The Liturgy of the Word begins with a time of repentance from sin to prepare ourselves to hear God's word and receive him in the Eucharist. This penitential rite is followed by a brief time of worship, including on Sundays or special feast days the "Gloria," a hymn of glory to God. The word of God is then proclaimed. First is a reading from the Old Testament or New Testament (other than the Gospels), or both, followed by responsorial verses (usually from one of the psalms), and then a reading from one of the four Gospels. These readings are selected by the Catholic church as part of a cycle, so that readings from the whole Bible will be proclaimed on Sundays over a three-year period, and on weekdays over a two-year period. A sermon or homily on the readings is then given. The Second Vatican Council taught:

> The sermon . . . should draw its content mainly from scriptural and liturgical sources. Its character should be that of a proclamation of God's wonderful works in the history of salvation, that is, the mystery of Christ, which is ever made present and active within us, especially in the celebration of the liturgy. (SC, no. 35)

In the early church, catechumens (those preparing for entry into the church) withdrew from Mass at this point of the service. They had not yet been initiated through baptism into the great mystery of faith that is the heart of the second part of the Mass, the Eucharist. The Liturgy of the Eucharist begins on Sundays and special feast days with the Nicene Creed, a profession of our faith accepted by the Catholic church at the Council of Nicea in A.D. 325 and completed at the First Council of Constantinople in A.D. 381. It is important to reaffirm and profess each week the common faith that is the foundation of Christianity (see Eph 4:5, 6, 13). The Prayer of the Faithful, following the homily or Nicene Creed, presents to God the prayers and petitions of the gathered community, so they may be offered to God the Father in union with Jesus Christ, who constantly intercedes for us to the Father (Heb 7:25). In the Offertory of the Mass, the priest offers to God the prayers of the community, and the bread and wine, which we pray will become the body and blood of Christ. It is important to realize that at this point all the participants also offer themselves to God, both as a community and as individuals. Catholics gathered at Mass offer to God all that we are and all that we have done in the past day or week, humbly asking him to accept and purify this offering, and to unite it with the eternal offering of Jesus himself.

From this point on, the Mass moves to the great Eucharistic Prayer during which the solemn Consecration of bread and wine takes place. First, the celebrant prays that the Holy Spirit would make this offering of bread and wine acceptable an offering "in spirit and truth" (Jn 4:23, 24). This is called the *epiclesis* or invocation of the Holy Spirit. Soon following this are the words of consecration, the words of Jesus himself, "This is my body...," "this is the cup of my blood...," "Do this in memory of me...." Catholics believe that at this point, by God's sovereign power and will, the bread and wine truly become the body and blood of Jesus Christ. At this climactic moment of the Mass the whole congregation reflects on the mystery of God's coming among us and worships him in our midst.

After the Consecration, the saving death and resurrection of Christ is commemorated explicitly, and another *epiclesis* is offered, this time calling down the Holy Spirit on the congregation that, through receiving the Body of the Lord, it might become more deeply the body of Christ. Then prayers are offered for the whole church, the pope and bishops, and all its members, living and deceased. We express our hope that we will also one day share the joy of eternal life united with God and his angels and saints. This time of worship and petition ends with another elevation of the Host, Christ's Body, and the chalice of his Blood, at which time the priest declares, "Through him, with him, and in him, in the unity of the Holy Spirit, all honor and glory are yours almighty Father, forever and ever," and all the people respond with the great "Amen!"

In immediate preparation for receiving the Body and Blood of Jesus Christ, the congregation prays the Lord's Prayer together and usually at this point greets one another with a sign or kiss of peace, to express unity, peace and reconciliation with each other (Mt 5:23, 24) and with the Lord. All Catholics who are not living in a state of serious unrepented sin then are encouraged to approach the altar to receive the Lord's Body and Blood in Holy Communion. What a tremendous, precious time when Jesus Christ approaches us personally, and individually enters each person's heart through the sacramental reality of his own Body and Blood! At least a few moments are devoted to prayer and reflection after communion, a time in which the Lord lives within us in the most personal, intimate way that is possible in this life. The Mass draws to a conclusion with the final prayers, dismissal, and sometimes a closing hymn. The word Mass originates in the Latin words of dismissal, *Ite missa est.* "Go, the Mass is ended" literally means "Go, you are dismissed," or better "Go, you are sent forth"—sent forth into the world to live out what has been celebrated and received in the liturgy.

Living in Union with God: Helps to Union

Prayer, the sacraments, and the study of God's word in the Bible and authentic Christian tradition are the basic ways that God has given humanity to grow in union with him. However, God has also provided many helps to assist us in living a fuller, richer Christian life. Let us look at some of these helps to deeper union with the Lord.

The Liturgical Year. Catholics understand that time is one of God's greatest gifts and so seek ways to consecrate time to God. The Catholic church sets aside special times to offer God praise and worship and to commemorate his mighty works and those people who have been powerful instruments of his work in the world. The time we live in is traditionally designated "A.D."—*Anno Domini* or "Year of the Lord." Each year, the Catholic church joins with many Christians to celebrate the major events of our redemption in Jesus Christ. The liturgical year begins with the first Sunday of Advent, a season which prepares us for the coming, or advent, of Jesus Christ among us. This season reaches its climax in the feast of the birth of Christ, Christmas. The day of Christmas had been observed by Gentiles in the Roman Empire as the feast of *Sol Invictus,* the unconquered Sun, which begins to shine for a longer time every day after the winter solstice, which begins around December 21. Christians knew that the true unconquered Son was the Son of God, Jesus Christ, who is the light of the world shining ever more brightly since his birth as a man. Hence, Christians have reclaimed time for God by established feasts such as Christmas to replace former pagan customs.[2] The Christmas season continues with the feast of Mary, Mother of God, on January 1, consecrating the entire new year to her prayers; it concludes with the feast of the Baptism of the Lord. This is followed by Epiphany, the feast of the manifestation of Christ to the nations, celebrated January 6, or the Sunday nearest that date.

The next major liturgical observance for Catholics is Lent, followed by Easter, the Ascension, and Pentecost. Lent began as a period for the instruction and preparation of catechumens (those who would enter the church at Easter) and became a time of penance and renewal for the whole church. The forty days of Lent emulate Jesus' forty days of temptation in the desert, or the wandering of Israel for forty years in the Sinai desert. The Catholic church in the United States observes Lent by abstaining from meat every Friday (for those between ages

14 and 69), and also fasting (eating solid foods only at one full meal and two smaller meals, maximum) and abstinence from meat for those between 21 and 59 on Ash Wednesday and Good Friday. These are minimal sacrifices observed by all, but the faithful are urged by church teaching to seek other ways during Lent to prepare one's heart for the great feast that lies ahead. The last week of Lent, known as Holy Week, commemorates the events of Jesus' life from the time of his triumphal entry into Jerusalem (Palm Sunday) until his resurrection on Easter morning (preceded by Holy Thursday, commemorating Jesus' Last Supper, and Good Friday, recalling Jesus' suffering and death at the hands of men). The joyous feast of Christ's resurrection, Easter Sunday, is the greatest Christian feast and the climax of the liturgical year. Its vigil St. Augustine called the "mother of all vigils." It is the Christian Passover of Jesus Christ from death to life, and with this the passing over of God's people from the bondage of sin to the freedom of God's sons and daughters through the resurrection of Jesus. The Catholic church also celebrates the ascension of Jesus into heaven on Ascension Thursday, forty days after Easter.

The third great Christian feast of the liturgical year is Pentecost, from the Greek word for fifty since it occurs fifty days after Easter. This feast commemorates the sending of the Holy Spirit upon the apostles and the birth of the church. After this, there is a long period of ordinary time in which the Catholic church remembers the events and teaching of Jesus' public ministry, culminating in his teaching on the end of time and on his second coming, as the liturgical year draws to a close.

Within this framework of the major events of Christ's life and the coming of the Holy Spirit, feasts of the saints (holy men and women who have served God in an exemplary way), are interspersed throughout the year. Some of these feasts honor Mary, the Mother of God, such as the feasts of the Annunciation (March 25), the Visitation (May 31), the

Immaculate Conception (Dec. 8), and the Assumption of Mary into heaven (August 15). The Catholic church prescribes readings for Mass taken from the Bible for every day of the year and for the feasts of saints.

The liturgical year, based upon the events of Jesus Christ's life and readings from the sacred Scriptures, is an important way that Catholics continually are enabled to reflect upon and live out the mysteries of our salvation in Jesus Christ.

The Liturgy of the Hours. Not only is every day dedicated to God, but in the Catholic tradition certain hours of the day are set aside for prayer and reflection on God's word. The Liturgy of the Hours, or the Divine Office, is the official daily liturgical prayer of the whole Catholic church. It is comprised mainly of the recitation of psalms, readings from the Bible, and some selections from distinguished church Fathers and conciliar statements of the past.

The Liturgy of the Hours developed first from the regular prayers said by all Christians at certain times of the day (see the *Didache,* St. Hippolytus, Tertullian) and was fostered and developed further by the founders and leaders of the monastic movement, so that "the whole course of the day and night is made holy by the praises of God" (SC, no. 89). In its present form for broad use, it consists of: (1) an office of readings for the day, which may be said at any time; (2) morning prayer; (3) mid-day prayer; (4) vespers or evening prayer; and (5) a brief night prayer (compline). Those who have received the sacrament of Holy Orders and those who are vowed to religious life usually are required to pray the Liturgy of the Hours daily, but lay persons are also invited to pray it. The liturgical renewal that has taken firm hold in the church since the Second Vatican Council urges parishes to have public recitation of morning prayer and evening prayer, so that lay people can attend. Even though the Liturgy of the Hours may be prayed alone, it was originally designed to be sung, chanted, or recited together by groups of Christians, whether in monastery, rectory, convent, or parish. Praying the Liturgy of the Hours enables Christians to join in the heartbeat of the prayer life of God's people, the universal church.

Prayer and Devotion to Mary and the Saints. The previous chapter on the church introduced us to the concept of the communion of saints. Through our baptismal covenant, Catholics enter into a living, committed relationship not only with God but also with all of God's people in the church of Jesus Christ. It is a great mystery, yet a truth, that the church consists of all those who have died in union with Jesus Christ, as well as the living. The Letter to the Hebrews exhorts us that since we are "surrounded by so great a cloud of witnesses," from Abel to the present (Heb 11), we should lay aside every burden and sin and "run with perseverance the race that is set before us" (Heb 12:1). The Book of Revelation recounts John's inspired vision of a great multitude of people in white robes, the martyrs, standing before the throne of God worshiping (Rv 7:9-17) with their prayers rising like incense up to God's throne (Rv 8:3, 4).

An important aspect of both the Jewish and Christian tradition has been to honor and praise the godly men and women who have gone before us (see Sir 44). One reason for this, as the Letter to the Hebrews relates, is to receive encouragement from their example and to imitate their virtues. Another reason that the Catholic tradition insists upon this is that we may receive help from their prayers as they remember our particular needs before the throne of God. Because of their lives of faith and obedience, Catholics believe that Mary and the other saints are particularly close to God, God's special friends. Just as we might ask a friend here on earth (especially holy or godly persons) to pray for us and our needs, the Catholic church teaches that it is proper and good to ask those recognized by the church as saints to pray for us and for our needs. (The process by which the Catholic church formally recognizes a deceased person as a saint is called "canonization.") We are all part of God's family, whether we are living here on earth or living with the Lord, and even the death of our bodies does not divide our unity in Jesus Christ. We continue to support each other.

Thus, another help for growing in union with God is our relationship with Mary and the saints. We can both imitate their lives, and ask them to pray to the Lord for us and for our intentions. As the Second Vatican Council taught:

> The Church has always believed that the apostles, and Christ's martyrs who have given the supreme witness of faith and charity by the shedding of their blood, are quite closely joined with us in Christ. She has always venerated them with special devotion, together with the Blessed Virgin Mary and the holy angels. The Church too has devoutly implored the aid of their intercession. (LG, no. 50)

The Catholic church cautions that the honor given the saints and Mary and their intercession for us in no way contradicts or detracts from the adoration given to God alone. We must always approach God with our needs through Jesus Christ, "the one mediator between God and men" (1 Tm 2:5), in the power of the Holy Spirit. (see LG, nos. 51, 60, 62)

Devotion and Devotions. The Catholic tradition recognizes that there is a proper devotion that a Christian may have to one of the saints, to Mary, or to a certain mystery of faith. Praying and reflecting on any of these may inspire a person and draw him closer to God. Often Catholics are led to seek the prayers of a particular saint before God's throne. Just as in a family there are special bonds between certain members, in God's family there often develop special bonds of spiritual unity and friendship among members of the church. It should not surprise us, then, that nearly every Catholic has an attraction, bond, or devotion to some saint or mystery of our faith. The message of the gospel is so rich that it touches different people in different ways and leads us each to discern a saint or Christian symbol that especially embodies the gospel and brings it alive for us. Some people may identify with the poverty and joy of St. Francis of Assisi and St. Clare; the zeal for God of St. Ignatius of Loyola or St. Catherine of Siena; the wisdom of St. Thomas Aquinas, St. Augustine or St. Theresa of Avila; the missionary fervor of St. Paul, St. Dominic, St. Thérèse de Lisieux, St. Francis Xavier, and countless others; the practical wisdom and holiness of St. Benedict, St. Frances de Sales or St. Jeanne de Chantal; the brilliance and steadfastness of St. Thomas More; the humor of St. Philip Neri; the zeal for reform of St. Charles Borromeo; the love of the poor of St. Vincent de Paul and many others. The diversity of these canonized saints, who represent all of the saints in heaven, indicates the richness of God's work in the church and calls us forth to follow and imitate Christ as they did. The lives of all the saints echo the words of St. Paul: "Be imitators of me, as I am of Christ" (1 Cor 11:1).

Our devotion to Mary, the saints, or to mysteries such as the Cross of Christ or the Sacred Heart of Jesus gives rise to special prayers or devotions directed to them. It is beyond the scope of this short catechism to present the wide variety of Catholic devotions. They include prayers such as consecration and novenas to Our Lady, the rosary, and a plethora of prayers to the saints, to Mary, and to Jesus and the Holy Spirit under various titles.

Probably the most widespread and popular Catholic devotion is recitation of the rosary. Though not absolutely essential to a Catholic's spiritual life and growth, millions of Catholics have benefited through the ages by prayerful reflection on the fifteen mysteries of the life of Christ and his mother commemorated in the rosary and by the rhythmic recitation of the prayers of the rosary (the Apostles' Creed, the Lord's Prayer, the Hail Mary, and the Glory Be to the Father) which quiets our spirit and helps us to pray. Pope Paul VI, in his apostolic letter on Devotion to the Blessed Virgin Mary, highly recommended the rosary, comparing it with the liturgy: "... like the liturgy, it is of a community nature, draws its inspiration from Sacred Scripture, and is oriented toward the mystery of Christ. . . ."[3]

Another reason that the rosary has gained special prominence among Catholic devotions is because in one of the most widely accepted apparitions of Mary, at Fatima, Portugal, in 1917, Mary told the children that she was the "Lady of the Rosary," and asked them to pray the rosary daily. Since that time, praying the rosary either as individuals or in families or groups has become a characteristic of the prayer life of many Catholics. Recent popes have heeded the request of Mary at Fatima by consecrating Russia to her Immaculate Heart, a solemn prayer for the full conversion of that vast and powerful territory, and by encouraging Catholics to pray the rosary and to consecrate themselves and their families to Mary, who is the spiritual Mother of all Christians.

Sacramentals. Sacramentals are another type of help to growing in union with God. As their name implies, sacramentals usually are related to one of the seven sacraments. Like the sacraments, sacramentals make use of material objects to remind us of God and to put us into contact with him through our senses. They differ from the sacraments in that their effectiveness in drawing us closer to God depends more on our personal faith and devotion, whereas Christ acts in the sacraments in a more sovereign way, even when the faith of some people approaching the sacrament may be weak or lacking.

Sacramentals include such things as blessed (or holy) oil, water, or salt, that Catholics can use in prayer and blessing every day. Objects connected with the sacraments, such as the altar, the baptismal font, the crucifix or cross, and the paten and ciborium used at Mass, are sacramentals because they remind us of God and of his presence in the sacraments. Some sacramentals are related to devotion, such as the rosary, the scapular, medals, pictures, and statues of Mary and the saints. The Eastern Christian use of icons or sacred images is an ancient and venerable form of sacramental. Sacramentals are signs that point to God and remind Catholics of his presence. They help us to proclaim the richness of the mystery of Jesus Christ, who desires to use all things he has created to lead us to recognize him and to praise him for his glory revealed in them.

Fasting and Abstinence. Another means to union with God is self-denial. Catholics deny themselves of food, drink, sleep or comfort, not because the body is evil or demands punishment, but: (1) as a form of prayer of petition to God; (2) to remind us of God's goodness and of our utter dependence on him; and (3) to detach ourselves temporarily from some good things of the world in order to focus more fully on God and to hear him speak to us more clearly.

Jesus himself said that his followers would fast after he (the bridegroom) was no longer with them on earth (Mk 2:18, 19). Fasting was observed in the primitive church (Acts 13:2; 14:23; 2 Cor 11:27), and one of the earliest Christian writings outside the Bible, the *Didache,*[4] records that the early Christians fasted on Wednesdays and Fridays. In later times, special periods of fasting and abstinence from food and drink were established by the church, both in the East and West, especially the penitential season of Lent preceding Easter.

The Catholic church has always taught the importance of penance and self-denial, even though it has established different specific guidelines at times. Although the requirements of fasting and abstinence for Catholics are not as rigorous today as in the past, this is intended to allow us to be more responsible in this area, undertaking penances voluntarily. Pope Paul VI's Apostolic Constitution on Fast and Abstinence (February 17, 1966) reaffirms that penance is essential to Christianity, for all Christians are called by Jesus to take up the cross daily to follow him (Mt 16:24; Lk 14:27; Mk 8:34). As the Constitution states: "By divine law all the faithful are required to do penance."

Penance not only involves fasting and abstinence, but also prayer and charity, especially giving alms, or money to those in need. Pope Paul VI emphasized that this ancient Jewish triad of prayer, fasting, and almsgiving, soon accepted by Christianity, is the fundamental way that the Catholic church teaches its members to deny themselves in order to grow in love for the Lord and others.

Indulgences. As stated above, one way that Christians repent of sin is through prayer. Because the Catholic church attaches such importance to prayer and to other penitential acts done in faith, it declares that special graces, called indulgences, may come to a baptized person who offers certain prayers or who does certain penitential works with intention of receiving these graces.

The Catholic church has always recognized that prayer and other penitential acts done in faith call down the mercy of God. God not only forgives sin when Christians pray and repent, but he also desires to remove the effects or consequences of sin. All sin has consequences: disruption of the society around us, damage to the life and character of the one who sins, as well as offending our Creator. The sinner normally experiences the consequences of his or her sin as a punishment that comes upon the person either in his life or after death in purgatory. (Note, however, that not all trial or suffering is a direct result of sin, as Jesus himself taught. See Jn 9:3.) Traditional Catholic theology calls this "temporal punishment due to sin." However, God, in his mercy, removes some of the consequences of sin when a baptized person prays to God for the removal of this punishment or undertakes penitential acts. The Catholic church declares that a Christian does receive a special share in the "infinite merits of Christ," called an indulgence, for the removal of the consequences (temporal punishment) due to sin when certain prayers are offered or penitential actions are done. Christians not only can seek these indulgences for themselves but also for others in the body of Christ, even for the deceased who may still be suffering the consequences of their own sin in the purifying fire of purgatory (see 1 Cor 3:10-15; 2 Mc 12:43-46).

The Catholic understanding of indulgences has been clouded by certain abuses in the past, such as the selling of indulgences that was rightly denounced by Martin Luther in the sixteenth century. Probably it is best today to keep the understanding of indulgences fairly simple: prayer and penance calls down the mercy of God; the Catholic church simply recognizes the value of certain prayers and acts of penance in calling down God's mercy when it designates them indulgences. The Catholic church designates certain indulgences as "plenary" (removing all effects of sin that result in God's just punishment) or "partial" (removing part, but not all, of these consequences of sin).

In studying carefully the Catholic church's teaching on indulgences, it is inspiring to discover that at its root is the redeeming work of Jesus Christ and the body of Christ in action. Christians are called to pray for themselves and for others, even for those departed from life on earth, that the infinite merits of Jesus Christ and of all the saints united with him would free us from the bondage of sin and all its effects.[5]

The Work of the Holy Spirit

Now that we have considered some aspects of Catholic worship and devotion, the final section of this chapter will be devoted to the source and foundation of all Christian prayer: God's work in us through the Holy Spirit. The Catholic church teaches that it is impossible to pray or have a life of true devotion without the Holy Spirit. Jesus said that true worshipers must worship "in Spirit and truth" (Jn 4:23, 24). In addition, the work of the Holy Spirit is not limited to the sacraments of baptism and confirmation. As the Gospel of John teaches, the Spirit's working is free and even surprising to us, at times. Jesus said:

> "The wind blows where it will. You hear the sound of it
> but you do not know whence it comes
> or whither it goes; so it is with every one who is born of the
> Spirit." (Jn 3:8)

One of the surprises of the Holy Spirit in the Catholic church is the rise of the pentecostal movement or the charismatic renewal shortly after the close of the Second Vatican Council. Many Catholics see this as God's response to Pope John XXIII's prayer at the council for the Holy Spirit to renew his wonders in our time, as by a "new Pentecost." Pope Paul VI and Pope John Paul II have both recognized and endorsed the Catholic charismatic renewal as a genuine work of the Holy Spirit.

How has this new working of the Holy Spirit come about? Many confirmed Catholics have felt a need to pray for a fuller release or empowerment of the Holy Spirit in their lives that they might love, serve, and witness to Christ more effectively. They desire Christ and the Holy Spirit to come alive in them as a reality, rather than just a concept or doctrine. God has been responding to the prayer of such Catholics in an evident and powerful way. In response to prayer, the Holy Spirit has come into the lives of millions in a new way, bringing gifts, graces, deeper virtue, and the love of God.

How is this extra-sacramental working of the Holy Spirit to be understood theologically by Catholics? St. Thomas Aquinas spoke of a new sending or sendings of the Holy Spirit in the lives of Catholics in addition to the visible sendings of the Holy Spirit in the sacraments. St. Thomas wrote in his *Summa Theologia:*

> There is an invisible sending (of the Holy Spirit) also with respect to an advance in virtue or an increase of grace. . . .

> Such an invisible sending is especially to be seen in that kind of increase of grace whereby a person moves forward into some new act or new state of grace: as, for instance, when a person moves forward into the grace of working miracles, or of prophecy, or out of the burning love of God offers his life as a martyr, or renounces all of his possessions, or undertakes some other such arduous thing. (*Summa Theologia* I, q. 43, a. 6)

Fr. Francis Sullivan, S.J., draws the following conclusion from St. Thomas's teaching:

> I conclude from this teaching of St. Thomas that there is no reason why Catholics, who believe that they have received the Holy Spirit in their sacramental initiation, should not look forward to new "sendings" of the Spirit to them, which would move them from the "state of grace" in which they already are into some "new act" or "new state of grace." Now if we recall that in biblical language, "sending the Spirit," "pouring out the Spirit," and "baptizing in the Spirit" are simply different ways of saying the same thing, the conclusion follows that it is quite in accord with traditional Catholic theology for baptized and confirmed Christians to ask the Lord to "baptize them in the Holy Spirit." What they are asking for, in the language of St. Thomas, is a new "sending" of the Holy Spirit, which would begin a decisively new work of grace in their lives. As we have seen from the examples which St. Thomas gives, (working miracles, prophecy, etc.) he would obviously not be surprised if such a new work of grace involved a charismatic gift.[6]

Fr. Sullivan goes on to explain that this new sending of the Holy Spirit is more than the conferral of a new gift (or gifts) of the Spirit, but "a new way of the Spirit's indwelling in the soul . . . a real innovation (making new) of the person's relationship with the indwelling Spirit."[7]

This is one Catholic understanding of what is commonly

termed being "baptized in the Holy Spirit," or the "release of the Spirit." Far from being only a Protestant or Pentecostal phenomenon, the Second Vatican Council and recent popes have affirmed the validity and importance of this manifestation of the Holy Spirit and of the charisms or gifts of the Spirit that often accompany it. As the Second Vatican Council taught:

> It is not only through the sacraments and Church ministries that the Holy Spirit sanctifies and leads the people of God and enriches it with virtues. Allotting His gifts "to everyone according as He wills" (1 Cor 12:11), He distributes special graces among the faithful of every rank. By these gifts He makes them fit and ready to undertake the various tasks and offices advantageous for the renewal and upbuilding of the Church, according to the words of the Apostles: "The manifestation of the Spirit is given to everyone for profit" (1 Cor 12:7). These charismatic gifts, whether they be the most outstanding or the more simple and widely diffused, are to be received with thanksgiving and consolation, for they are exceedingly suitable and useful for the needs of the Church. (LG, no. 12)

What are these charismatic gifts, or manifestations of the Holy Spirit, spoken of by the Second Vatican Council? They may be divided into three general categories, although the activity of the Holy Spirit in the lives of Christians is not limited to these. They are the "Isaian gifts" of the Holy Spirit, the "Pauline gifts," and the "fruit of the Spirit." The prophet Isaiah listed seven gifts to be possessed by the Messiah, and which are now shared by God's messianic people, the church: ". . . the Spirit of the LORD shall rest upon him, / the spirit of wisdom and understanding, / the spirit of counsel and might, / the spirit of knowledge and the fear of the LORD. / And his delight shall be in the fear of the LORD" (Is 11:2-3).

These seven gifts—wisdom, understanding, counsel, fortitude, knowledge, piety and fear of the Lord—have traditionally been recognized by Catholics as manifestations of the Holy Spirit's indwelling in the believer—charisms of the Holy Spirit.

St. Paul presents another set of gifts of the Spirit, most fully set forth in 1 Corinthians 12:4-11:

> Now there are varieties of gifts, but the same Spirit;
> and there are varieties of service, but the same Lord;
> and there are varieties of working, but it is the same God who inspires them all in every one. To each is given the manifestation of the Spirit for the common good. To one is given through the Spirit the utterance of wisdom, and to another the utterance of knowledge according to the same Spirit, to another faith by the same Spirit, to another gifts of healing by the one Spirit, to another the working of miracles, to another prophecy, to another the ability to distinguish between spirits, to another various kinds of tongues, to another the interpretation of tongues. All these are inspired by one and the same Spirit who apportions to each one individually as he wills.

This is the list of the gifts of the Spirit (see also Eph 4) that the Dogmatic Constitution on the Church says "are to be received with thanksgiving and consolation, for they are exceedingly suitable and useful for the needs of the Church" (no. 12). St. Thomas Aquinas called these gifts the "graces freely given" (*gratiae gratis datae*) by God to the church. The designation of these as "extraordinary" gifts is later terminology. Paul's lists of these workings of the Holy Spirit are not complete or exclusive; there may be other gifts of the Spirit in addition to these.

Finally, St. Paul also describes the "fruit of the Spirit" in his Letter to the church in Galatia. This "fruit" is the sign of the Holy Spirit's working in a person's character, as God transforms each of us to his likeness in our thoughts, attitudes, and actions. Paul writes:

> . . . the fruit of the Spirit is love, joy, peace, patience, kindness, goodness, faithfulness, gentleness, self-control; against such there is no law. (Gal 5:22, 23)

The value of all these workings of the Spirit are always determined by the way they are used and their end, or purpose. They must be used in love, or else they are worthless (1 Cor 13), and their highest purpose is the "common good" (1 Cor 12:7) or "building up the body of Christ" (Eph 4:11-12). They are never to be considered personal property or causes for boasting. They are free gifts of God.

The Holy Spirit's presence in our lives is not limited to these gifts and fruits. Christians are called to relate to the Holy Spirit as a person—the person of God who guides us (Acts 16:6-8); speaks to us (see Acts 10:19; 13:2; 21:11; 28:25); consoles us (Acts 9:31); sends us forth (Acts 13:4); warns (Acts 20:23); prompts (Acts 21:4), and teaches us the truth (Jn 16:13). As Catholics grow in personal relationships with the Holy Spirit, they will realize the importance of being led by the Holy Spirit in all decisions and actions. "If we live by the Spirit, let us also walk by the Spirit" (Gal 5:25).

A final note on workings of the Holy Spirit is the importance of the Spirit in creating and safeguarding the unity of Christians and the Church. After St. Paul listed the various gifts of the Holy Spirit (1 Cor 12:4-11), he proceeded to describe the church as a body with many parts or members, each member having its own particular gift and place in the body (1 Cor 12:12-27). Each Christian has a particular gift and place in the church. Many of the problems in the church in Corinth, and in the church of Jesus Christ today, stem from

Christians not understanding or not accepting their particular gift and role in the body of Christ. They may have an individualistic perspective, not understanding that in God's eyes and plan they are not just individuals, but part of a whole church, a people, for whom they should have personal concern. The gifts of the Spirit are given as they are so "that there may be no discord in the body, but that the members may have the same care for one another" (1 Cor 12:25). The Holy Spirit calls Catholics to consider our lives and our gifts as belonging first to God, and then to each other in the church.

In this view of the church, there is to be no contention between those who are called by God to serve as leaders in the church, especially the ordained, and those who have other gifts and callings. There is not an hierarchical church (the ordained) opposed to or set apart from a charismatic church (those not ordained who possess certain gifts). There is only one church of Jesus Christ, whose members all are charismatic, possessing gifts of the Holy Spirit of various types for the common good (LG, nos. 8, 12). God has sent the Holy Spirit to his people in power and with an abundant variety of gifts and manifestations. Catholics seek the presence of the Spirit and all of his gifts to serve one another for the glory of God!

EIGHT

Living as a Catholic Christian

Jesus Christ as the Model and Source of the Christian Life

> THE LORD JESUS, the divine Teacher and Model of all perfection, preached holiness of life to each and every one of his disciples, regardless of their situation: "You therefore are to be perfect, even as your heavenly Father is perfect" (Mt 5:48). He himself stands as the Author and Finisher of this holiness of life. For He sent the Holy Spirit upon all men that he might inspire them from within to love God with their whole heart and their whole soul, with all their mind and all their strength (cf. Mk 12:30) and that they might love one another as Christ loved them (cf. Jn 13:34; 15:12)... Thus it is evident to everyone that all the faithful of Christ of whatever rank or status are called to the fullness of the Christian life and to the perfection of charity. (LG, no. 40)

This statement of the Catholic bishops at the Second Vatican Council summarizes well what the Christian life and Christian morality is all about. Regardless of whether one is married or single, ordained or professing religious vows or not, all are called to the same holiness of life and perfect charity that comes from following Jesus Christ. The summation of all Catholic moral teaching is this: be like Jesus Christ. As a follower of Jesus Christ, learn to live like him, act like him, think like him, love like him. Jesus Christ is the incarnate Word of God, God himself in human form. He is God come among us to show what life is all about and how to live. He has also come to share the very life of God with us. All we need to do to receive this new, divine life that will enable us to live like Jesus Christ, is to turn to him and ask for it. "Behold, I stand at the door and knock; if anyone hears my voice and opens the door, I will come in to him and eat with him, and he with me" (Rv 3:20).

Jesus taught how we are to live in such a simple way: "You shall love the Lord your God with all your heart, and with all your soul, and with all your mind. This is the great and first commandment. And a second is like it, You shall love your neighbor as yourself" (Mt 22:37-39); or as Jesus added in the Gospel of John, "love one another as I have loved you" (Jn 15:12). This is so simple and yet so difficult! It is important to begin a chapter on Christian morality in this way because too often Christians lose sight of the goal or ask the wrong questions. We often begin by asking what God's law is—what we can and can't do. This is to miss the whole point of the Christian life. The call of Jesus Christ is basically a positive one: a call to love, a call to true freedom. It is primarily a call to become like Jesus Christ, not just to avoid sin or vice or even just to practice certain virtues. As we set our eyes on Christ and pray earnestly for his grace, we will see ourselves freed from sin and increase in virtue because we will grow to be more like him. The goal of the Christian life is "to grow up in every way into him who is the head, into Christ . . ." (Eph 4:15).

The Catholic bishops of the United States have taught:

> Christian morality defines a way of living worthy of a human being and of an adopted son of God. It is a positive

> response to God, by growing in the new life given through Jesus Christ. It is supported and guided by the grace and gifts of the Holy Spirit. . . .
>
> Sustained by faith, man is to live a life of love of God and of his fellow man. This is his greatest responsibility, and the source of his greatest dignity. A man's holiness, whatever his vocation or state of life may be, is the perfection of love of God.[1]

All are called to holiness, and holiness means the perfection of our love of God.

Freedom from Sin

Why can't we love God, others, and ourselves as we would like? Sin is the reason. Sin not only injures and disfigures us but it offends God, our good, all-loving Father. The horror and stupidity of sin is that instead of accepting God's love and favor, we turn our backs on him and cut ourselves off from the source of life and mercy. Sin is like slapping Jesus in the face, or driving nails further into his pierced hands. Christians must detest sin, realizing what it really is and what it does to us.

The first chapter of this catechism described the original sin of the first human persons, which resulted in the separation or alienation of the entire human race from God and his love. The state of original sin led to personal sin, individual acts done knowingly and deliberately that violate God's will and law. This is sometimes called formal sin. The Catholic church has long recognized seven root or "deadly" sins that are at the heart of most personal sin: pride, greed, lust, anger, gluttony, envy and sloth (laziness). All personal, or formal, sin offends God and harms our relationship with him. However, Scripture and the Catholic church recognize a distinction between personal sin that is "mortal" or "deadly," (see 1 Jn 5:16-17), which separates one from the friendship of God or deepens one's alienation from God,[2] and less serious offenses against

God that injure our relationship with him but do not totally sever it. These latter are called "venial sins" in Catholic theology. In human relations, too, we understand that we can offend or hurt others in ways that either damage our relationship with another person or bring it to an end.

The good news for the human race is that God has not left us trapped in the bondage of sin but has forgiven and reconciled mankind to himself through his Son, Jesus Christ. Since the coming of Christ, God offers this forgiveness and reconciliation to each person living on earth. If there remains a breach in the relationship between God and any person, it is not God who is responsible for it. God has done his utmost to bring each of us back to his friendship by becoming a man and dying a shameful, painful death on a cross in order to conquer sin (Rom 8:3; 2 Cor 5:21). God invites every person, each of us, back into loving union with him.

With the coming of Christ, two ways of life have been set before each person: the way of life (obedience to God; accepting his invitation to friendship) and the way of death (rebellion against God; refusal to accept his love and enter into friendship with him). This distinction is found in the earliest Christian writings of the first and second century (the *Didache*, the *Epistle of Barnabas*, and others). It is even found in the Old Testament:

> I call heaven and earth to witness against you this day, that I have set before you life and death, blessing and curse; therefore choose life, that you and your descendants may live, loving the LORD your God, obeying his voice, and cleaving to him; for that means life to you and length of days . . . (Dt 30:19-20; see also Dt 30:15-19)

The Old Testament passage reveals that from God's earliest dealings with his people, Israel, he set forth the same choice: to love and obey him and find life or to rebel against him and die. In Jesus Christ, the choice is made clearer, for Jesus himself is "the way, and the truth, and the life" (Jn 14:6); the person who believes in him and faithfully follows him will enjoy eternal life and happiness with God (Jn 14:1-6, 23-24).

Modern theology speaks about this choice as a person's "fundamental option." This theory stresses that the basic orientation of a person's life is either *toward God*, through obedience to God in response to his grace, or *away from God*, due to serious sin. According to this moral theory, it is possible for a person oriented toward God to offend God in small ways, and yet remain in God's friendship. The person's fundamental option for God may not change despite some failures and shortcomings. However, many small sins do weaken our relationship with God and may lead us to fall into more serious sin that separates us from God's friendship; this changes our fundamental option. Christians cannot take venial sin lightly. On the other hand, it is possible for those who have rejected God, whose fundamental option is against God, to do some genuinely good things through the abundance of God's grace in the world. This does not necessarily mean that they are in a proper relationship with God, but it is a sign that God may be at work in their lives to lead them to conversion—to change their fundamental option away from rebellion and towards him. This grace offered to them by God may eventually make them choose to turn away from their sins—to repent—and to accept God's friendship through believing in and following Jesus Christ.

The Enemies of God: the World, the Flesh, and the Devil

Despite Christ's definitive victory over sin on Calvary, there still remain enemies to God's salvation that seek to lure people away from the way of life in Christ. Catholic theology has traditionally identified the three greatest enemies of God's salvation as the "world," the "flesh," and the devil.

The "world" in this sense is not the created order that the

Bible proclaims to be "very good" (Gn 1:31), nor the world which God loved so much that he came to save (Jn 3:16). Rather, it is a biblical term for that world or world-system of human ideas and values that are opposed to God and his rule (see Jn 17:9; 1 Jn 2:15). The "world" here can refer to false values or ideologies in human society or to idolatrous, inordinate attraction or attachment to things or ideas in the world, even though these things may be good in themselves. Especially in Western society, the greatest manifestation of the world is materialism, the ceaseless pursuit of material things and the insatiable desire for more. The world lures us to desire power, money, possessions, status, and success, for their own sake and not for the glory of God and for the advancement of his kingdom.

The "flesh" is not our physical flesh or bodies, which are good because they are created by God, but flesh in the Pauline sense of the allurements of our fallen human nature. As Paul wrote to the church in Galatia:

> Now the works of the flesh are plain; fornication, impurity, licentiousness, idolatry, sorcery, enmity, strife, jealousy, anger, selfishness, dissension, party spirit, envy, drunkenness, carousing, and the like. I warn you, as I warned you before, that those who do such things shall not inherit the kingdom of God.... those who belong to Christ Jesus have crucified the flesh with its passions and desires. (Gal 5:19-21, 24)

As Jesus taught: "If any man would come after me, let him deny himself and take up his cross and follow me" (Mt 16:24). Christians must learn to recognize, renounce, and break from attractions and passions of the flesh and instead follow Jesus by submitting our emotions and passions to his rule.

The final enemy of Christians is the devil, or Satan (Rv 12:9), "that ancient serpent. . . the deceiver of the whole world," the fallen angel, Lucifer, who first rebelled against

God and now only lives to lure all other rational creatures into the same eternal misery of rebellion and separation from God. Jesus confronted the devil himself (Mt 4:1-11; Mk 1:12-13; Lk 4:1-13) and the hosts of demons and evil spirits, until Satan put it into the heart of Judas Iscariot to deliver Jesus up to death (Lk 22:3; Jn 13:27). Although Satan was defeated and all his power broken by Jesus' death and resurrection, in the mystery of God's plan, Satan and other evil spiritual powers are still allowed to tempt humanity until Christ's glorious second coming (Rv 20). For this reason, Christ and the apostles Peter, James, and Paul call Christians to prayer, watchfulness, and spiritual warfare. Jesus prayed for his followers that the Father would "keep them from the evil one" (Jn 17:15). Peter warned: "Be sober, be watchful. Your adversary the devil prowls around like a roaring lion, seeking someone to devour. Resist him, firm in your faith . . ." (1 Pt 5:8-9). James confirms: "Resist the devil and he will flee from you. Draw near to God and he will draw near to you" (Jas 4:7-8). And finally, Paul instructs:

> Finally, be strong in the Lord and in the strength of his might. Put on the whole armor of God, that you may be able to stand against the wiles of the devil. For we are not contending against flesh and blood, but against the principalities, against the powers, against the world rulers of this present darkness, against the spiritual hosts of wickedness in the heavenly places. Therefore, take the whole armor of God. . . . (Eph 6:10-13)

The devil is real, but Christians who are aware of his presence have no reason to fear him or evil spirits. Jesus Christ has overcome all evil, and we need only draw near to Christ in prayer and faith, and daily put on the "whole armor of God" (truth, righteousness, the gospel of peace, faith, the word of God, and prayer—Eph 6:14-18) to find protection from Satan and the spiritual powers of evil. Catholics also rely on the intercession of Mary ("her seed" has been sent to crush the head of Satan [Gn 3:15]), of St. Michael the Archangel, and of all the angels and saints to protect us in our battle against Satan and his demons.

Some theologians prefer to think of the biblical teaching about Satan and evil spirits as mythical—a story which personified evil in the world. Primitive people, they say, may have accepted this personification of evil as literally true, but modern man understands that Satan, demons, and other spiritual realities spoken of in the Bible are mainly symbolic. In the twentieth century, biblical scholar Rudolph Bultmann led the way in this task of "demythologizing the Bible." However, recent popes, such as Paul VI, and great Christian thinkers, like C.S. Lewis, have strongly reaffirmed and illustrated the reality of Satan and evil spirits.[3] Lewis argues that Satan's most effective strategy today in luring people to damnation is to make people believe that he doesn't exist, or exists only as a comical figure with horns and hoofs.[4] And yet, ironically, at the same time that some people are denying the existence of Satan and evil spirits, fascination with the occult has become rampant and even popular in Western society. The Catholic teaching and tradition on the occult or any form of spiritism (including astrology) is clear: *avoid* it; have nothing to do with it. Even seemingly harmless or entertaining forms of the occult, such as ouija boards or seances, are ways that Satan and evil spirits open people to their influence. Christians have no need for such dangerous diversions or "entertainment." Why live in the twilight, in possible danger of deception? Christ, our Light, has come to dispel all darkness!

Claiming Our Freedom: Repentance and Conversion

How do we accept God's offer of forgiveness and the free gift of new life in Christ? The first step is to renounce sin and all evil and turn toward God, which is called repentance. The word is taken from the Greek *metanoia,* which literally means to "change your mind" about the way you are living and accept God's judgment and will.

Some people fear that God will not forgive their sins, the serious wrongdoing of their past life. The Bible, both the New and the Old Testaments, confirm that our turning away from sin is God's deepest desire. He is eager, even longing, to forgive us. The prophet Isaiah says, "though your sins are like scarlet, / they shall be as white as snow" (Is 1:18), and Psalm 103 reminds us that "as far as the east is from the west, / so far does he remove our transgressions from us" (Ps 103:12). Jesus told the parable of the lost sheep and concluded that there is more joy in heaven over one repentant sinner than over ninety-nine who have no need of repentance (Lk 15:3-7).

Some people view repentance as a negative or painful experience. On the contrary, it is sin that is negative. Repentance is joyful, because we know we have a loving Father ready to forgive us and receive us back into his love whenever we repent, no matter how serious the sin or how many times we fall. The parable of the prodigal son beautifully illustrates this (Lk 15:11-32). Jesus told Peter that his forgiveness was to be unlimited—"seventy times seven" (Mt 18:22). Is Peter to be more forgiving than God himself? The only sin beyond God's mercy is the sin "against the Holy Spirit" (Mk 3:28-29), which probably means attributing God's work to Satan, thus refusing to believe that there is a loving God who desires to love, heal, and forgive us.

Along with repentance comes conversion. As we turn away from sin, we must turn toward God in Jesus Christ by believing in him and submitting our lives to him and to his plan for us. This conversion to God may occur in different ways. Some people tell of a sudden conversion experience in which they radically turned away from sin and turned to God in a single, momentous event. Conversion also may be more gradual, as a person breaks from the life of sin to God's life and his will in progressive stages. Even for those who have a radical conversion experience, conversion to Christ actually never ceases.

Christians are always in need of deeper, ongoing conversion—turning our lives over to God more fully every day. Our minds and hearts need constantly to be conformed to the mind and heart of Jesus Christ. As Jesus himself taught: "If any man would come after me, let him deny himself and take up his cross daily and follow me. For whoever would save his life will lose it; and whoever loses his life for my sake, he will save it" (Lk 9:23-24).

Conversion is a process of losing our lives for Jesus Christ more completely every day, that we may find our lives in him.

Christian Character and Virtues

Christians are called to be "other Christs," to possess the same character and virtues that Jesus Christ had. This is not something we can earn or achieve by our own efforts. We must ask God in prayer to form his character in us, especially seeking the specific virtues we lack. We can cooperate with God's grace by seeking to assume the character and virtues of Christ through discipline and by our decisions to act or think in certain ways, while always realizing that ultimately only God can develop our character and infuse virtues. All goodness and virtue comes from God; it is his gifts that we must ask for and then act upon us as his grace is offered to us.

Paul said that he considered everything else to be rubbish compared with the "surpassing worth of knowing Christ Jesus" (Phil 3:8). Of his own life he said, ". . . the life I now live in the flesh, I live by faith in the Son of God" (Gal 2:20).

At baptism, Christians receive the Holy Spirit, the gift of God's sanctifying grace, and also certain virtues essential to Christian life called "infused virtues." The most important of these infused virtues are faith, hope, and charity (or love). These are the so-called "theological virtues" that St. Paul says will remain after all other gifts of God pass away (1 Cor 13:13). These virtues are called "theological" because they are the central attributes of God himself. Paul notes that "the greatest of these is love" (1 Cor 13:13), because love is the very essence of God's nature (see 1 Jn 4:8). As one author has put it, "charity is the source, center, and goal of every virtue, for every virtue centers in the loving orientation of man to God... Charity perfects the virtues, gives them life, and directs them to God."[5]

Faith is another indispensable Christian virtue, because it is the only proper orientation toward God through which we are justified, considered righteous in God's sight (Rom 4:24-25), and sanctified, that is, made holy or like God. As the Council of Trent of the Catholic church taught:

> Faith is the beginning of human salvation, the foundation and root of all justification; without which it is impossible to please God (Heb 11:6) and to enter the fellowship of His sons. (Decree on Justification, Chap. 8)

Finally, hope is the firm confidence God gives to a person that he or she will persevere in faith and love and so attain eternal life and happiness with God. Hope is not only personal but also communal. It is the hope of the whole Christian people in Christ's desire to save us as a people, bringing all who are faithful to God and his grace to the glory of heaven. We also hope in God's mercy and blessings for his people in this life on earth, although this is not the ultimate goal of hope. St. Paul said, "If for this life only we have hoped in Christ, we are of all men most to be pitied" (1 Cor 15:19). The Letter to the Hebrews expresses God's desire that "each one of you... show the same earnestness in realizing the full assurance of hope until the end, so that you may not be sluggish, but imitators of those who through faith and patience inherit the promises" (Heb 6:11, 12). St. Paul expresses confidence given to the Christian through hope, saying that, "we rejoice in our hope of sharing the glory of God" (Rom 5:2) and "For in this hope we were saved. Now hope that is seen is not hope. For who hopes for what he sees? But if we hope for what we do not see, we wait for it with patience" (Rom 8:24-25).

Besides the virtues of faith, hope, and charity, there are other virtues that reflect aspects of these central virtues or which remove obstacles to love of God and others. Four of this type are known as the moral virtues or "cardinal virtues": prudence, justice, fortitude, and temperance. Prudence enables one to choose correctly how to best carry out the will of God. Justice inclines us to give to others at all times what is due to them by right.[6] There are many forms of justice—social, legal, distributive—which are specific applications of this same virtue in different circumstances. In all instances, justice must be balanced and expanded by charity. Fortitude, or courage, enables the Christian to do what is right and required in the Christian life, whatever the cost or consequences. Temperance, or self-control, is a virtue which enables us to control our bodily desires and appetites, especially our sexual powers and appetite for food and drink. Temperance is needed to channel properly all our passions and desires for good and godly purposes.

We recognize under different names other virtues such as the Beatitudes (Mt 5:2-12), and the "fruit of the Spirit"—"love, joy, peace, patience, kindness, goodness, faithfulness, gentleness, self-control" (Gal 5:22-23). All of these are attributes of God himself that he wishes to instill in his people to make us more like him. These virtues develop in the lives of Christians as they are practiced, until they become mature habits, intrinsic parts of the Christian character. If we lack any of these virtues, we should pray for them and seek to practice them in our daily lives.

Christian virtue expresses itself visibly in many ways. Traditional Catholic teaching has spoken of works of mercy which are concrete expressions of virtue. Some of these works serve the physical and practical needs of others (the "corporal works of mercy")—to feed the hungry; to give drink to the thirsty; to clothe the naked; to shelter the homeless; to visit the imprisoned; to care for the sick; and to bury the dead. Jesus spoke of the great reward for some of these works in his sermon on the last judgment (Mt 25:31-36). Likewise, there are also works of mercy that meet the spiritual needs of others (the "spiritual works of mercy")—to admonish the sinner; to instruct the ignorant; to advise the perplexed; to comfort the unhappy; to bear wrongs patiently; to forgive all injuries; and to pray for the living and the dead. These works also are commanded or encouraged by the Bible in many places and hold a venerable place in Catholic moral tradition.

Grace and Free Will

All Christian virtues and character flow from God and his grace. Through baptism and the other sacraments, we come to share the very life of God, which Catholics call "sanctifying grace." God's grace precedes every good thought or action, and even every inclination to the good ("prevenient grace"). God offers us the power each day, at every moment of our lives, to avoid sin and to do his will in particular circumstances ("actual grace"). Finally, God offers the grace of final perseverance, the ability to continue to follow Jesus Christ to the end of our lives so we will be able to share eternal life with him in heaven. God freely offers all that is necessary for a life that is rich and fruitful—the grace that can transform each person into the image of Jesus Christ, forming his character within us.

God's grace is never forced upon anyone. It must be sought after and freely accepted. When we do accept it and embrace it, we are able to do God's will and the Christian virtues flourish in our lives. In view of this, one might ask whether any virtues or good works are due to our own human will or effort or whether they are entirely the work of God. The New Testament makes it clear that no Christian can boast of any good work as being his own doing or can glory in himself, rather than in the Lord (Eph 2:8-10; 1 Cor 1:31; 2 Cor 10:17). God, through his grace, is the primary source and author of every virtue and good work.

On the other hand, the active cooperation of the human will with God's grace is essential. When Jesus invites us to "Come, follow me" and commands us to love God and each other, there is a presupposition that people are free to choose whether to accept or reject Jesus' invitation, to obey him or not. Thus, good works and virtues are primarily God's work, the result of his grace, and secondarily ours. The Catholic church has always maintained the reality of free will that makes possible real human responsibility for our choices and actions. Without genuinely free will, to talk about Christian morality would be relatively meaningless, since no one would be responsible for his actions.

Another extreme, incorrect view would be to view Christian morality as a purely human work. God's grace is essential. Jesus himself said, "apart from me you can do nothing" (Jn 15:5). Every good human act is both a result of God's action, his grace, and the free response of the human will to God's grace in performing the act.

Conscience

Conscience is the core of a person's being, the faculty by which he makes practical judgments about whether particular acts are morally right or wrong. The Christian desires to hear the voice of God in his or her conscience so that these judgments will be correct and in accordance with God's will. The conscience listens and judges, and then the person's will acts, either according to what the conscience dictates or in opposition to it. Human freedom and moral sensitivity rest in the conscience, as the Pastoral Constitution on the Church in the Modern World beautifully expresses:

> Deep within his conscience man discovers a law which he has not laid upon himself but which he must obey. Its voice, ever calling him to love and to do what is good and to avoid

> evil, tells him invariably at the right moment: do this, shun that. . . his conscience is man's most secret core, his sanctuary. There he is alone with God whose voice echoes in his depths. By conscience, in a wonderful way, that law is made known which is fulfilled in the love of God and of one's neighbor. . . Hence the more a correct conscience prevails, the more do persons and groups turn aside from blind choice and try to be guided by the objective standards of moral conduct. (no. 16)

As this passage indicates, the dictates of a person's conscience must be obeyed, because it is the only internal source a person has to judge what is right and wrong. The Second Vatican Council's Declaration on Religious Freedom states that:

> In all his activity, a man is bound to follow his conscience faithfully, in order that he may come to God, for whom he was created. It follows that he is not to be forced to act in a manner contrary to his conscience. Nor, on the other hand, is he to be restrained from acting in accordance with his conscience, especially in matters religious. (no. 3)

Since each person is bound to follow the dictates of his conscience, whether correct or incorrect, it is essential that the conscience be properly formed and informed. The individual's conscience may always err, but one is not guilty of negligence or sin if he or she has done his best to form his conscience according to God's will. However, if a person is ignorant or in error in a moral decision because of negligence in seeking the truth, God holds the person responsible for this. As the Second Vatican Council teaches:

> Conscience frequently errs from invincible (unavoidable) ignorance without losing its dignity. The same cannot be

> said of a man who cares but little for truth and goodness, or of a conscience which by degrees grows practically sightless as a result of habitual sin. (GS, no. 16)

How, then, is a person's conscience formed correctly? First, the Catholic church believes that there are reliable, objective sources through which God reveals his will. They include divine revelation, natural law, official church teaching, and human law. These will be discussed in detail in the next section of this chapter. The practice of the Christian virtues and works of mercy previously discussed also form the conscience according to God's will, as does the continual effort to follow the leadings of the Holy Spirit in everyday life.

Also a person can assist in the formation of conscience through fostering proper dispositions and attitudes. For example, one must desire to know the truth and be willing to accept it, whether it is immediately agreeable or not. Catholics must seek to have a positive attitude toward legitimate authority and be willing to be taught by the church. A person must be open and docile to the direct guidance that God may give through the Holy Spirit. The conscience cannot be formed properly if one is not genuinely open to the truth and to all the ways God has established to reveal the truth.

Let us take a specific case in which a person must make an important moral decision and is unsure about what is right and wrong in the matter. Suppose a married person is deciding whether to use artificial contraceptives. How does the person properly form the conscience? First, the person should pray earnestly for God's guidance, asking God to reveal his perfect will and praying for the desire and power to do only what would be most pleasing to him. All selfish desires and attitudes must be put aside. Then the person should consult the objective sources of God's revelation in order to find out what God desires. In most cases, there is something in the Bible, Christian tradition, the natural law, or the teaching of the church that relates to the decision being made. To be responsible in forming one's conscience entails being diligent in seeking out the truth from these sources. This may require study and consultation with reliable sources. For the issue of artificial contraception, Catholics have a long-standing tradition, based on natural law, of rejecting artificial means of contraception. This tradition was confirmed by Pope Paul VI in his encyclical letter, *Humanae Vitae.*

Finally, once the person has prayed for God's guidance and sought out God's truth from objective sources of revelation, the person is ready to think prayerfully about the right or best thing to do. In this reflection, Catholic theology has taught that the person must consider three aspects of the decision:

1) The object: Does the act itself conform to the moral law? Is the act good in itself according to God's revelation through objective sources?

2) Circumstances: Are there any relevant circumstances that may affect the degree of rightness or wrongness of the act?

3) The end or purpose: Is the intention behind performing the act a genuinely good one? Does the act have a good end or purpose?

All three of these aspects must be positive for the act or decision to be assuredly a good one.

A certain modern school of thought, often called "situation ethics," holds that the moral value of an act may be determined almost entirely by the situation or circumstances. Catholic teaching rejects this view. Even though circumstances may affect the decision or may lessen or increase the person's culpability (blameworthiness) for a wrong act, circumstances cannot make an act right which is wrong or evil in itself (the object) or which is done with an evil or selfish intention (the end or purpose). For example, a married person may consider using artificial contraceptives because of certain circumstances (e.g., having a large family already with a low income). Yet, if the use of this means of birth regulation is wrong or objectionable in itself, then it cannot be morally justified.

I have chosen this controversial example of a moral decision to illustrate the important personal responsibility involved in forming one's conscience and making a moral choice. Catholics, and all Christians, are bound to do what their conscience dictates in this matter and in all decisions of right and wrong, but in forming their conscience they are obliged to seek God's will in prayer and to follow the will of God as it is revealed in the Bible, authentic Christian tradition, natural law, and church teaching.

Church Teaching: Dissent or Acceptance?

What about the possibility of dissent from or disagreement with a teaching of the Catholic church? It is important here to distinguish the different degrees of authority of a church teaching. In the Catholic tradition, some moral and religious teachings have been formally defined by dogmatic definitions of ecumenical councils or popes. These are to be accepted by Catholics as part of our Christian faith. Further, there are other teachings of the church which are considered matters of faith because they have been consistently believed by Christians from the time of the early church until recent times. These must be accepted as part of the faith of the church, even though they have not been formally defined by a pope or ecumenical council. Many moral teachings of the Catholic church fall into this latter category, such as the condemnation of abortion, homosexual acts, and masturbation. A Catholic may go through a period of questioning or struggling with such teachings in order to fully understand them, but the end result of this process of conscience formation should be to recognize and embrace personally the truth of a teaching presented by the Catholic church as a dogmatic definition or a matter of faith. Those who finally reject a matter of Christian belief considered essential by the Catholic church are faced with a serious choice.

They must decide whether they can submit their personal judgments to the church's teaching or whether they must, in honesty, cease to consider themselves Catholic Christians. The Catholic church has always strongly emphasized preserving the unity of its members based on a common faith, and has warned against false teaching. (See Eph 4:5, 14-15; Phil 1:27; Gal 1:6-9; 1 Tm 6:3-5; 2 Tm 4:2-4; Ti 1:9-2:1; 2 Pt 2:1-3; Lk 10:16.)

However, not all teachings of the Catholic church are presented as dogmatic definitions or matters of faith. In fact, most of what is presented in the "ordinary magisterium" (usual or everyday teaching office) of the bishops or popes is considered "religious teaching"—teaching which should be heeded and morally accepted with an obedient attitude ("religious assent") but which may be rejected in certain circumstances if a person's responsibly formed conscience dictates. Nonetheless, Catholics should only decide to oppose even a religious teaching of their church with reluctance, and only after careful study and prayerful discernment. Their presupposition is that what the pope and united bishops teach is true, even in their ordinary magisterium. As the Catholic bishops of the United States have taught in the Basic Teachings on Catholic Religious Education:

> The conscience of the Catholic Christian must pay respectful and obedient attention to the teaching authority of God's Church. It is the duty of this teaching authority, or Magisterium, to give guidance for applying the enduring norms and values of Christian morality to specific situations of everyday life. (Art. 17, p. 18)

There is, however, room for legitimate differences of opinion and a plurality of views within the Catholic church in matters on which Scripture and the apostolic tradition are not clear in their teaching or which are not considered matters of faith or specified by a dogmatic definition (LG, no. 25). The underlying principle here is beautifully expressed in the ancient Catholic saying: "let there be unity in what is necessary, freedom in what is unsettled, and charity in everything."[7]

What attitudes should be fostered toward the church's teaching in the area of morality? It is important for Catholics to realize that the moral guidance provided by the church and by the Scriptures is not to be viewed as a set of arbitrary restrictions, but as a gift of God. Thank God that he has chosen to reveal his will to his people, with clear guidance! Even when the demands of God's will are challenging and oppose our own selfish and sinful desires, we should rejoice. Should it surprise us that the demands of the moral teachings of the church are often as difficult and challenging as the demands and call of Jesus himself? This would only make sense, since the church's moral teachings and guidance are extensions and practical applications of Jesus' teaching. What most of us need to develop is a greater love for the law of God and a desire to form our conscience according to it. The longest of the psalms of the Old Testament, Psalm 119, is a psalm praising God's law and thanking him for giving it to us:

> Oh, how I love thy law! / It is my meditation all the day. / Thy commandment makes me wiser / than my enemies, for it is ever with me. . . . / Thy word is a lamp to my feet / and a light to my path. (Ps 119:97, 98, 105)

The laws of God are not just restrictions, but the source of true freedom and peace. Jesus said, "'If you continue in my word, you are truly my disciples, and you will know the truth, and the truth will make you free'" (Jn 8:31-32). Christian freedom, genuine freedom, is not found in doing whatever we want, but in doing God's will. Jesus was the freest person who has ever lived, because he was most obedient to the will of his Father. Our consciences will find their freedom and peace when they are formed according to God's law and will. Let us consider now the sources of moral guidance that he has graciously provided.

God's Guidance in Moral Living

God has a clear plan for how we should live. In the Declaration on Religious Freedom of the Second Vatican Council, the Catholic church teaches:

> ... that the highest norm of human life is the divine law—eternal, objective, and universal—whereby God orders, directs, and governs the entire universe and all the ways of the human community, by a plan conceived in wisdom and love. Man has been made by God to participate in this law, with the result that, under the gentle disposition of divine Providence, he can come to perceive ever increasingly the unchanging truth. (no. 3)

The Catholic church always has taught that good and evil, right and wrong, are not arbitrary, subjective concepts, but are realities clearly determined by the Creator of all, God himself.[8] Some people are offended by the idea that there is a God who establishes rules for human life and behavior. Should it surprise us that the God who created the human race would also determine, and then reveal, the ways by which we would find true fulfillment and happiness? Truly, God "desires all men to be saved and to come to the knowledge of the truth" (1 Tm 2:4), as Paul wrote to Timothy. The truth about morality, like all Christian truth, is a truth that liberates, a truth that sets us free (Jn 8:32).

Natural Law

Of course, it would be strange, indeed, if God created people to live a moral life, and then made it difficult or impossible for them to discover or to understand his will for their lives. Catholics believe that God reveals his plan and his will for human life in a variety of ways, so that no one can claim total ignorance of it. There are certain objective sources of the knowledge of God's will for human living (moral norms) that are accessible to all people. The most basic and universal level of understanding God's plan for human life is through "natural law." Natural law does not mean laws of nature, such as gravity, but the ways God created man to act and interrelate that may be discovered or deduced from observing human nature itself. These are universal principles that apply to people of all times, places, cultures, and situations. Even sin, the rebellion of mankind against God, cannot totally obscure our recognition of the truths of natural law.

C.S. Lewis lucidly explains and illustrates the principle of natural law in the first section of *Mere Christianity,* where he describes the universal "law of fair play" that everyone naturally recognizes and wishes others to abide by, even when we would like to make exceptions for ourselves! Whenever we say, "that's not fair!" we assume the existence of a universal moral law. I would refer anyone interested to *Mere Christianity* for a simple, convincing explanation of natural law.[9]

An example of natural law is the fact that man and woman were created by God as two different sexes in order to procreate. This points to the natural purpose and meaning of sexuality and indicates that homosexuality and masturbation are distortions of the natural law in this area. The apostle Paul commented that when a certain group of people rejected the truth about God that was plain to them by nature:

> For this reason God gave them up to dishonorable passions. Their women exchanged natural relations for unnatural, and the men likewise gave up natural relations with women and were consumed with passion for one another.... And since they did not see fit to acknowledge

> God, God gave them up to a base mind and to improper conduct. (Rom 1:26, 28)

On the other hand, Paul taught in the following chapter of Romans that non-Jews (or non-Christians) who sincerely seek God and live according to the natural law will be rewarded, even though they have not received the law of God revealed in the Old and New Testament:

> When Gentiles who have not the law do by nature what the law requires, they are a law to themselves, even though they do not have the law. They show that what the law requires is written on their hearts, while their conscience also bears witness and their conflicting thoughts accuse or perhaps excuse them on that day when, according to my gospel, God judges the secrets of men by Christ Jesus. (Rom 2:14-16)

The law of God, his will for human life and morality, is not totally unknown to anyone, for God has written on the human heart what his law requires, and it is known to us through our conscience. However, the natural law only presents us with God's plan indirectly, like a shadow of the full reality. It would be easy to confuse or to miss the fullness of God's plan if all we had were the natural law to rely on. Hence, God has provided a second important source for knowing God's will which clarifies and completes what can be perceived from the natural law. This is divine revelation.

Divine Law

Through the inspired authors of the Bible, God has revealed more fully his plan for living, the divine law. To his people of the Old Covenant, Israel, God revealed the Decalogue, or the Ten Commandments (see Ex 20:2-17; Dt 5:6-22). A summary form of the Ten Commandments should be kept in memory by all Catholics; an explanation of the meaning of each of these commandments is very important, suited to the age or condition of the hearer. There are many other laws conveyed by God in the Old Testament, but these are the essential commandments that are binding for all people at all times. Jesus himself enjoined the rich young man to keep these commandments in order to attain eternal life (Mt 19:16-19). He further explained that his mission was to fulfill the teaching of the law and the prophets, not to abolish it. "For truly, I say to you, till heaven and earth pass away, not an iota, not a dot, will pass from the law until all is accomplished" (Mt 5:18).

Jesus not only taught the law of Moses, he fulfilled it by radicalizing it. In chapter five of Matthew's Gospel, Jesus explains that it is not enough to obey the commandments in our actions, but even our thoughts must be conformed to God's law or else we are sinning.

Jesus Christ is the fulfillment of the law, the revealer and full revelation of God's will for human life. When asked what is the greatest commandment of the law, Jesus summarized God's law and his plan for our lives in two points:

> "You shall love the Lord your God with all your heart, and with all your soul, and with all your mind. This is the great and first commandment. And the second is like it, You shall love your neighbor as yourself." (Mt 22:37-39; cf. Dt 6:4-5; Lev 19:18)

In the Gospel of John, Jesus radicalizes the second commandment, making it "new." "A new commandment I give to you, that you love one another; even as I have loved you, that you also love one another" (Jn 13:34). The Christian life is basically a life of love—love of God and love of every other human being. Jesus himself revealed this love fully by living it perfectly, not merely speaking about it. The real norm for human life is Jesus himself, because he is the fullness of God's revelation in the flesh—"the image of the invisible God" (Col 1:15).

In his Sermon on the Mount, Jesus presented another radical dimension of Christian life, the Beatitudes:

> "Blessed are the poor in spirit, for theirs is the kingdom of heaven.
> Blessed are those who mourn, for they shall be comforted.
> Blessed are the meek, for they shall inherit the earth.
> Blessed are those who hunger and thirst for righteousness, for they shall be satisfied.
> Blessed are the merciful, for they shall obtain mercy.
> Blessed are the pure in heart, for they shall see God.
> Blessed are the peacemakers, for they shall be called sons of God.
> Blessed are those who are persecuted for righteousness' sake, for theirs is the kingdom of heaven." (Mt 5:3-10)

Rather than posing these commandments, Jesus presents them as promises for those who possess these virtues. In his moral teaching, he always wishes to call people forth to the perfection of holiness and discipleship. He does not call people to meet certain minimum standards of conduct, but to perfection: "You, therefore, must be perfect, as your heavenly Father is perfect" (Mt 5:48). Perhaps one can be saved by avoiding sin, by keeping the commandments, but why stop there? "The young man said to him, 'All these [the commandments] I have observed; what do I still lack?' Jesus said to him, 'If you would be perfect, go, sell what you possess and give to the poor, and you will have treasure in heaven; and come, follow me'" (Mt 19:20-21). Following Jesus is what Christianity is about; keeping the commandments is but one of the necessary and expected consequences of following Jesus.

The Teaching Office of the Church

How is this precious revelation found in Scripture to be interpreted correctly and applied properly to new circumstances? Catholics believe that God provides authoritative interpretation and application of the Bible and authentic Christian tradition through the official teaching office (*magisterium*) of the Catholic church. This is a third objective source of moral guidance for Catholics. Even when the Bible does not explicitly address an issue, Catholics can ask, "What does the Christian tradition—such as the Fathers of the church and other great Catholic thinkers—have to say about it?" and, "Have the popes or ecumenical councils of Catholic bishops ever taught definitively about this matter?" On certain moral issues of current concern, there is a unanimous consensus of the Christian tradition from the early church until recent times. Abortion, for instance, has been universally rejected by Christians from the second through the twentieth century, until recently when some Christians have questioned this tradition. Some disputed moral issues have been settled by the formal teaching of a pope or an ecumenical council of bishops, for example, such acts as masturbation, fornication, adultery, homosexual acts, and other sexual vices. These throughout the centuries have been condemned by the ordinary teaching of the church and by formal judgments of the *magisterium*.[10]

The teaching office of the church has the dual role of protecting the truth of revelation from error or distortion and of "developing a deeper understanding of revelation and applying this revelation to the various issues and situations of human life." These have been called the "protective aspect" and "creative aspect" of the church's teaching role in the area of morality.[11]

Besides the essential work of the pope, bishops, and priests in defending and interpreting the true Christian way of life, teachers and parents play a vital role in passing on this saving truth to others, especially to young people. Without parents and teachers actively understanding and explaining the Christian way of life and the church's teaching on specific moral questions, the work of the pope and the bishops would be in vain. Few would actually hear what the *magisterium* and tradition of the church has to say without parents, pastors, and teachers passing this on to others, especially to youth.

Many Catholics wonder whether there is a comprehensive list of Catholic teachings on moral issues, and what church teachings Catholics are bound to believe. Although there is no definitive list of official pronouncements on moral teaching, many of them are summarized in documents such as *To Live in Christ Jesus* (1976) or *Basic Teachings for Catholic Religious Education* (1973) published in the United States by the National Conference of Catholic Bishops. Teachings on specific areas of morality may be found in reliable reference books of Catholic moral teaching or in specific documents, such as the Declaration on Certain Questions Concerning Sexual Ethics (1975), Declaration on Abortion (1974), or the Declaration on Euthanasia (1980), from the Sacred Congregation for the Doctrine of the Faith, the Catholic church's official doctrinal office in Vatican City.

Human Law

A final source of moral guidance for Christians is human law, which includes both church law and civil law. Jesus himself respected civil law and civil authority, as long as it did not violate God's law (see Mt 22:17-21; 23:1-3). He also observed many of the laws and traditions of Judaism (church law), except where their observance had grown legalistic and had violated the supreme law of love (see Lk 13:10-17; 14:1-6).

Human law, especially church law, can actually be an aid to observing the law of God. Because of fallen man's inclination to sin, human law can curb our tendency to sin and help us to follow God's will and the promptings of the Holy Spirit.

Church law applies the laws of God to specific areas of Christian and human life. We must beware of legalism and avoid this by being aware that the higher gospel values, such as charity, always direct, and sometimes supersede, the observance of human (even church) laws. Normally, though, "obedience to church laws gives us an opportunity in practical daily ways to obey the Lord and His church."[12]

Civil laws are necessary to protect the common good and to maintain essential aspects of the common good, such as justice and order. As long as they do not violate God's laws, Christians should observe civil laws as honestly and fully as possible. This is done out of respect to the authority of civil government, which comes from God, and in order to set a good example of obedience to others (Rom 13:1-7).

We have seen that God makes known his will for human conduct in a variety of ways: through natural law, divine revelation, the teaching office of the church, and human law. When God's will, revealed through those channels, is consistently observed and followed, the result is the development in a person of Christian character and virtue—the character and virtue of Jesus Christ himself.

Living According to God's Will

Studying the principles of how to form our consciences and live according to God's will should lead us to consider the specific things we are to do and to avoid in our daily lives as Catholic Christians. The basic command of Jesus is our primary task each day: to love the Lord with our whole heart, mind, soul, and strength, and to love those around us, our neighbor, as Christ has loved us. We are called to love all people, but this love begins with those around us, especially those we have a commitment to through the sacraments and our common life in the body of Christ, the church.

There is an order to love. If we are married or living with our family, we are called to love our spouses, children, parents, brothers and sisters with a committed love that is sealed by the sacrament of matrimony. We are also especially called to love the members of the new family that God has given us in Jesus Christ, the church. The New Testament teaches the vital peace of the "love of the brethren" (*philadelphia*) in the Christian life, love of those with whom we are united in Christ through baptism (see Heb 13:1; 1 Thes 4:9; 1 Pt 1:22; 3:8). As St. Paul instructed the Galatians: "let us do good to all men, and especially to those who are of the household of faith" (Gal 6:10). An important part of Christian witness to the world that Christ has come is the love we have for one another in the body of Christ. As Jesus told his apostles, "By this all men will know that you are my disciples, if you have love for one another" (Jn 13:35).

These teachings remind us of the communal nature of Christianity, including Christian morality. No one can attain salvation or live the Christian life totally on their own. God has formed us into a people, the church, so that we can learn how to love another and extend that love to all men. We also cannot live a moral life according to God's will on our own. Not only do we need teaching and guidance from the leaders in the church to show us how to live, we also need support and encouragement, and sometimes correction and admonition, from other Christians to spur us on to live according to God's will each day. Sin and grace are social and communal, as well as individual. If one member of the body of Christ is rebelling against God, or even on the borderline of sin, it affects other Christians. We need to pray for each other, for we all are sinners. We must also call one another back to righteousness and God's will when we fall. ". . . speaking the truth in love, we are to grow up in every way into him who is the head, into Christ . . ." (Eph 4:15). Likewise, when one member of the body of Christ accepts God's grace and grows in holiness, it strengthens and encourages other Christians, so that we can all imitate that example and grow more fully into the image of Christ.

We realize that "genuine Christian love . . . demands the avoidance of particular kinds of behavior that are always wrong and the practice of other kinds of Christian behavior that are always right."[13] The Catholic bishops of the United States summarized some of our practical obligations of love towards God, neighbor, and ourselves:

> Towards God the Christian has a lifelong obligation of love and service. The Will of God must be put first in the scale of personal values, and must be kept there throughout life. One must have toward God the attitude of a son to an all-good, all-loving Father, and must never think or live as if independent of God. He must gladly give to God genuine worship and true prayer, both liturgical and private.
>
> Man must not put anyone or anything in place of God. This is idolatry, which has its variations in superstition, witchcraft, occultism. Honoring God, man is never to blaspheme nor perjure himself. Honoring God, one is to show respect for persons, places and things related specially to God.
>
> Atheism, heresy and schism are to be rejected in the light of man's duties to God.
>
> Towards his fellow man the Christian has specific obligations in love. Like Christ, he will show that love by concern for the rights of his fellow man—his freedom, his housing, his food, his health, his right to work, etc. The Christian is to show to all others the justice and charity of Christ—to reach out in the spirit of the beatitudes to help all others, to build up a better society in the local community and justice and peace throughout the world. His judgment and speech concerning others are to be ruled by the charity due all sons of God. He will respect and obey all lawful authority in the home, in civil society, and in the Church.
>
> Many are the sins against neighbor. It is sinful to be selfishly apathetic towards others in their needs. It is sinful

to violate the rights of others—to steal, deliberately damage another's good name or property, cheat, not to pay one's debts. Respecting God's gift of life, the Christian cannot be anti-life and must avoid sins of murder, abortion, euthanasia, genocide, indiscriminate acts of war. He must not use immoral methods of family limitation. Sins of lying, detraction and calumny are forbidden, as are anger, hatred, racism and discrimination. In the area of sexuality, the Christian is to be modest in behavior and dress. In a sex-saturated society, the follower of Christ must be different. For the Christian there can be no premarital sex, fornication, adultery, or other acts of impurity or scandal to others. He must remain chaste, repelling lustful desires and temptations, self-abuse, pornography and indecent entertainment of every description.

Towards self the follower of Christ has certain duties. He must be another Christ in the world of his own day, a living example of Christian goodness. He must be humble and patient in the face of his own imperfections, as well as those of others. He must show a Christlike simplicity towards material things and the affluence of our society. The follower of Christ must be pure in words and actions even in the midst of corruption.

To be guarded against is the capital sin of pride, with its many manifestations. So too with sloth—spiritual, intellectual and physical. The Christian must resist envy of others' success and of their financial and material possessions. He is not to surrender self-control and abuse his bodily health by intemperance in drugs, alcohol, food.

Obviously, this listing does not cover all morality or all immorality. But it indicates the practical approach which will help the Christian to form a right conscience, choose always what is right, avoid sin and the occasions of sin, and live in this world according to the Spirit of Christ in love of God.[14]

Thanks be to God for revealing to us, his people, the way of life, and blessing us with the power to know it and to live it through the Holy Spirit. This chapter has considered norms for living as a Christian that are applicable to all times. The following chapter will discuss more specifically the challenges and opportunities of Christian life in the world today.

NINE

Catholics in the World

THE CHRISTIAN WAY OF LIFE and moral decisions are not carried out in a vacuum but within the world. This chapter will consider some principles of Catholic living and decision-making today. A primary source for this study is the longest document of the Second Vatican Council, the Pastoral Constitution on the Church in the Modern World, *Gaudium et Spes.*

Characteristics of the World Today

Our first task as Catholics considering how to live in the world today must be that of discerning what is really going on in the world, "scrutinizing the signs of the times and of interpreting them in the light of the Gospel. . . . Today the human race is passing through a new stage of its history. Profound and rapid changes are spreading by degrees around the whole world (GS, no. 4)."[1] Rapid change is certainly a primary characteristic of the twentieth century. Some of these changes may be attributed to science and technology, others to political or social causes. Our age is a time of progress and uncertainty, in which the human race looks forward to the future with expectancy and hope of the good that may come from change, but also with misgivings, unrest, and even fear of a future that may hold frustration, bondage and disaster.

The bishops of the Second Vatican Council pointed out many troubling imbalances in the modern world: "an abundance of wealth, resources, and economic power" held by some, while a "huge proportion" of humanity is "tormented by hunger and poverty"; a keener awareness of freedom, in contrast to "new forms of social and psychological slavery"; a growing sense of the interdependence of mankind and of the need for unity, opposed by the reality of growing tension among men and nations because of "political, social, economic, and ideological disputes (GS, no. 4)."

Accompanying this is the irony that while many people continue to search for a better world, their own personal lives are often in disarray because they have neglected the betterment of their own spirit. While it is true that some have come to realize their need for "a more personal and explicit adherence to faith" in God, "on the other hand, growing numbers of people are abandoning religion in practice (GS, no. 7)." Indeed, religion (and Christianity in particular) is often viewed as being antithetical to progress, science, and other human endeavors, or is simply seen as outmoded and irrelevant to the present situation of humanity.

In the final analysis, the Second Vatican Council sees the world today in a position of dangerous paradox, with the future of the human race hanging in the balance depending upon the choices we make.

> ...the modern world shows itself at once powerful and weak capable of the noblest deeds or the foulest. Before it lies the path to freedom or slavery, to progress or retreat, to brotherhood or hatred. Moreover, man is becoming aware that it is his responsibility to guide aright the forces which he has unleashed and which can enslave him or minister to him. (GS, no.9)

The Heart of the Problem

Although the external circumstances of the modern world have undoubtedly changed, the Catholic church teaches that the root of problems today remains the same now as always. The Catholic bishops at the Second Vatican Council taught:

> The truth is that the imbalances under which the modern world labors are linked with the more basic imbalance rooted in the heart of man. For in man himself many elements wrestle with one another. . . . (GS, no. 10)
>
> Although he was made by God in a state of holiness, from the very dawn of history man has abused his liberty, at the urging of personified Evil (Satan). Man set himself against God and sought to find fulfillment apart from God. . .
>
> Often refusing to acknowledge God as his beginning, man has disrupted also his proper relationship with his own ultimate goal. At the same time he became out of harmony with himself, with others, and with all created things.
>
> Therefore man is split within himself. As a result, all of human life, whether individual or collective, shows itself to be a dramatic struggle between good and evil, between light and darkness. Indeed, man finds that by himself he is incapable of battling the assaults of evil successfully, so that everyone feels as though he is bound by chains. (GS, no. 13, cf. no. 37)

The basic problem of human life in the world, today and always, is *sin:* rebellion against God and his plan. That is the heart of the problem we face. The rebellion against God is becoming increasingly blatant in the world today. In Western society, many people have dropped any pretense of being God-fearing, and have openly turned to pornography, sexual promiscuity and homosexuality, the occult, rebellion against authority, and a host of other evils clearly condemned by sacred Scripture and Christian tradition.

An increasing number of people profess to be atheists—denying the very existence of God. The Pastoral Constitution on the Church in the Modern World devotes three sections (nos. 19-21) to this problem. Atheism has many forms: the theoretical atheism of existential philosophers and others; the "systematic atheism" which asserts absolute human independence from God or even the notion of God; and political atheism "... which anticipates the liberation of man especially through his economic and social emancipation. This form (of atheism) argues that by its very nature religion thwarts such liberation by arousing man's hope for a deceptive future life, thereby diverting him from the constructing of the earthly city" (GS, no. 20). There is also a sort of "practical atheism," subtly promoted by secular humanism, by which a person's attention and concern is so fully directed to life in this world that the question of God is never adequately considered or addressed. Many people today dismiss belief in God simply because he doesn't seem necessary for one to be a good person, which is the highest moral ideal that they can accept or imagine.

The Catholic church continues to affirm and teach that the root of all the problems of mankind is the rejection of God, whether through knowing denial of God, through ignorance, or through the rebellion against him that Christians call sin. Without the grace and power of God, the human person is bound to fall into all manner of sin against himself, his neighbor, and the created world. Without the knowledge of God, humanity is blind to the ultimate source of redemption and help when facing the difficult struggles and challenges of life in the world.

God's Solution: Jesus Christ

Man proposes many solutions to the myriad of pressing problems and inequities of the world: social engineering;

peace talks and summit meetings; political, social, and economic solutions of various sorts. While those may be necessary to help resolve certain problems, Christians must remember that the world's ills cannot be solved by human efforts alone. Without the help of God and the guidance of his Holy Spirit, all of these efforts remain incomplete and destined to fail.

Sin has only one remedy: the redemptive love and mercy of God that comes to us through the Savior Jesus Christ. The Pastoral Constitution on the Church in the Modern World constantly reverts from its analysis of the situation of the human race today to the ultimate solution of this situation: Jesus Christ (see GS, nos. 3, 10, 22, 31, 32). In him alone, the Council says, "can be found the key, the focal point, and the goal of all human history" (GS, no. 10). Pope John Paul II also affirmed the primacy of Jesus Christ in his first encyclical letter, *Redemptor Hominis* (The Redeemer of Man):

> In Christ and through Christ God has revealed Himself fully to mankind and has definitely drawn close to it. At the same time, in Christ and through Christ man has acquired full awareness of his dignity, of the heights to which he is raised, and of the surpassing worth of his own humanity, and of the meaning of his existence. All of us who are Christ's followers must therefore meet and unite around him. (nos. 30, 31; Chap. 11)

The fundamental solution to the struggles of this age is for humanity to discover its true identity, which is only fully revealed in the person of Jesus Christ. In Christ, each person has been given the opportunity to be transformed from within and reborn in the image of God, our Creator. As Pope John Paul II said in his address to the world at Christmas, 1985:

> Christ is born so that we may be reborn, new men in the New Man . . . the more human world of which Christ the Lord . . . is the first-fruit, is a world inhabited by a *new people*, which goes forward "with sobriety, righteousness, and

> godliness" towards the full joy of Heaven. A people that knows how to be *sober* with regard to the resources of the universe and wise in the use of the energies of its own mind, for it knows how to resist the false mirage of progress that is indifferent to moral values, and looks only to the immediate and material advantage.
>
> A people, too, that is inspired by *justice* in its thoughts, resolutions and deeds, a people even aiming at the goal of a more authentic community of persons, in which every individual will feel accepted, respected and esteemed.
>
> A people, finally, that in *godliness* transcends itself in opening itself to God, from whom it expects the constant support needed for traveling forward, along the road of true progress, towards the goal of meeting with Christ, the Redeemer of man and Lord of history.[1]

The human race cannot become this "new people" by its own efforts, but only by the power of God coming to us through Jesus Christ and the Holy Spirit. As the Second Vatican Council expressed this truth:

> . . . if anyone wants to know how this unhappy situation [of the world today] can be overcome, Christians will tell him that all human activity, constantly imperiled by man's pride and deranged self-love, must be purified and perfected by the power of Christ's cross and resurrection. For redeemed by Christ and made a new creature in the Holy Spirit, man is able to love the things themselves created by God . . . He can receive them from God, and respect and reverence them as flowing constantly from the hand of God. (GS, no. 37)

From Christ, we also learn to bear the sufferings and hardships that come from following God and his will:

> Undergoing death itself for all of us sinners, He taught us by example that we too must shoulder that cross which the

> world and the flesh inflict upon those who search after peace and justice. Appointed Lord by His resurrection and given plenary power in heaven and on earth, Christ is now at work in the hearts of men through the energy of the Holy Spirit. He arouses not only a desire for the age to come, but... He animates, purifies and strengthens those noble longings by which the human family strives to make its life more human and to render the whole earth submissive to this goal. (GS, no. 30)

The Extraordinary Synod of Bishops in 1985 also affirmed the centrality of the cross of Christ. The Final Report of that Synod stated:

> ... in the present day difficulties God wishes to teach us more deeply the value, the importance and the centrality of the cross of Jesus Christ... When we Christians speak of the cross we do not deserve to be labeled as pessimists, but we rather found ourselves upon the realism of Christian hope. (Section D2)

It is evident from these statements that Jesus Christ imparts the desire to make this world more fully human, abounding in peace and justice. This will entail suffering, but Jesus gives us the perfect example, especially through his death on the cross, of enduring suffering for the sake of God's kingdom. Through his cross and resurrection, Jesus also provides grace and the power of the Holy Spirit to guide and strengthen us as we seek to follow God's will in the midst of temptation and trial.

The Dignity of the Human Person

The Second Vatican Council and Pope John Paul II reiterate that a central goal of the Catholic church's efforts in this world is to promote and safeguard the dignity of each human person. The Catholic church is convinced that the solution to the problems of human society depends upon a correct understanding and appreciation of the unsurpassable worth of each human life. The Pastoral Constitution on the Church in the Modern World affirms the belief that,

> By no human law can the personal dignity and liberty of man be so aptly safeguarded as by the Gospel of Christ that has been entrusted to the Church. For this gospel announces and proclaims the freedom of the sons of God, and repudiates all the bondage which ultimately results from sin. (no. 41)

The Catholic church has always taught and defended the inestimable value of every human life, believing that each human person "by his interior qualities . . . outstrips the whole sum of mere things." Each person, from the moment of conception, possesses "a spiritual and immortal soul" (GS, no. 14) destined for eternal life. Thus, one human life is more valuable in God's eyes than all other created things combined. As the noted Christian author, C.S. Lewis reflected in his address, "The Weight of Glory,"

> It is a serious thing to live in a society of possible gods and goddesses, to remember that the dullest and most uninteresting person you talk to may one day be a creature which, if you saw it now, you would be strongly tempted to worship, or else a horror and a corruption such as you now meet, if at all, only in a nightmare. All day long we are, in some degree, helping each other to one or other of these destinations. It is in light of these overwhelming possibilities, it is with the awe and circumspection proper to them, that we should conduct all our dealings with one another, all friendships, all loves, all play, all politics.
>
> There are no *ordinary* people. You have never talked to a mere mortal. Nations, cultures, arts, civilization—these are mortal, and their life is to ours as the life of a gnat. But it is

> immortals whom we joke with, work with, marry, snub, and exploit—immortal horrors or everlasting splendours . . .
>
> Next to the Blessed Sacrament itself, your neighbor is the holiest object present to your senses. If he is your Christian neighbor he is holy in almost the same way, for in him also Christ . . . Glory Himself, is truly hidden.[2]

In addition to an immortal soul, each person possesses an intellect that is able to perceive truth and wisdom; a moral conscience, which senses an internal law telling the person how to live; and the gift of free will by which each person chooses his or her path of life, including whether or not to submit to God and his call.

The Catholic church asserts that there are certain rights and obligations that necessarily follow from the fact of the dignity of the human person.

> There is a growing awareness of the exalted dignity proper to the human person, since he stands above all things, and his rights and duties are universal and inviolable. Therefore, there must be made available to all men everything necessary for leading a life truly human, such as food, clothing, and shelter, the right to choose a state of life freely and to found a family, the right to education, to employment, to a good reputation, to respect, to appropriate information, to activity in accord with the upright norm of one's own conscience, to protection of privacy and to rightful freedom in matters religious, too. (GS, no. 26)
>
> These rights are possessed equally by all. (no. 29)

As well as expressing these rights, the Second Vatican Council also listed some violations of human dignity that threaten fully human life:

> . . . whatever is opposed to life itself, such as any type of murder, genocide, abortion, euthanasia, or willful self-

> destruction, whatever violates the integrity of the human person, such as mutilation, torments inflicted on body or mind, attempts to coerce the will itself; whatever insults human dignity, such as subhuman living conditions, arbitrary imprisonment, deportation, slavery, prostitution, the selling of women and children; as well as disgraceful working conditions, where men are treated as mere tools for profit, rather than as free and responsible persons; all these things and others of their like are infamies indeed. They poison human society, but they do more harm to those who practice them than those who suffer from the injury. Moreover, they are a supreme dishonor to the Creator. (GS, no. 27)

The Relationship of Society to the Person

The Catholic church understands that the basic purpose of human society and government is to serve the individual person: safeguarding and promoting the human rights of each one and protecting against the threats to life itself. *Gaudium et Spes* expresses the principle well:

> . . . the social order and its development must inceasingly work to the benefit of the human person if the disposition of affairs is to be subordinate to the personal realm and not contrariwise, as the Lord indicated when He said that the Sabbath was made for man, and not man for the Sabbath. (no. 26)

Social institutions and bodies, including churches and governments, ultimately exist for the service of individual persons and must therefore respect and safeguard their rights and dignity. *Gaudium et Spes* reiterates, "For the beginning, the subject, and the good of social institutions is and must be the human person, which for its part and by its very nature stand completely in need of social life" (no. 25). The latter part of this quotation implies that while social institutions exist for the good of the individual person, and not vice versa, persons cannot isolate themselves from others and ignore the needs of society or the church. Social life, and especially life within the body of Christ, the church, is an essential need of human nature and a major vehicle by which each person discovers his or her own identity and grows into a son or daughter of God. As was noted previously, it is God's plan to call together humanity and to save us as a people, not as isolated individuals. Love of neighbor is just as essential to the Christian life as love of God (see 1 Jn 4:20, 21), and to love others we must first enter into social relationships with them (see GS, nos. 24, 32; LG, no. 9).

Building strong Christian social relationships also has practical benefits. It is by working together that Catholics are most effective in renewing the social order and proclaiming the gospel of Jesus Christ to others. The Pastoral Constitution warned against an individualistic attitude or approach to restoring the social order to Christian standards:

> Profound and rapid changes make it particularly urgent that no one, ignoring the trend of events or drugged by laziness, content himself with a merely individualistic morality. It grows increasingly true that the obligations of justice and love are fulfilled only if each person, contributing to the common good, according to his own abilities and the needs of others, also promotes and assists the public and private institutions dedicated to bettering the conditions of human life. . . .
>
> Let everyone consider it his sacred obligation to count social necessities among the primary duties of modern man, and to pay heed to them. (GS, no. 30)

The Pastoral Constitution on the Church in the Modern

World strongly encourages all Christians, especially lay persons, whose sphere of activity it properly is, to become actively involved in the affairs of society according to their vocation and abilities. It is not enough to be a "Sunday Catholic." The Constitution explicitly denounces the dichotomy between daily life in the world and our faith and calls this false division one of "the most serious errors of our age" (no. 43). Instead, the bishops of Vatican II counseled:

> Laymen should... know that it is generally the function of their well-formed Christian conscience to see that the divine law is inscribed in the life of the earthly city.... laymen are not only bound to penetrate the world with a Christian spirit. They are also called to be witnesses to Christ in all things in the midst of human society. (GS, no. 43)

A Catholic Understanding of the World and Christian Hope

Some Catholics are hesitant when they hear exhortations from the church to get involved in the world and its affairs. This hesitancy may be the result of bad past experiences, of unconcern, selfishness, or being too busy with personal affairs; or it may stem from a genuine lack of understanding about whether and how Christians are supposed to relate to the world.

One possible source of misunderstanding is the different possible meanings of "the world" that were discussed in the last chapter. The world can either be viewed as the arena of God's activity (Mk 16:15) that he loves and has redeemed at a great cost (Jn 3:16), or it may be understood as an evil place dominated by values opposed to God (Jn 15:18; 1 Jn 2:15, 16) or even by Satan himself (Jn 12:31; 14:30; 16:11).

The Pastoral Constitution on the Church in the Modern World instructs Catholics concerning the negative usage of this term, as when St. Paul says: "Do not be conformed to this world. . ." (Rom 12:2). The Constitution explains:

> By world is here meant that spirit of vanity and malice which transforms into an instrument of sin those human energies intended for the service of God and man. . . (GS, no. 37)

This understanding sheds light on the well-known maxim that Christians are to be in the world, but not of the world (see Jn 17:14-18). This means that although Christians are physically on earth, they are not to submit themselves to the false values or powers of the world that are opposed to God.

The Catholic approach to the world and human society cannot be characterized simply as either optimistic or pessimistic, but rather as marked by realism and Christian hope. Christian hope affirms that all who consciously commit their lives to Jesus Christ and conform every area of their lives to his teaching will find peace and ultimate victory over all evil (Rom 8:22-25). This hope, implanted by the Holy Spirit, was the force that has motivated the great martyrs, missionaries and saints of the church to endure willingly (even joyfully) their hardships and sufferings on account of the gospel. Catholics today also are challenged by the gospel and church teaching to sacrifice their lives (their time, energy, money) so that the world and human society can be transformed according to God's will and plan. However, this can only occur if they first have been changed and transformed from within by the Holy Spirit. Only through God's grace can we view and approach the many disturbing realities of the world with true Christian courage and hope (see Col 1:24-29).

Vocation of Prayer and Penance

There are different ways Catholics can take active responsibility for the world—different callings or vocations. Some are called to influence the world through a contemplative life of prayer and penance. This is not a passive approach, or an escape from the world, but a time-honored Catholic vocation based upon the realization that the course of human events is profoundly affected by prayer, as well as influenced by the prophetic lifestyle of the contemplative. As T.S. Eliot wrote in his choruses from "The Rock":

> Even the anchorite who meditates alone,
> For whom the days and nights repeat the praise of God,
> Prays for the Church, the Body of Christ incarnate.[3]

Some Christians mistakenly view the contemplative vocation as useless to society, despite Jesus' teaching about Martha and Mary (Lk 10:38-42). It is hard to determine whether this view flows from a modern Western orientation toward action, from a lack of faith in the power of prayer, or both. In either case, it is essential for Catholics to grasp the importance of prayer for the direction and transformation of human society. Even those who are called by God to very active involvement in the world need to pray. In order to act according to God's will, we first must listen to what God has to say about how to act, seeking the guidance of the Holy Spirit, and also draw strength from the Lord for our activity.

We also need to pray because there is spiritual opposition to the accomplishment of God's will in the world—opposition that can only be overcome by spiritual means and not by human effort alone. The ministry of Jesus and other writings of the New Testament underscore the reality that "we are not contending against flesh and blood, but against the principalities, against the powers, against the world rulers of this present darkness, against the spiritual hosts of wickedness in the heavenly places" (Eph 6:12). In response to this realization, Paul exhorts the church to "Pray at all times in the Spirit, with all prayer and supplication. To that end keep alert with all perseverance, making supplication for all the saints..."

(Eph 6:18). Jesus himself spent many hours in prayer and fasting in his warfare against Satan, a warfare that ultimately led to his death "when the devil... put it into the heart of Judas Iscariot, Simon's son, to betray him" (Jn 13:2). At another time, Jesus told his apostles that "this kind [of demon] cannot be driven out by anything but prayer [and fasting]" (Mk 9:29). To repeat, one of the most pressing needs of the Catholic church in our day is recognition of the reality of Satan and his opposition to God's kingdom, and the need for prayer and other spiritual means to combat him. The Catholic church recognized this principle when it proclaimed St. Thérèse de Lisieux, a cloistered contemplative nun, the patroness of missionaries. Although she never set foot in mission territory, her fervent desire for the conversion of the world to Christ and her zealous prayer for this is recognized by Catholics as having a tremendous missionary impact.

Reflecting on the magnitude of evil in the world should indicate that this evil is not simply the product of human weakness or perversity alone, but is instigated and fostered by a malevolent being that is more than human, even grotesquely inhuman. Yet, salvation means that we have been freed by the Lord's death and resurrection from the power of Satan, sin, and death in our lives. As the Second Vatican Council proclaims:

> From bondage to the devil and sin, He delivered us, so that each one of us can say with the Apostle: the Son of God "loved me and gave Himself up for me" (Gal 2:20). By suffering for us He not only provided us with an example for our imitation. He blazed a trail, and if we follow it, life and death are made holy and take on a new meaning.(GS, no. 22)

Bringing Christ to the World

The basic message that the Catholic church brings to the world today must be this same message of liberation and hope for humanity in Jesus Christ that is recorded in the Scripture. When Pope John Paul II asked in his first encyclical letter, *Redemptor Hominis,* what Christians are called to do in this moment of history, he answered:

> Our response must be: Our spirit is set in one direction, the only direction for our intellect, will, and heart is towards Christ, our Redeemer, towards Christ, the redeemer of man. We wish to look toward Him—because there is salvation in no one else but Him—the Son of God—repeating what Peter said, "Lord, to whom shall we go? You have the words of eternal life." (*Redemptor Hominis,* no. 7)

How do Catholics bring Christ to the world? There are two basic approaches that will be discussed here. The first is evangelization: the proclamation of the good news of Jesus Christ in order to lead others to conversion and faith in him so that they may be saved and enjoy eternal life with God. This always has been the primary task of the disciples of Jesus, his church.

A second approach to bringing Christ to the world is to seek the transformation of the social order (including the political, economic, and cultural spheres of man's activities), so that this social order truly reflects and operates according to God's will, as revealed most fully by Jesus Christ and his teaching.

Both these approaches are important for Catholics, but the first has priority. Society is made up of individual persons and therefore will not reflect God's will and Christian values fully unless the individuals who make up the society personally embrace Christ. Only when this happens will they be able to discern God's will through the grace and truth that comes fully through Jesus Christ alone. It is true that the grace of Christ may be available to those who are not explicitly Christian, (this point is disputed by theologians), but certainly the fullness of God's plan for human society will not be achieved unless people come to know, love, and serve the Savior of the human race, Jesus Christ. Hence, evangelization of persons precedes and makes possible the transformation of society according to the fullness of God's will and plan.

Evangelization

The great commission for all Christians to evangelize is based on Jesus' parting words to his followers in Matthew's Gospel (Mt 28:19-20).

The charter for evangelization for Catholics today is the apostolic exhortation of Pope Paul VI, December 8, 1975, entitled On Evangelization in the Modern World (*Evangelii Nuntiandi*). This is a short document that should be studied by every mature Catholic applying the great commission of Jesus to the world today. The document explains, first, the meaning of evangelization:

> ... to evangelize is first of all to bear witness, in a simple and direct way, to God revealed by Jesus Christ, in the Holy Spirit, to bear witness that in His Son God has loved the world—that in His Incarnate Word He has given being to all things and has called men to eternal life (no. 26)....
>
> Evangelization will also always contain—as the foundation, center and at the same time summit of its dynamism—a clear proclamation that, in Jesus Christ, the Son of God made man, who died and rose from the dead, salvation is offered to all men, as a gift of God's grace and mercy.... (no. 27)

But what is meant by "salvation"? The document goes on to explain that our evangelization does not announce an "imminent (this-worldly) salvation" that meets material and spiritual needs of life on earth alone, but the church announces:

> ... a salvation that exceeds all those limits in order to reach fulfillment in a communion with the one and only divine Absolute (God): a transcendent and eschatological sal-

> vation, which indeed has its beginning in this life but which is fulfilled in eternity. (no. 27)

In other words, Catholics must witness to the reality of God's love as shown in Jesus Christ and in the gift of eternal life that God has offered to every person. How does one witness? Witness does not mean reciting doctrine or abstract truths. A witness has first-hand, personal knowledge of that to which he testifies. In order to evangelize, Catholics first must know the reality of God's love and of the power of the death and resurrection of Jesus Christ in their own lives. True evangelization requires genuine faith and conversion on the part of the evangelizer. As the Catholic bishops affirmed at the Extraordinary Synod in 1985, in the document, "Message to the People of God, Final Report":

> The evangelization of non-believers in fact presupposes the self-evangelization of the baptized and also, in a certain sense, of deacons, priests and Bishops. Evangelization takes place through witnesses. The witness gives his testimony not only with words, but also with his life. We must not forget that in Greek the word for testimony is *martyrium.* In this respect, the more ancient churches can learn much from the new churches, from their dynamism, from their life and testimony even unto the shedding of their blood for the Faith. (Section II, B, a), 2, pp. 50-51)

The world needs to confront the reality of Christ, the "power of God and the wisdom of God" (1 Cor 1:24), as he is present in the world changing peoples' lives. As the apostle Paul puts it, "the kingdom of God does not consist in talk but in power" (1 Cor 4:20). That is what is at the heart of evangelization—the testimony or witness of people, through both word and example, to God's transforming power and love in their lives. Many Catholics, it appears, need to be evangelized themselves, to encounter God personally before they can become true evangelizers and carry out Jesus' commission to "Go therefore and make disciples of all nations . . ." (Mt 28:19).

The 1985 Extraordinary Synod of Bishops proclaimed:

> Every baptized man and woman, according to his or her state in life and in the church, receives the mission to proclaim the Good News of salvation for man in Jesus Christ (Message to the People of God, III);

and

> Evangelization is the first duty not only of the Bishops but also of priests and deacons, indeed, of all Christians. (Final Report II, B, a), 2, p. 50) . . . The Church makes herself more credible if she speaks less of herself and ever more preaches Christ crucified (cf. 1 Cor 2:12). . . . (Final Report, II, A, 2, p. 45)

The primary mission of the church in the world, today as always, is evangelization: to witness in the power of the Holy Spirit to God's love as revealed in Jesus Christ, so that all people will come to know, love, and serve God, and receive the gift of eternal life.

Finally, it must be stressed that evangelization is only the first stage of an ongoing, life-long growth in believing in and following Jesus Christ. The Catholic church has always emphasized that the proclamation of God's word (*kerygma,*) or the act of evangelization, must be followed by an ever fuller instruction in the Christian life (known as catechesis, or *didache,* meaning teaching) that contributes to the person's growth in holiness.

As Pope John Paul II wrote in his apostolic exhortation on catechesis in our time, *Catechesi Tradendae:*

> . . . within the whole process of evangelization, the aim of catechesis is to be the teaching and maturation stage, that is to say, the period in which the Christian, having accepted by

faith the person of Jesus Christ as the one Lord and having given Him complete adherence by sincere conversion of heart, endeavors to know better this Jesus to whom he has entrusted himself: to know His "mystery," the kingdom of God proclaimed by Him, the requirements and promises contained in His Gospel message, and the paths that He has laid down for anyone who wishes to follow Him.

It is true that being a Christian means saying "yes" to Jesus Christ, but let us remember that this "yes" has two levels: It consists in surrendering to the word of God and relying on it, but it also means, at a later stage, endeavoring to know better and better the profound meaning of this word. [no. 20]

... Finally, catechesis is closely linked with the responsible activity of the Church and of Christians in the world. A person who has given adherence to Jesus Christ by faith and is endeavoring to consolidate that faith by catechesis needs to live in communion with those who have taken the same step. Catechesis runs the risk of becoming barren if no community of faith and Christian life takes the catechumen in at a certain stage of his catechesis. [no. 24]

... the truths studied in catechesis are the same truths that touched the person's heart when he heard them for the first time. Far from blunting or exhausting them, the fact of knowing them better should make them even more challenging and decisive for one's life. [no. 25][4]

A strong community of faith is necessary to foster this growth in Christ.

Transforming the Social Order

The Second Vatican Council also teaches that Catholics have a responsibility to work for the betterment of human society—to serve as a "leaven" (1 Cor 5:6) in order to transform every sphere of human activity, so that they all may attain the full purpose and life that God intends. The church "serves as a leaven and as a kind of soul for human society as it is to be renewed in Christ and transformed into God's family" (GS, no. 40).

But how, practically, do the church and its members seek to transform human society? As the Pastoral Constitution on the Church in the Modern World instructs:

> Christ, to be sure, gave His church no proper mission in the political, economic, or social order. The purpose which He set before her is a religious one. But out of this religious mission itself came a function, a light, and an energy which can serve to structure and consolidate the human community according to the divine law. As a matter of fact, when circumstances of time and place create the need, she can and indeed should initiate activities on behalf of all men. This is particularly true of activities designed for the needy, such as the works of mercy and similar undertakings. (GS, no. 42)

The history of the Catholic church abounds in examples of Catholics of every vocation initiating works of mercy and other services as a response to the call of the gospel. There is no foundation to the view that the church has been or should be separated from the world, if by this is meant a detachment from the needs and concerns of human beings and human society. The very first sentence of *Gaudium et Spes* declares:

> The joys and the hopes, the griefs and the anxieties of the men of this age, especially those who are poor or in any way afflicted, these too are the joys and hopes, the griefs and anxieties of the followers of Christ. (GS, no. 1)

Christ's ministry, carried on by his church, involves healing the sick, feeding the hungry, encouraging the lonely and discouraged, freeing the oppressed. In Luke's Gospel, Jesus applied the prophecy of Isaiah (61:1-2) to himself. "The Spirit of the Lord is upon me, / because he has anointed me to preach good news to the poor. / He has sent me to proclaim release to the captives / and recovering of sight to the blind, / to set at liberty those who are oppressed . . ." (Lk 4:18).

The Catholic church carries on this mission of Jesus Christ in the world. *Gaudium et Spes* firmly rejects the false view of considering the Christian life as an escape from involvement in this world by focusing solely on life in the world to come. Rather, it is precisely through our involvement in this world (specifically through love of our neighbor, even our enemies) that we attain eternal life in heaven. The Second Vatican Council was direct about this:

> This Council exhorts Christians, as citizens of two cities, to strive to discharge their earthly duties conscientiously and in response to the gospel spirit. They are mistaken who, knowing that we have here no abiding city but seek one which is to come, think that they may therefore shirk their earthly responsibilities. For they are forgetting that by the faith itself they are more than ever obliged to measure up to those duties, each according to his proper vocation . . .
>
> This split between the faith which many profess and their daily lives deserves to be counted among the most serious errors of our age.
>
> Therefore, let there be no false opposition between professional and social activities on the one part, and religious life on the other. The Christian who neglects his temporal duties neglects his duties toward his neighbor and even God, and jeopardizes his eternal salvation.
>
> Christians should rather rejoice that they can follow the example of Christ, Who worked as an artisan. In the exercise of all their earthly activities, they can thereby gather their humane, domestic, professional, social and technical enterprises into one vital synthesis with religious values, under whose supreme direction all things are harmonized unto God's glory. (GS, no. 43)

The Catholic church affirms that all human activities and enterprises are to be carried out for the glory of God.

The principle stated here is clear: Christians, especially the laity, have a responsibility for the life and affairs of the world (see Chapter Four). The Second Vatican Council acknowledges that in practice there may be legitimate differences of opinion among Christians about specific actions to be taken, or even disagreements in judging what is a truly Christian activity or response. Pope John Paul II and the Second Vatican Council have both taught that the gospel of Jesus Christ cannot be equated with any particular social, political, or economic system. The gospel stands in judgment over all human thought and activity.

The pastors of the Catholic church strive to assist God's people by giving positive guidance and direction to the members of the church about social issues and the concerns of the world. Since 1890, the popes have issued a series of social encyclicals that have provided authoritative direction to Catholics about the social issues of the day. These encyclicals include *Rerum Novarum* of Pope Leo XIII (1891), *Quadragesimo Anno* of Pope Pius XI (1931), *Mater et Magistra* (1961) and *Pacem in Terris* (1963) of Pope John XXIII, *Populorum Progressio* of Pope Paul VI (1967) and *Laborem Exercens* of Pope John Paul II (1981).

The Pastoral Constitution on the Church in the Modern World admits that the Catholic church, including its pastors and members, has failed at times to be faithful to the Spirit of God in carrying out its mission in the world, and seeks "to struggle against [these defects] energetically." The Constitution further states that:

> The Church also realizes that in working out her relationship with the world she always has great need of the ripening which comes from the experience of the centuries. (GS, no. 43)

This is a very important statement, because it acknowledges that there is an authentic development or "ripening" that takes place, through the guidance of the Holy Spirit, in the relationship of the Catholic church and its teaching on the social, economic, political, and cultural life of the world. For this reason, some Catholic teaching on social or political issues is liable to change. Essential doctrines of the Catholic faith do not change, but the church's understanding of how it should relate to the world and apply its teaching to the life of human society does deepen and mature through the on-going guidance of the Holy Spirit. Until the Lord comes again, the Catholic church and individual Catholics are still liable to err in their efforts to live the gospel in the world and to transform it according to God's plan. However, we can also expect to see an even greater wisdom and maturity in these efforts due to the Holy Spirit's guidance.

There are many examples of this growth or deepening of the Catholic church's teaching regarding issues and affairs of the world. The principles governing many of these issues, such as the Catholic church's view of political life, culture, socio-economic activity, and peace in the world, are found in the second part of the Pastoral Constitution on the Church in the Modern World of the Second Vatican Council. Other issues are addressed in various official church documents, such as the two instructions on liberation theology published by the Sacred Congregation for the Doctrine of the Faith in Rome in 1984, and 1986.[5] Such instructions are not necessarily the Catholic church's final word on these matters but they represent the ever-deepening Catholic understanding of the gospel of Christ, as we seek to live and apply the gospel practically in the world through the guidance and empowerment of the Holy Spirit.

Marriage and Family Life

While it is true that there are many areas in which Catholic doctrine has developed in the course of centuries, what is striking about the Catholic church's teaching on some areas, such as marriage and family life, is its consistency. The Pastoral

Constitution on the Church in the Modern World singles out marriage and family life as one area of special concern for the church in the world today. There were few topics that Jesus spoke so clearly and strongly about as the sacredness of marriage:

> But Jesus said to them, "... from the beginning of creation, 'God made them male and female.' 'For this reason a man shall leave his father and mother and be joined to his wife, and the two shall become one.... What therefore God has joined together, let man not put asunder.'"
>
> And in the house the disciples asked him again about this matter. And he said to them, "Whoever divorces his wife and marries another, commits adultery against her; and if she divorces her husband and marries another, she commits adultery." (Mk 10:5-12)

The most adequate image of the sacredness and indissolubility of the marriage bond is the bond of love between Christ, the bridegroom, and his bride, the church (Eph 5:21-33).

The bond of marriage must be sacred and indissoluble because it is the basis for the most important and most basic human social group: the family. The simple fact is that God wills every person to enter the world and be prepared to participate in society through the family. As the Second Vatican Council put it, "the family is the foundation of society" (GS, no. 52).

The family is also essential to the life of the church, because from the family new church members are presented for baptism, and within the family people are educated and trained in the knowledge and practice of their faith. The Dogmatic Constitution on the Church, *Lumen Gentium,* calls the family the "domestic church" because, "In it parents should, by their word and example, be the first preachers of the faith to their children" (no. 11). Indeed, parents remain primary teachers of faith and morality for their children throughout their lives. *Gaudium et Spes* calls the family "a kind of school of deeper humanity" (no. 52), and insists that both the father and the mother are important in raising children in Christ.

> The active presence of the father is highly beneficial to their formation. The children, especially the younger among them, need the care of their mother at home. This domestic role of hers must be safely preserved, though the legitimate social progress of women should not be underrated on that account. (no. 52)

In Western society, it is evident that the traditional structure of the family is being seriously challenged from many quarters. In paragraphs 47-53 of the Pastoral Constitution on the Church in the Modern World, and in Pope John Paul II's apostolic exhortation on the Role of the Christian Family in the Modern World, (Familiaris Consortio, Nov. 22, 1981), the Catholic church presents extended teaching on principles of family life and reaffirm its uncompromising stand against divorce, civil marriage, abortion, sterilization, infanticide, artificial contraception and "a contraceptive mentality," as well as other threats to family life such as "a mistaken theoretical and practical concept of the independence of spouses to each other; serious misconceptions regarding the relationship of authority between parents and children; the concrete difficulties that the family experiences in the transmission of values, etc."[6] Pope John Paul II comments that:

> At the root of these negative phenomena there frequently lies a corruption of the idea and the experience of freedom, conceived not as a capacity for realizing the truth of God's plan for marriage and the family, but as an autonomous power of self-affirmation, often against others, for one's own selfish well-being. (FC, no. 6)

The source of life and success for Christian marriage and the family is Jesus Christ and his example of self-sacrificial love. Marriage and family life only works according to God's plan when all involved are actively seeking to sacrifice and lay down their lives for one another by the grace of God.

> ... sacrifice cannot be removed from family life, but must in fact be wholeheartedly accepted if the love between husband and wife is to be deepened and become a source of intimate joy. (FC, no. 34)

Sacrifice is not enough, however. Wisdom, God's wisdom, is necessary for successful married and family life. The biblical teaching on marriage must be re-examined with greater seriousness by Catholics. God has an order and plan for family life. This wisdom from God is to be found in the Scripture and Catholic tradition. Biblical texts concerning the proper order of family life, such as Ephesians 5:21ff; 6:1-4, cannot be lightly dismissed as culturally conditioned or out-moded, as scholarly studies such as Stephen B. Clark's, *Man and Woman in Christ* (Ann Arbor, MI: Servant Publications, 1980) have convincingly demonstrated.

One of the primary Christian and Catholic values that is under the most severe attack today is the importance and value of motherhood. While affirming "the equal dignity and responsibility of women with men," Pope John Paul II has taught:

> While it must be recognized that women have the same right as men to perform various public functions, society must be structured in such a way that wives and mothers are *not in practice compelled* to work outside the home, and that their families can live and prosper in a dignified way even when they themselves devote their full time to their own family.

> Furthermore, the mentality which honors women more for their work outside the home than for their work within the family must be overcome. This requires that men should truly esteem and love women with total respect for their personal dignity, and that society should create and develop conditions favoring work in the home.... (FC, no. 23)

Familiaris Consortio adds that the ultimate affront to the dignity of women is anything that would lead to "a renunciation of their femininity or an imitation of the male role" (FC, no. 23). In the same document, Pope John Paul II promotes "the fullness of true feminine humanity" which would include the essential duties of motherhood and family life within the home, as well as valued service and activity outside the family circle. Likewise, men are called to respect and promote the dignity and rights of women, and as fathers and husbands, to reveal the fatherhood of God within the family by "ensuring the harmonious and united development of all the members of the family" and "manifesting towards his wife a charity that is both gentle and strong like that which Christ has for the church" (no. 25).

Living according to biblical and authentic Catholic teaching is not easy for Catholic married couples and families in most places. The genuine values that guide Catholic life are unpopular in many societies, and secular attitudes have even heavily infiltrated the Catholic church itself. Families who desire to live in fidelity to the teaching of Scripture and the Catholic church and who wish to resist the encroachment of other secular values into their homes often find it necessary to seek out support and encouragement from other families with similar values. New communities of Christians are forming to provide such support, and Catholic parishes are challenged to provide clear teaching and support for families who wish to stand firm and live according to Catholic values, as a light and witness to the gospel in the midst of an increasingly confused and post-Christian world. With sound Catholic teaching and mutual support, these families can hope to carry out the fourfold mission of the Catholic family expressed by the Synod of Bishops in 1981:

1. forming a community of persons;
2. serving life;
3. participating in the development of society;
4. sharing in the life and mission of the church (FC, no 17).

Those aspects of the task of the Catholic family, are described in detail in "The Role of the Christian Family in the Modern World" of John Paul II.

The sad reality is that the widespread abandonment of traditional Christian norms of marriage and family life in Western society is resulting in increasingly deeper personal and social problems. Catholics faithful to their tradition and biblical teaching must pray that the Holy Spirit will use this situation to reveal to people the error of infidelity and experimentation, and lead them back to authentic biblical and Catholic values in marriage and family life.

TEN

Mary

THE DOGMATIC CONSTITUTION on the Church of the Second Vatican Council closes with a chapter on Mary in order to highlight her crucial role in God's plan of salvation. Christians need to understand Mary and her unique place in God's saving plan. Then Mary can assume the role God wants her to play in our own lives and we can honor Mary as God intends. A proper understanding of Mary is also very important for Catholics in discussions and relationships with other Christians, and even with non-Christians. God desires Mary to be a source of Christian unity, not an obstacle to unity.

This chapter will present some of the fundamental Catholic beliefs about Mary, but it is by no means exhaustive. A fuller understanding may be obtained by examining the teachings on Mary of ecumenical councils (such as Chapter 8 of *Lumen Gentium* from Vatican II), papal teachings (such as Pope Paul VI's apostolic exhortation, *Marialis Cultus,* Feb. 2, 1974), teachings of Catholic bishops (such as the U.S. Catholic bishops' pastoral letter, *Behold Your Mother: Women of Faith,* Nov. 21, 1973), and many other writings on Mary by the great saints and theologians of the Catholic church.

Mary in the Bible

A basic question to begin with might be, Why do Catholics honor Mary at all? The answer is simple. Catholics honor Mary because God has honored her by choosing her to be the mother of God incarnate, Jesus Christ. This role of Mary was prefigured and foretold in the Old Testament, as the Second Vatican Council explains:

> The books of the Old Testament recount the period of salvation history during which the coming of Christ into the world was slowly prepared for. These earliest documents, as they are read in the Church and are understood in the light of a further and full revelation, bring the figure of the woman, Mother of the Redeemer, into a gradually sharper focus.
>
> When looked at in this way, she is already prophetically foreshadowed in that victory over the serpent which was promised to our first parents after their fall into sin (cf. Gn 3:15). Likewise she is the Virgin who is to conceive and bear a son, whose name will be called Emmanuel (cf. Is 7:14; Mi 5:2-3; Mt 1:22-23). She stands out among the poor and humble of the Lord, who confidently await and receive salvation from Him. With her, the exalted Daughter of Sion, and after a long expectation of the promise, the times were at length fulfilled and the new dispensation established. (LG, no. 55)

In the New Testament, even though Mary is not spoken of at length or in great detail, she is mentioned at many of the crucial points of the life of Christ and of his church. The infancy narratives, especially in the Gospel of Luke, focus on God's call to Mary to accept her role in his plan (see the Annunciation, Lk 1:26-38), and on the conception and birth of Jesus that resulted from her unqualified "yes" to God: "I am the [servant] handmaid of the Lord; let it be to me according to your word" (Lk 1:38).

Mary's response to God is seen more fully in her great prayer of praise, the Magnificat (Lk 1:46-55), in which she acknowledges the honor God had given her—"for all generations will call me blessed" (Lk 1:48)—but immediately directs all praise back to God—"for he who is mighty has done great things for me, / and holy is his name" (Lk 1:49).

Mary's response to God resulted in hardship and suffering for her. She gave birth to Jesus in a stable, then had to flee to Egypt to escape Herod's wrath (see Mt 2:13-14; Lk 2:6-7). When Mary and Joseph presented Jesus in the temple, Simeon prophesied that her heart would be "pierced with a sword" (Lk 2:35). She witnessed her Son's terrible death. Mary also experienced the normal anxieties of a mother, such as when they left behind the twelve-year-old Jesus in Jerusalem (see Lk 2:41-50). Yet the Bible always shows Mary to be a woman of faith in the midst of these trials. "But Mary kept all these things, pondering them in her heart" (Lk 2:19, 51).

Mary appears in the New Testament at certain times during Jesus' public ministry. In John's Gospel, Jesus worked his first public miracle, at Cana, at Mary's request (see Jn 2:1-12). Mary followed Jesus during his public ministry as is indicated when the crowd told Jesus that his mother and brothers were there to see him (see Mt 12:46-50; Mk 3:31-35; Lk 8:19-21). Jesus' response that his mother and brothers are "those who do the will of God" was not a rebuke of Mary, for she herself had totally dedicated herself to following the will of God (see Lk 1:38).

Mary followed Jesus right to the foot of the cross, where Jesus gave her to the "beloved disciple," John, to be his mother (Jn 19:25-27). The final glimpse we have of Mary in the New Testament is the scene of her praying with the apostles in the upper room, ready to receive with them the outpouring of the Holy Spirit on Pentecost—the birth of the church (Acts 1:14; 2).

Deepening Understanding of Mary: Christian Tradition

It should not surprise us that the church, as it has reflected more deeply on Mary's role in God's plan, has been led to deeper insight into the truth about her. We even see this process begun in the New Testament, in which the later Gospels, Luke and John, have a fuller treatment of Mary and her importance than the earlier Gospels, Mark and Matthew. The Holy Spirit was responsible for this deepening understanding.

Catholics believe that the Holy Spirit continues to unfold and deepen our understanding of the truths of faith found in the Bible. He has done so as Christians have pondered and prayed about these truths over the ages. As a result of this process, the Catholic church has recognized and defined certain beliefs about Mary that are found implicitly in the Bible (not in their full form), doctrines which the universal church came to accept and believe with overwhelming consent through the guidance of the Holy Spirit. Here we will examine four of the doctrines about Mary that the Catholic church teaches as matters of faith.

1. Mary as Mother of God. All Catholic doctrines concerning Mary are related to and emerge from our understanding of her Son, Jesus Christ. The Holy Spirit impelled the early Christians to honor and address Mary as the Mother of God, *theotokos* in Greek (literally "God-bearer"). They reasoned that if Jesus were truly God, as well as man, and if Mary were truly his mother, it would be perfectly fitting to speak of Mary as the God-bearer or Mother of God.

A great disturbance arose in the church of the fifth century A.D. when the bishop of Constantinople, Nestorius, prohibited use of the title *theotokos* for Mary, on the grounds that it implied that Mary gave birth to God—to the *divine* nature of Jesus. However, soon afterwards the Council of Ephesus (A.D. 431) condemned Nestorius' rejection of *theotokos*. This great council of Catholic bishops taught that it is right and good for Christians to address and honor Mary as Mother of God, understanding this to mean that she gave birth to the one, undivided person of Jesus Christ, who is both fully God and fully man. Only Jesus' humanity came from the flesh of Mary while his divine nature came through the power of the Holy Spirit "overshadowing" Mary (Lk 1:35). Nonetheless, since Mary gave birth to the one person of Jesus, the Catholic church has held continually that Mary should be honored as the Mother of God.

2. Mary's Perpetual Virginity. Church leaders of the fourth century and earlier taught that Mary remained a virgin throughout her life. God preserved Mary's virginity in the conception and birth of Jesus. Catholics believe that throughout her life, Mary embraced this unique vocation of virgin mother to which God first called her through the angel Gabriel. Mary abstained from sexual relations and bore no other children after the birth of Jesus.

The biblical data concerning this doctrine is neutral, as even ecumenical studies have concluded.[1] Matthew 1:25 states that, "...he...knew her not until she had borne a son; and he called his name Jesus." The Greek word translated "before" or "until" does not imply that Mary had sexual relations with Joseph *after* the birth of Jesus.[2] The use of the term "the brother" or "brothers" of Jesus is also ambiguous. The word could mean blood brothers, but it could also refer to other close relatives, such as cousins. Hence, the Bible neither clearly confirms nor denies whether Mary remained a virgin. In such cases, Catholics have always sought to understand the Scripture according to what the Holy Spirit has led the church as a whole to believe. Until fairly recently—until after the Protestant Reformation—the consensus of the Christian people was that Mary remained a virgin throughout her life.[3]

There is good reason for belief in Mary's perpetual virginity, besides the testimony of Christian tradition. It is a full response to God's unique call to Mary. It is a sign of her total consecration to God and of respect for the fact that God himself had dwelt and grown within her womb. What other human child would be worthy of sharing that dignity? Mary's perpetual virginity also helps us to realize that through her call to be the Mother of Jesus, Mary was also being called by God to be the mother of all Christians, who have been made Christ's body through baptism. Perhaps God's call and gift to Mary of perpetual virginity may be understood best by those who, like Mary, have embraced celibacy in order to become spiritual fathers and mothers of God's people in the church.

3. Mary's Immaculate Conception. If a great dignitary, like a president or the pope, were to come to live in your home for a time, how carefully would you clean and prepare for that guest? If God planned to live for a time as a human being within the womb of a woman and then be taught and formed by this woman after his birth, how carefully would God prepare that woman for this awesome responsibility and privilege? The Catholic doctrine of the Immaculate Conception states that in view of Mary's role of bearing and raising the Son of God, God prepared her for this by freeing her from original sin from the moment of her conception in the womb of her mother, Anne. God prepared Mary to be a vessel without a trace of sin, not because of her own virtue or merit but because of her unique role in his plan of salvation.

There are some common questions that this teaching raises. First, if Mary was conceived without sin, did she really need a Savior? Put simply, was Mary saved? The Catholic church teaches that Mary actually was the first to be saved by the grace of her Son, Jesus. God first applied to Mary the grace that he knew and foresaw that Jesus would gain by his life and death on the cross. The official definition of Mary's Immaculate Conception, promulgated by Pope Pius IX in 1854, states:

> The Blessed Virgin Mary, in the first instant of her conception, by a singular grace and privilege of almighty God, and in view of the foreseen merits of Jesus Christ, the Savior of the human race, was preserved free from all stain of original sin.[4]

Second, does this doctrine state that Mary never sinned? Although Mary was freed from original sin at the moment of her conception, it is conceivable in theory that Mary could have sinned during her life. She had free will and was tempted as we all are. However, Catholic tradition overwhelmingly affirms that in reality Mary always responded to the grace of God to resist sin and thus remained without sin throughout her life.

Mary's freedom from original sin certainly aided her in avoiding sin throughout her life, but it did not guarantee it. Even Eve, who was born without sin, succumbed to the temptation of Satan. Thus, Mary is the new Eve, who reversed the effects of the disobedience of the first Eve by her perfect obedience to God, as St. Irenaeus first observed in the second century.[5] Just as sin entered the world through Eve and her unbelief and rebellion, salvation entered the world through Mary by her faith and perfect obedience to God and his will.

A striking confirmation of the truth of the Immaculate Conception of Mary occurred just four years after its definition as a Catholic dogma of faith by Pope Pius IX in 1854. On the Feast of the Annunciation in 1858, a beautiful Lady appeared to a simple peasant girl, Bernadette Soubirous, at Lourdes, France. The Lady told her, "I am the Immaculate Conception." At the time, Bernadette did not even know what "Immaculate Conception" meant, but repeated these words to a trusted friend.[6] Today many Catholics, including the recent popes, believe that Bernadette had an authentic experience of Mary at Lourdes. The hundreds of medically verified healings and other miracles that have occurred at Lourdes since 1858, through Mary's intercession, point to the reality of Mary as the Immaculate Conception.

4. The Assumption of Mary into Heaven. This doctrine, formally defined by Pope Pius XII in 1950, after millions of petitions for its definition had been received by the Vatican, declares that Mary, "having completed the course of her earthly life, was assumed body and soul to heavenly glory."[7] This definition affirms that Mary experienced immediately at the end of her time on earth the resurrection of the body that is promised to all faithful followers of Jesus. The doctrine of the Assumption of Mary into heaven flows from and completes the concept of her Immaculate Conception. Since Mary was preserved from sin by a unique gift and grace of Christ, she was able to experience the immediate union of her whole being with God at the end of her life. Sin could not in any way obstruct her full and immediate union with the Lord in heaven.

The Assumption of Mary is a source of hope for us because it foreshadows what will one day happen to each faithful Christian. The raising of Mary, body and soul, into heaven anticipates what will happen at the final judgment to all who are to be saved. All who are saved by the grace of Christ will one day live in perfect joy with the Lord with transformed, glorified bodies. Reflecting on Mary's assumption helps us to turn our thoughts toward our ultimate goal and to pray that we, too, will one day experience the resurrection of the body and the life of eternal glory that Mary has already entered into fully through the grace of her Son, Jesus Christ.

The Five "M's" of Mary

In addition to these four official teachings about Mary that all Catholics are bound to believe as articles of faith, there are many other aspects of Catholic belief about Mary that are helpful in understanding her role in God's plan and in approaching her in prayer. One way of remembering some important truths about Mary is to think of five of her attributes that begin with the letter "M": member, model, mother, mediatrix, and messenger. The first three of these "M's" are mentioned in one paragraph of the chapter on Mary in the Dogmatic Constitution on the Church of the Second Vatican Council:

> . . . Therefore, she is also hailed as a pre-eminent and altogether singular *member* of the Church, and as the

Church's *model* and excellent exemplar in faith and charity. Taught by the Holy Spirit, the Catholic Church honors her with filial affection and piety as the most beloved *mother*..." (LG, no. 53) [Emphasis mine]

1. Mary as a Member of the Church. The Second Vatican Council included its discussion of Mary in the last chapter of the Dogmatic Constitution on the Church in order to emphasize that Mary is a member, albeit "a pre-eminent and altogether singular member," of the church. This attribute of Mary is a reminder that however much we might rightfully honor and exalt Mary for her response to God and for her role in God's saving plan, she remains fully human and is not to be adored by Christians.[8] Mary is not a goddess, but a fully human servant of God whom he has highly favored through his mercy and grace. This fact can enable Catholics to identify more fully with Mary and to realize that the holiness and full consecration to God that she exhibited is something which is possible for every Christian. It is, in fact, the goal of the Christian life.

2. Mary as Model. The last statement above implies that Mary provides an ideal model for each individual Christian of a life of discipleship, consecration, and holiness. God calls each person to make the unconditional "yes" to him and to his will that Mary expressed at the Annunciation and proceeded to live out until the end of her life. Catholics honor Mary because she is the model disciple, the perfect, most faithful follower of her Son, Jesus Christ. Thus, she is a model of true discipleship for each Christian.

Mary is not only a model for individual Christians but she is a model for the church as a whole. The church is called to be God's presence in the world through its faithfulness to the gospel and to following Jesus as he guides the church through the Holy Spirit. Mary manifested God's presence most perfectly by pondering the events and words that constituted her call and experience and by carrying out faithfully everything

God told her. Because the church has not attained the perfection of discipleship that Mary attained, we continue to look to her as the best example of what we, as the church, are called by God to be and to do.

As the Second Vatican Council's Dogmatic Constitution on the Church notes:

> As St. Ambrose taught, the Mother of God is a model of the Church in the matter of faith, charity, and perfect union with Christ... the followers of Christ still strive to increase in holiness by conquering sin. And so they raise their eyes to Mary who shines forth to the whole community of the elect as a model of the virtues.... (LG, nos. 63, 65)

3. Mary as Mother. Mary is not only a model, she is much more—she is our mother. Mary is the Mother of God, but also by God's grace and call she is the spiritual mother of the church and of each Christian. The basis of this is found in the Gospel of John, chapter 19. As his last act before his death, Jesus told the beloved disciple, who represents all of Jesus' disciples, "Behold, your mother" (Jn 19:27). Christian tradition from the earliest times confirms that Mary is, indeed, the mother in the order of grace of the church and of each Christian.

4. Mary as Mediatrix. Because Mary is our mother, she is committed to pray and intercede for each of her children and for the church as a whole. Catholic tradition has ascribed a number of different titles to Mary to describe her role of intercession. As the Second Vatican Council explains:

> By her maternal charity, Mary cares for the brethren of her Son who still journey on earth surrounded by dangers and difficulties, until they are led to their happy fatherland. Therefore the Blessed Virgin is involved by the Church under the titles of Advocate, Auxiliatrix, Adjutrix, and Mediatrix. These, however, are to be so understood that

> they neither take away from nor add anything to the dignity and efficacy of Christ the one Mediator. For no creature could ever be classed with the Incarnate Word and Redeemer. . . . (LG, no. 62)

The Dogmatic Constitution on the Church goes on to explain that just as Jesus' priesthood is shared in various ways by members of the church, he also gives us a share in his unique role as mediator (1 Tm 2:5-6)—one who prays or intercedes on behalf of others before the Father. The Catholic church has long held that because of her sinlessness and close union with her Son, Mary has been given a role of mediation or intercession before God above any other human being. In that role, Catholics speak of Mary as Mediatrix.[9]

Is it not appropriate that God should have given a special role of mediation or intercession to the mother of the church? Who on earth pleads for a person as effectively and fervently as that person's mother? The church, as God's family, has been blessed by God with Mary as a mother to mediate and intercede for all Christians in order to lead them to her divine Son, Jesus Christ. The Second Vatican Council's concluding statement on Mary as Mediatrix affirms:

> The Church does not hesitate to profess this subordinate role of Mary. She experiences it continuously and commends it to the hearts of the faithful, so that encouraged by this maternal help they may more closely adhere to the Mediator and Redeemer [Jesus Christ]. (LG, no. 62)

5. Mary as Messenger. Mary's role as messenger has become more prominent in recent times. This refers to the appearances, or apparitions, of Mary that have been reported by Catholics at various times throughout the church's history, and notably more often in the past 150 years. In these appearances, Mary usually presents a prophetic message. The message is sometimes directed toward an individual or local church, but sometimes Mary's words are intended for the whole church or for a large segment of the church.

How does the Catholic church view these apparitions of Mary and their accompanying messages? The church does not require its members to believe in the authenticity of any apparitions or particular messages, since these are private revelation. As Pope John Paul II explained in an address at Fatima, on May 13, 1982:

> The Church has always taught and continues to proclaim that God's revelation was brought to completion in Jesus Christ, who is the fullness of that revelation, and that "no new public revelation is to be expected before the glorious manifestation of the Lord" (*Lumen Gentium,* no. 4). The Church evaluates and judges private revelations by the criterion of conformity with that single public revelation.[10]

Therefore, private revelations such as appearances of Mary must conform fully to the standard of public revelation that comes from Jesus Christ if they are to be accepted and heeded.

It is noteworthy that recent popes have visited and preached at some sites of Mary's reported appearances, such as Lourdes, France, and Fatima, Portugal, and that the messages of Mary presented at these and other sites have been judged by the Catholic church to be in full conformity with biblical teaching and authentic Catholic tradition. Numerous miracles have also been confirmed at some of these sites, such as a multitude of medically verified physical healings at Lourdes. Just as God sent angels as messengers of his word in the Old Testament, it appears that he has chosen in this age to speak particular words of encouragement, instruction, and warning through Mary.

Most of the reported appearances of Mary in recent times have followed the same, biblically-based pattern. Mary appears to simple, humble, and usually poor people. The appearances are accompanied by an outpouring of the Holy Spirit, manifesting itself by the good fruit of joy, thanksgiving, worship and praise of God, and deepened trust in the Lord even in the midst of persecution or oppression. Often healings and other miracles accompany such apparitions.

The effects of such apparitions of Mary and her messages have been profound. Mary's appearance to a poor Mexican peasant, Juan Diego, in 1531, as Our Lady of Guadalupe led to the conversion to Christianity of an estimated eight million native people within seven years. Thousands of people who have visited Lourdes since her appearance there in 1858 to Bernadette Soubirous have been healed and turned to Jesus Christ. In 1917, Mary appeared to three children (ages seven to ten) at Fatima, Portugal, and called for prayer, especially the rosary, and consecration of Russia to her immaculate heart. She warned, "If my requests are heard, Russia will be converted and there will be peace. If not, she will spread her errors throughout the entire world, provoking wars and persecution of the Church. . ."[11] At that time, Russia was a poor country torn by civil war, and this prediction seemed almost laughable. But history has proven it true. Mary's appearance at Fatima reminds Christians that the things we do now and our prayers and faith have consequences for our own salvation and for that of the world. As Pope John Paul II stated in his homily at Fatima on May 13, 1982:

> If the church has accepted the message of Fatima, it is above all because that message contains a truth and a call whose basic content is the truth and call of the gospel itself.
>
> "Repent, and believe in the Gospel!" (Mk 1:15): these are the first words that the Messiah addressed to humanity. The message of Fatima is, in its basic nucleus, a call to conversion and repentance, as in the Gospel . . .

At Fatima, Mary promised a sign of the validity and truth of her appearances there. It is estimated that about one hundred thousand people witnessed this sign—the sun dancing in the sky at mid-day. Many secular observers witnessed this sign, and have not been able to explain it. It has often been ignored, but never effectively denied.[12]

There are many more reported appearances of Mary. The Catholic church has always been wary about placing undue emphasis on these private revelations, but many of them have been accepted as legitimate by the local bishops, whose role it is to discern their validity. In the most widely accepted apparitions, Mary has consistently called Christians to prayer, repentance, and conversion to God. Sometimes she has warned of serious consequences for the world if this message remains unheeded. Mary always has presented herself in authentic apparitions as a messenger or servant of God. Although she has affirmed traditional Catholic titles for herself and encouraged the use of Marian prayers, such as the rosary, her focus is always unmistakably centered on Jesus Christ. The most recent reported appearances of Mary, in Medjugorge, Yugoslavia, repeat many of the themes of the message of Mary at Fatima and affirm the basic truths of the gospel and Catholic Christian teaching.

Conclusion

Catholics are encouraged to foster a proper devotion to Mary, the Mother of God. We honor her, as God honors her, for her special role in his plan of salvation. We imitate her faithfulness as the model disciple of Jesus Christ. We approach her as the spiritual mother that Jesus has given to each Christian and to his church, and we continually ask her, as our mother, to pray and intercede for us before the throne of God. We also must carefully weigh the meaning of the many urgent prophetic words that have come to the church in our time through her reported appearances.

Mary should have a special place in the life of each Christian. Although the form of our relationship with Mary may differ somewhat from person to person, the Catholic church recommends certain forms of honor and devotion, especially the rosary, prayed either individually or in families and groups; and the observance of the feasts of Mary that occur throughout the church year, such as the feast of the Annunciation (March 25), the Assumption (August 15), the Immaculate Conception (December 8), and the Mother of God (January 1). Through a proper relationship and devotion to Mary, Catholics grow ever deeper in their love of God and their following of her Son, Jesus Christ.

ELEVEN

The Life of the Age to Come

Eternal Life

CHRISTIANS BELIEVE THAT THE BRIEF span of our lives on earth is a prelude and a preparation for life after death, everlasting life in the age to come. As persons created in God's image, we are spiritual beings as well as physical ones. This means that we, like God, are all destined to live forever.

For Christians, the real question is not whether we will live forever, but how? No one would look forward to an eternity of suffering or boredom. Christianity is truly good news because it proclaims that God offers to all people a life of unsurpassable joy and peace that will last forever. Christians claim that the truth of this message is confirmed because one man underwent death, a terrible death, but was raised from the dead and returned to announce the reality of eternal life with God. The resurrection of Jesus Christ remains the ultimate reason for our Christian belief in eternal life. As St. Peter exclaimed in the opening of his First Letter:

> Blessed be the God and Father of our Lord Jesus Christ!
> By his great mercy we have been born anew to a living hope

> through the resurrection of Jesus Christ from the dead, and to an inheritance which is imperishable, undefiled, and unfading, kept in heaven for you, who by God's power are guarded through faith for a salvation ready to be revealed in the last time. (1 Pt 1:3-4)

Accepting God's Offer

Eternal life with God is an absolutely free gift. There is nothing that any person could do to merit, earn, or deserve an eternity of happiness with God. Catholic theology teaches that without the gift of God that Scripture calls grace, human beings remain in the bondage of original sin and fall into ever deeper rebellion against God and his plan. The result of this sin is death—eternal separation from God. As St. Paul wrote, "the wages of sin is death, but the free gift of God is eternal life in Christ Jesus our Lord" (Rom 6:23).

Salvation is also a gift that must be accepted through our cooperation with God's grace and our freely given response to the work of the Holy Spirit in our lives. From this perspective, eternal life or salvation is not simply a gift that we receive at the end of our lives when we die. Eternal life begins now as we choose to accept God's grace and his gift of the Holy Spirit. After all, salvation and eternal life actually are just ways of talking about sharing in or possessing the life of God himself. Catholics understand that although God's life in us reaches its completion or fullness when we are totally united with the Lord after death, it begins for us in this life with faith in God (Jn 17:3) and baptism (Rom 6:3-4).

The sacrament of baptism inaugurates that work of God in us by which the Father delivers us from the dominion of darkness (Satan's kingdom, into which each person is born because of original sin), and into the kingdom of light, the kingdom of his beloved Son, Jesus Christ (see Col 1:13).

Baptism is only the beginning of the Christian's road to

eternal life. The Gospel of John also stresses the necessity of believing in Jesus (Jn 3:16) and the Father (Jn 5:24); eating Jesus' flesh and blood in the Eucharist (Jn 6:54), and following Jesus, the Good Shepherd (Jn 10:27-28), throughout our lives. The result of responding to God's call in this way is that the Christian progressively becomes an entirely new creation (2 Cor 5:17) freed from the bondage of Satan and sin. Catholics call this process of freedom from sin and growth in Christ sanctification. St. Paul teaches that even here on earth the faithful follower of Christ experiences a foretaste of the glory of reigning in the heavens with Jesus Christ. "But God, who is rich in mercy, out of the great love with which he loved us, even when we were dead through our trespasses, made us alive together with Christ . . . and raised us up with him, and made us sit with him in the heavenly places in Christ Jesus. . . ." (Eph 2:4-6).

On the other hand, those who reject God's offer and continue to live in sin experience even here on earth a foretaste of the pain of eternal separation from God. It is unfortunately true that while the road to heaven is like heaven itself, the road to hell resembles hell. We see many people entrapped by the lies of Satan, seeking self-fulfillment, happiness, and pleasure apart from God and his laws, and instead becoming locked into deeper disappointment, isolation, and hopelessness. The writings of many modern atheist existentialists, such as Camus and Sartre, reflect the sadness and "quiet desperation" of those who attempt to live without God, struggling to accept the meaninglessness and absurdity of their lives with some semblance of dignity.

Christian Hope and Eternal Life

While life apart from God leads to despair, Christianity proclaims a message of hope. Christian hope is a fundamental virtue that enables us to look forward confidently to receiving the fullness of God's gift of eternal life and happiness. Christians experience the same trials and struggles in this world as anyone else, but their hope in God and his salvation transforms their attitude towards life. St. Paul wrote:

> For this slight momentary affliction is preparing for us an eternal weight of glory beyond all comparison. . . . For we know that if the earthly tent we live in is destroyed, we have a building from God, a house not made with hands, eternal in the heavens. . . . He who has prepared us for this very thing is God, who has given us the Spirit as a guarantee. (2 Cor 4:17; 5:1, 5)

Or as the Letter of James says so succinctly: "Blessed is the man who endures trial, for when he has stood the test he will receive the crown of life which God has promised to those who love him" (Jas 1:12).

Death

As these passages indicate, the Holy Spirit enables Christians to view and approach death in a way totally different than those without the knowledge of God. As St. Paul wrote to the Thessalonians:

> But we would not have you ignorant, brethren, concerning those who are asleep, that you may not grieve as others do who have no hope. For since we believe that Jesus died and rose again, even so, through Jesus, God will bring with him those who have fallen asleep. (1 Thes 4:13, 14)

Death, for most, is a fearful experience. However, for those perfected in faith, hope, and love, death holds no fear. St. Paul speaks of his own death in a matter-of-fact way and even expresses his preference to die so that he can be fully united with the Lord: "My desire is to depart and be with Christ, for that is far better. But to remain in the flesh is more necessary on your account" (Phil 1:23, 24). Paul also writes:

> So we are always of good courage; we know that while we are at home in the body we are away from the Lord, for we walk by faith, not by sight. We are of good courage, and we would rather be away from the body and at home with the Lord. So whether we are at home or away, we make it our aim to please him. (2 Cor 5:6-9)

While St. Paul speaks of the Christian's approach to death in terms of faith and hope, St. John says that death holds no fear for Christians because we know the love of God:

> So we know and believe the love God has for us. God is love, and he who abides in love abides in God, and God abides in him. In this is love perfected with us, that we may have confidence for the day of judgment.... There is no fear in love, but perfect love casts out fear. (1 Jn 4:16-18)

People are often bound by fear because they are seriously ill or near death and are given hollow and empty words of encouragement or hope. "Hang in there, Joe, you've pulled through in the past, you'll pull through this one, too!" It seems a law of human behavior that when we don't have a solution to a problem we deny or attempt to deny its reality. Western society increasingly attempts to hide or deny the reality of death, because it has forgotten that there is a solution, and only *one* solution to it—the resurrection of Jesus Christ.

The Reality of the Resurrection

Why does faith in the resurrection of Jesus provide Christians with such unshakeable hope? Christ has been raised, and Christians believe that they, too, will share in his resurrection and eternal life. As St. Paul wrote, answering the sceptics of his age (and ours) who deny the reality of the resurrection:

> But in fact Christ has been raised from the dead, the first fruits of those who have fallen asleep. For as by a man came death, by a man has come also the resurrection of the dead. For as in Adam all die, so also in Christ shall all be made alive. (1 Cor 15:20-22)

The resurrection of the dead is not a symbol or a myth. The resurrection is a reality that all will experience. The great Christian martyrs and saints could approach death with courage, even joy, because of their faith in the resurrection. During their lives on earth they knew the goodness and mercy of the Lord and so came to believe that the same merciful, loving God would not abandon them to eternal death but would raise them up to eternal life, as he first raised Jesus, the beloved divine Son of God.

Therefore, Christians believe that death is not a final end of life, but a completion of the mission of life on earth. The goal of this life is to come to know God through faith, hope, and love, so that one may see him face-to-face after death (see 1 Cor 13:12, 13). Traditional Catholic theology calls this the beatific vision—the direct vision of God that brings perfect and ultimate happiness. Until Christ comes again, human beings can only attain this goal by passing through the veil of death. Through our faith, we are able to exclaim with St. Paul:

> "Death is swallowed up in victory."
>
> "O death, where is thy victory? / O death, where is thy sting?" The sting of death is sin, and the power of sin is the law. But thanks be to God, who gives us the victory through our Lord Jesus Christ. (1 Cor 15:54-57)

The Bible consistently teaches that what people should fear

is not death, but sin. Serious sin brings with it the consequences of eternal punishment, as St. Paul says, the "sting of death is sin." In Matthew's Gospel, Jesus warns, "... do not fear those who kill the body but cannot kill the soul; rather fear him who can destroy both soul and body in hell" (Mt 10:28). The result of sin is not merely physical death but the ultimate death of eternal separation from God and the pains of hell.

The warnings of the Bible about the consequences of sin are urgent and must not be overlooked or minimized. However, at the heart of the gospel is the proclamation that sin no longer has power over those who know and follow Jesus Christ. The good news is that Jesus has conquered sin, and along with it the power of death:

> But if we have died with Christ, we believe that we shall also live with him. For we know that Christ being raised from the dead will never die again; death no longer has dominion over him. The death he died, he died to sin, once for all, but the life he lives he lives to God. So you also must consider yourselves dead to sin and alive to God in Christ Jesus. (Rom 6:8-11)
>
> There is therefore now no condemnation for those who are in Christ Jesus. For the law of the Spirit of life in Christ Jesus has set me free from the law of sin and death. (Rom 8:1-2)

What Happens at Death?

The Letter to the Hebrews says that: "... it is appointed for men to die once, and after that comes judgment" (Heb 9:27). The Catholic church teaches that at the moment of death, each person will "appear before the judgment seat of Christ, so that each one may receive good or evil, according to what he has done in the body" (2 Cor 5:10; cf. Rom 2:6). This is known, in Catholic theology, as the "particular judgment," to distinguish it from the "general judgment" or "last judgment" when Christ will "come again in glory to judge the living and the dead" (Nicene Creed).

As Romans 8:1-2 implies, at the particular judgment there is "no condemnation for those who are in Christ Jesus." For those whose lives have been fully in union with the Lord on earth, unstained by unrepented sin and sin's effects, the moment of death will be a moment of glorious reunion with the Lord and the beginning of a life of unspeakable joy that will last forever. "What no eye has seen, nor ear heard, / nor the heart of man conceived, what God has prepared for those who love him . . ." (1 Cor 2:9).

For those who die in the grace of Christ Jesus but with some remaining unrepented sin or the effects of sin in their lives, the Catholic church teaches that God, in his mercy, purifies the person of these sins so that they, too, may enter into the joy of heaven. This purification or purgation, known as purgatory, will be discussed more fully later in this chapter.

Those who have rejected God and the grace of Christ receive the consequences of this choice beginning even at the moment of death: eternal separation from God which Jesus often called hell (Mk 9:47; Mt 18:7-9; Lk 16:19-31).

What happens to the human person at death? We must acknowledge that there is a mystery connected with death which evades our comprehension and is not fully explained even by Christian revelation. Biologically, we know that the body stops functioning and soon begins to decay. Christians believe that the spiritual principle of the person, traditionally known as the soul, continues unchanged, is judged, and enters into one of the particular destinies described above.[1] We might also say, rightly, that the human person is judged and continues to exist, even though the person's body has ceased to function. This situation could not continue forever, though, because God created human beings as embodied spirits, creatures who by nature exist and relate by means of bodies. Jesus' resurrection testifies that God's plan includes resurrection and transformation of the body, which occurs for us at the Lord's second coming and final judgment. Until then, the exact nature of human existence after death remains unclear. This is part of the mystery of God's plan that we accept through faith without full understanding.

The Sacred Congregation for the Doctrine of the Faith has stated,

> Neither Scripture nor theology provides sufficient light for a proper picture of life after death. Christians must firmly hold the two following essential points: on the one hand they must believe in the fundamental continuity, thanks to the power of the Holy Spirit, between our present life in Christ and the future life (charity is the law of the Kingdom of God and our charity on earth will be the measure of our sharing God's glory in heaven); on the other hand they must be clearly aware of the radical break between the present life and the future one, due to the fact that the economy of faith will be replaced by the economy of fullness of life: we shall be with Christ and 'we shall see God' (cf. 1 John 3:2), and it is in these promises and marvellous mysteries that our hope essentially consists. Our imagination may be incapable of reaching these heights, but our heart does so instinctively and completely.[2]

Let us continue to explore the possible destinies for human life after the particular judgment: hell, purgatory, and heaven.

Hell

Many Catholics today have tremendous difficulty understanding or believing the Christian doctrine of hell. If God is the God of infinite love, mercy, goodness and compassion, how could he create or permit to exist a place or condition of endless torment and unhappiness? Some theologians today admit the possibility of hell's existence but claim that few people, if any, are there. Both reason and Christian revelation prevent us from dismissing the reality of hell. Jesus could not have been more clear about the matter. He told parables about eternal punishment, such as the rich man and Lazarus (Lk 16:19-31), the marriage feast (Mt 22:1-14), the wicked servant (Mt 24:45-51), the servants given talents (Mt 25:14-30), and others. He warned people directly about hell:

> ... if your hand causes you to sin, cut it off; it is better for you to enter life maimed than with two hands to go to hell, to the unquenchable fire. And if your foot causes you to sin, cut it off; it is better for you to enter life lame than with two feet to be thrown into hell. And if your eye causes you to sin, pluck it out; for it is better for you to enter the kingdom of God with one eye than with two eyes to be thrown into hell, where their worm does not die, and the fire is not quenched. (Mk 9:43-48)

Some people cannot reconcile sayings such as this with their image of Jesus—"gentle, meek, and humble of heart." Certainly Jesus is gentle but not when it comes to sin and warning his followers of the consequences of sin. When Jesus speaks of the consequences of sin and the reality of hell, the tone of his warning matches the danger involved. Although this text has been variously interpreted by scholars, it is difficult to escape its most evident meaning: nothing on earth is worth keeping (whether your hand, leg, eye, or life) if it means losing eternal life through sin.

Will many people end up in hell? Again the New Testament hands on some sayings from the Lord Jesus himself on this subject:

> "Enter by the narrow gate; for the gate is wide and the way is easy, that leads to destruction, and those who enter by it are many. For the gate is narrow and the way is hard, that leads to life, and those who find it are few." (Mt 7:13-14)

The Catholic church teaches that we cannot judge or determine whether any particular person has been condemned to hell, even Hitler or Judas Iscariot. The mercy of God is such that a person can repent even at the point of death and be saved, like the good thief crucified next to Jesus (Lk 23:39-43). On the other hand, the modern presupposition that few people will be condemned to eternal punishment finds no support in the New Testament and is in fact contradicted by sayings of Jesus himself.

What is the narrow "gate" and difficult "way" that leads to eternal life? *Jesus* is the "door" of his sheep (Jn 10:9), the "way, and the truth, and the life" (Jn 14:6), in whom alone salvation can be found (Acts 4:12). Jesus is the "life-preserver" that God has thrown into the troubled waters of human existence so that anyone who grabs onto him may be saved from eternal death.

Explaining Hell Today

Hell is the state of those who have decisively chosen to reject God and his wonderful plan for their existence. Hell, and eternal damnation in hell, is not God's idea or will but is the result of the choice of creatures with free will: angels and men who reject and rebel against God and his perfect love. Instead of asking why God could permit the existence of hell, we should rather ask why human beings could reject God and his will. Cases in point are attempts to kill whole races of peoples, slaughtering millions of innocent unborn children, or allowing the Son of God, Jesus Christ, to be tortured and crucified without just cause. To see the existence of hell as calling into question the love and mercy of God is to place blame in the wrong direction. All that God has done is to create angels and men in his own image, with the great gift of free will. God maintains such a great respect for the freedom of his creatures that he allows them to freely choose their own destiny, to opt either for things that lead to death or for things that lead to life. Through conscience, natural law, and revelation, God points out the way that leads to life, but he never forces anyone to choose that way. Thus the biblical teaching on judgment emphasizes that it is not God who actively condemns anyone to hell, but all are judged according to the choices they have made.

> For God sent the Son into the world, not to condemn the world, but that the world might be saved through him.... And this is the judgment, that the light has come into the world, and men loved darkness rather than light, because their deeds were evil. For everyone who does evil hates the light, and does not come to the light, lest his deeds should be exposed. But he who does what is true comes to the light, that it may be clearly seen that his deeds have been wrought in God. (Jn 3:17, 19-21; see also 2 Cor 5:10; Rom 2:4-8; Jn 12:47-48; Mt 12:36-37)

Jesus, of course, is the "light" spoken of by the Gospel of John (Jn 9:5). God's desire is that all people freely come into the light of Jesus Christ so that their sin may be exposed. If they repent of their sin, they are freed from it and thus are saved from the consequence of serious sin, eternal separation from God.

Is Hell a Place?

While hell may begin as an internal reality—such as growing alienation from God or a rejection of his love and plan—it culminates in an actual state or place of existence that lasts eternally (Mk 9:47-48; Mt 18:9). The Catholic church has always been somewhat guarded in describing what hell is like, lest it succumb to exaggeration or inaccuracy. Hell exists as a real state or a condition of being. It may be a physical, material place, since Christians believe in the resurrection of the body. Many great Christian writers have observed that the greatest pain of hell is the knowledge of the eternal loss of union with

God, along with the agonizing guilt of realizing that it is due to one's own choice. The "wailing and gnashing of teeth" often mentioned by Jesus may be seen as an expression of this eternal despair (Mt 22:13; 24:51; 25:30). "They shall suffer the punishment eternal destruction and exclusion from the presence of the Lord" (2 Thes 1:9). Jesus also often alludes to hell as a "place of torment" (Lk 16:28) and of "unquenchable fire" (Lk 3:17; Mt 3:12; 13:30; Mk 9:43, 48; Rv 14:11-12), which indicates that hell includes physical suffering. Great works of Christian literature such as Dante's *Inferno,* vividly portray both aspects of the pains of hell.

We must affirm, once again, that the primary reason that God sent his Son, Jesus, into the world was to save people from the pains of hell by showing them the way to eternal life in God. Yet, time and again, Jesus affirms in the Gospels that entry into the kingdom of heaven is not automatic. No one drifts into the kingdom of heaven, but it is possible to drift into hell (Mt 7:13). Mankind deserves only condemnation due to sin. God, out of sheer mercy and love, provides a way to life, Jesus Christ. Jesus shows us this way and constantly calls his followers to watchfulness and vigilance, lest they fall into sin which leads to eternal death. The way that Jesus has taught is the way of faith, discipleship, and constant repentance. We have a God of love and mercy, but we must accept this mercy through repentance:

> Or do you presume upon the riches of his kindness and forbearance and patience? Do you not know that God's kindness is meant to lead you to repentance? But by your hard and impenitent heart you are storing up wrath for yourself on the day of wrath when God's righteous judgment will be revealed. For he will render to every man according to his works: to those who by patience in well-doing seek for glory and honor and immortality, he will give eternal life; but for those who are factious and do not obey the truth, but obey wickedness, there will be wrath and fury. (Rom 2:4-8)

Purgatory

God exhibits both justice and mercy in his plan for the human race, and the doctrine of purgatory reveals this truth ideally. Purgatory is a stumbling block for many Christians in understanding the Catholic faith, and even many Catholics misinterpret it. The word purgatory, like incarnation or trinity, is not a biblical term, but the concept of God's work of purgation or purification is very biblical, as we shall see. Purgatory is not a second chance for a person to establish a right relationship with God or to repent for past sins after death. When a person dies, the time of free choice is over, and the person's eternal destiny rests entirely in God's hands.

How will God judge a person who has loved God and others, but somewhat selfishly or imperfectly? What happens to this person who has attempted to respond positively to God's grace even up to death, yet dies still in the bondage of some unrepented sin or the effects of sin in his or her life? According to strict justice, the person's sin would merit eternal separation from God, since the sinful cannot live eternally in the presence of the all-holy God. As the Book of Revelation explains, God's presence is so pure and holy that "nothing unclean shall enter it . . ." (Rv 21:27).

Catholics believe that the mercy of God is so great, his desire to save is so strong, and the infinite merit of Christ's death on the cross for sinners is so powerful, that God has a saving provision for those who die in this state of imperfect love, in a condition of sin that is not mortal or deadly. Rather than condemning them to eternal separation from him as their sins deserve, Catholics believe that God purges or purifies any remaining sin or the effects of sin that prevent the person from entering into full communion with God in heaven.

God's purification after death is called purgatory. Although the term is not found in the Bible, there are two or three texts in the Bible that refer to purgatory, according to ancient Christian tradition (2 Mc 12:46; 1 Cor 3:11-15; see Chapter Four).

Purgatory is reserved for those whose basic orientation in life is towards God and obedience to his will—not for those who are separated from God by rebellion or serious sin. These latter will not be purified, but suffer the pains of hell as the consequence of their life and choices on earth. God's mercy cannot override his respect for the freedom of choice that he gives to us. God's purification is available for those whose love is imperfect or who still suffer from the bondage or effects of sin, but God does not force anyone into heaven contrary to their free choices on earth.

What is purgatory like? As with all types of existence after death, there is a mystery involved here that requires us to approach it with faith and hope. It is notable that the biblical images of purification from sin often speak of fire as the purifying agent. The Catholic tradition concerning purgatory includes the notion of purgation from sin by the fire of God's love and holiness. Fire implies pain, and thus it should not surprise us if purgatory is painful. We know from our experience on earth that breaking from sin and overcoming all its ill effects in our lives is often painful, and usually takes time. Penance, prayer and discipline are necessary to receive God's full freedom and healing from sin while in this life. Purgatory is God's way of completing this process of deliverance and healing from sin and its effects—a process that begins here and now on earth. The goal of God's purifying work is always the same. God desires each person to share fully in his life and holiness and wills to set us free from anything that impedes or clouds that holiness. Purgatory attests that God completes what he begins. The victory of Jesus Christ over sin and its effects in our lives is perfect and complete when we come into his glorious presence in heaven.[3]

The Catholic church has taught since early in its history that this purification from sin, whether for ourselves or others, is significantly aided by prayer and penance. The Catholic doctrine of indulgences is based on the principle that every prayer, good work, or penance offered to God in faith for the remission of the effects of sin is effective.[4] That is, prayer, good works, and penances do foster God's work of purification of ourselves, others living on earth, and those in purgatory. Prayer and sacrifice for each other that we may be freed from sin are among the primary ways that the saints—members of the body of Christ whether on earth, in heaven, or in purgatory—can aid each other. Previously, the Catholic church even determined the length of time that a person's term in purgatory would be reduced if certain prayers were said, alms given, or penitential acts performed for the sake of the souls in purgatory or for the remission of sin of the living. (This penal idea of purgatory was an image that most people could easily understand.) There is no longer any length of time attached to indulgences—they are either partial or plenary (see Chapter Seven).

In conclusion, the existence of purgatory should not cause Christians to seek holiness any less fervently, wrongly presuming that God always will purify us after we die. It is far better to accept fully the grace God offers us now to repent and to turn to him for freedom and healing from sin and its effects, lest our hearts become hardened and we fall further away from God. If we are not advancing in holiness in this life, we are retreating from God. However, it is one of the greatest sources of hope and consolation for Catholics to know that even if we fall short of the complete holiness that God wants for us in this life, and even if we die without full healing and repentance from less serious sin and its effects in our lives, God in his mercy desires to purge and purify us so that we may enter into his all-holy presence without shame or fear. The pains of purgatory reflect the justice of God in punishing sin. However, the knowledge that the gift of eternal life is granted even to those who are not perfect in their love when they die reflects God's overwhelming mercy towards sinners.

Heaven

The goal of human existence, the purpose for which God created human beings, is eternal happiness with God, "For here we have no lasting city, but we seek the city which is to come" (Heb 13:14). Many people consider Christians to be escapists or utopians in looking forward to an eternity of happiness with God. They say it is a distraction from improving this world and serving humanity, a hollow promise that causes people to accept oppression and misery in this life, waiting for "the pie in the sky when you die." They say it is a foolish and false hope produced by our natural human incapacity to accept the certainty and finality of death.

Christian belief in heaven is not based on these things, but on faith and hope in the promises of Jesus Christ. Jesus reassured his followers:

> "Let not your hearts be troubled; believe in God, believe also in me. In my Father's house are many rooms; if it were not so, would I have told you that I go to prepare a place for you? And when I go and prepare a place for you, I will come again and will take you to myself, that where I am you may be also." (Jn 14:1-3)

Jesus also promises that his "sheep," his followers, hear his voice and receive eternal life from him (Jn 10:27, 28), and "inherit the kingdom prepared for you from the foundation of the world . . ." (Mt 25:34). He describes heaven as a joyous wedding feast (Mt 22:1-14; 25:1-13) and a great banquet (Lk 14:16-24) in which we celebrate the marriage of the Lamb of God, Jesus Christ, to his bride, the church (Rv 19:7-9).

Catholics believe that heaven is the fulfillment of the deepest yearnings of the human heart. St. Augustine wrote, "You have made us for Yourself, and our hearts are restless until they rest in You."[5] Heaven is the eternal sabbath day of rest in God after our six days of labor in this life. Yet, it would be wrong to think of heaven as something that exists only in the future for a Christian. Heaven begins in this life as we respond in faith to Jesus Christ and his grace. When we put God first in our lives and decide to give up all else in order to follow him, we experience the joy of discipleship that is the foretaste and beginning of the life of heaven. Jesus came that we may have life "and have it abundantly" (Jn 10:10), beginning now, and in its fullness in heaven.

Heaven is sharing in divine life and joy to the extent that we are drawn completely into the life of the Trinity. "In that day you will know that I am in my Father, and you in me, and I in you" (Jn 14:20). We aren't absorbed into the life of God in a way that we lose our individual identities, as in pantheism, but we find our true identity as we are immersed in God and his love. Catholics believe in the resurrection of the body, implying that heaven is a place and not just a vague state of existence. It is the place where we will not only see God face-to-face, but will perceive, with our own risen bodies, the risen and glorified bodies of Jesus, Mary and all others who have entered the life of heaven. All in heaven will be full of the joy of God, though our joy will be measured according to the capacity of each one of us to receive it. The more loving and generous we are on earth, the greater the joy of heaven for us, like cups of different sizes that are each completely full, but do not have the same capacities.

Limbo

Catholic theologians of the early church and the Middle Ages reflected on the eternal destiny of infants and very young children who died unbaptized, before the age that they could commit personal sin or make a responsible choice to believe in or follow God. Because they died without the sacrament of baptism, most theologians presumed that because of original sin, they could not enter the presence of God in heaven. On the other hand, it seemed unthinkable that they would be condemned for eternity to the punishment of hell, when they had no opportunity to choose responsibly for or against God in this life. As a result of this dilemma, Catholic theologians proposed the existence of a state of "natural blessedness" or happiness in which unbaptized infants would experience peace for eternity, but without the full joy of the kingdom of heaven.

The Catholic church has never formally recognized nor denied the existence of limbo in its official teaching, though it does teach that baptism, in some form, is necessary for salvation. Although this question appears to many people to be a trivial issue or based on mere speculation, the reality of millions of aborted unborn children and the shocking growth of infanticide every year should at least indicate the importance of this question today. If limbo does exist, as some theologians have proposed, abortion and infanticide not only are heinous crimes that bring spiritual death to those who perpetrate them, but they also deprive millions of innocent people, the unborn and infants, of the opportunity of the fullness of eternal life and joy with God. The blood of these martyrs surely cries out to the God of justice for retribution of this great evil.

However, many theologians today insist that God's mercy permits even unbaptized children to enter the kingdom of heaven, since the human heart will not truly be at peace and rest until it enters God's full eternal presence.

The Return of the Lord

Christians profess in the Nicene Creed that Jesus "will come again in glory to judge the living and the dead." In the Acts of the Apostles, as Jesus' followers were witnessing the ascension of Jesus, two messengers of Jesus asked, "Men of Galilee, why do you stand looking into heaven? This Jesus, who was taken up from you into heaven, will come in the same way as you saw Him go into heaven" (Acts 1:11). Jesus, in his risen glorified body, has been exalted to eternal kingship in the highest place of honor ("at the right hand of God"), and now is revealed to the world as the Lord of everything that has been created through him. Still, not everyone on earth recognizes or acknowledges this rule, or lordship, of Jesus Christ. We live in a period of history in which the reign or rule of God has been inaugurated or established on earth through the first coming of Jesus Christ but in which the human race still retains its freedom to ignore or to reject the kingship of Christ. Also in this age, Satan and his demons are permitted, for a time, to attempt to draw people away from the reign of God and into their own dominion of darkness.

Christian revelation proclaims that this period of human history will come to a close when the Son of Man returns, not in obscurity and humility as a baby in Bethlehem, but in glory and majesty as the king and judge of all. The Apostles' Creed proclaims, "He (Jesus) will come again in glory to judge the living and the dead."

There are a number of graphic descriptions of this second coming or parousia of Christ in the New Testament, all of which take their images from the apocalyptic, or revelational, literature of the Old Testament. Most of these descriptions use the imagery of the vision of Daniel in that apocalyptic book of the Old Testament:

> I saw in the night visions,
> and behold, with the clouds of heaven
> there came one like a Son of man,
> and he came to the Ancient of Days [God the Father]
> and was presented before him.
> And to him was given dominion and glory and kingdom,
> that all peoples, nations, and languages
> should serve him;
> his dominion is an everlasting dominion,
> which shall not pass away,
> and his kingdom one
> that shall not
> be destroyed. (Dn 7:13, 14)

The Bible indicates that a severe time of trial in the world, and particularly for Christians, will immediately precede the second coming of Christ. All three synoptic Gospels describe a time of tribulation on the earth and signs in the heavens. Various texts of the New Testament speak of the appearance of scoffers and false prophets who will lead many people away from the truth in the last days (Mt 7:15; 24:11, 24; Mk 13:22; 2 Pt 2:1-3; 1 Jn 4:1; Rv 16:13; 19:20; 20:10), and even the emergence of an anti-Christ or anti-Christs (1 Jn 2:18, 22; 4:3; 2 Jn 7). The Catholic church has never attempted to formally identify who these figures will be, but they will be identified by their activity of causing many to fall away from true faith in Christ and Christian love. As Matthew's Gospel attests: "And many false prophets will arise and lead many astray. And because wickedness is multiplied, most men's love will grow cold. But he who endures to the end will be saved." (Mt 24:11-13). However, not all will be bleak immediately before the Lord's coming. This passage in Matthew's Gospel concludes by predicting a great age of evangelism. "And this gospel of the kingdom will be preached throughout the whole world, as a testimony to all nations; and then the end will come" (Mt 24:14). When Jesus does return, it will be an unmistakable event, "And then they will see the Son of man coming in clouds with great power and glory" (Mk 13:26; see also Mt 24:30; Lk 21:27). No one will miss it, "For as the lightning comes from the east and shines as far as the west, so will be the coming of the Son of man" (Mt 24:27).

What will happen on earth when Jesus, the Son of man, comes? The Bible speaks of it as a time of great joy for the followers of Christ, an exaltant reunion. "Now when these things begin to take place, look up and raise your heads, because your redemption is drawing near" (Lk 21:28). St. Paul writes that when Christ descends from heaven ". . . the dead in Christ will rise first; then we who are alive, who are left, shall be caught up together with them in the clouds to meet the Lord in the air; and so we shall always be with the Lord. Therefore, comfort one another with these words" (1 Thes

4:16-18). Protestant Christians call this lifting up of the elect the rapture. The Catholic church does not define whether these images are to be taken literally or understood as poetic images or pointers to a reality beyond our imagination. The truth we must believe is that the bodies of both those living and those dead will rise at the second coming of Christ in order to receive their final reward or retribution, "For we must all appear before the judgment seat of Christ, so that each one may receive good or evil, according to what he has done in the body" (2 Cor 5:10).

This last judgment, or general judgment, will mark the time when human history comes to an end. Purgatory, God's provision for purification of sin after death, will also come to an end. The Gospel of Matthew vividly describes the judgment of the nations.

> "When the Son of man comes in his glory, and all the angels with him, then he will sit on his glorious throne. Before him will be gathered all the nations, and he will separate them one from another as a shepherd separates the sheep from the goats. . . ." (Mt 25:31-32)

God's judgment in Matthew is based on performance of the works of mercy such as feeding the hungry, clothing the naked, visiting the sick and imprisoned, and welcoming the stranger, emphasizing Jesus' words that "Not everyone who says to me, 'Lord, Lord,' shall enter the kingdom of heaven, but he who does the will of my Father who is in heaven" (Mt 7:21 ff).

The second coming of Christ also means that the physical universe and earth as we know it will come to an end. The New Testament envisions a destruction of the universe (Rv 21:1; 2 Pt 3:10-12), "Heaven and earth will pass away . . ." (Lk 21:33), but also contains the promise of "a new heaven and a new earth" (2 Pt 3:13; Rv 21:1), in which righteousness dwells and

God will reign forever. The Book of Revelation, especially in chapters 21 and 22, presents the most graphic and beautiful picture of this new Jerusalem:

> "Behold, the dwelling of God is with men. He will dwell with them, and they shall be his people, and God himself will be with them; he will wipe away every tear from their eyes, and death shall be no more, neither shall there be mourning nor crying nor pain anymore, for the former things have passed away. (Rv 21:3-4)

Part of the mystery of the new earth will be that our bodies will be raised and transformed. Chapter fifteen of St. Paul's First Letter to the Corinthians discusses the meaning of the resurrection of the body in detail. Paul points out that the body we are to possess will not be the same as the physical body that dies but will be a "spiritual body" that will be like the risen and glorified body of Jesus. "Just as we have borne the image of the man of dust [Adam], we also bear the image of the man of heaven [the risen Christ]" (1 Cor 15:49). Not only will our bodies be transformed, but so will the whole physical universe, ". . . the creation itself will be set free from its bondage to decay and obtain the glorious liberty of the children of God" (Rom 8:21; see also *Gaudium et Spes,* no. 34). As the triumphant Christ proclaims towards the close of the Book of Revelation, "Behold, I make all things new" (Rv 21:5).

This belief in the transformation of the earth affirms the value of our efforts to promote justice and other gospel values in this world. As the Second Vatican Council stated:

> Earthly progress must be carefully distinguished from the growth of Christ's kingdom. Nevertheless, to the extent that the former can contribute to the better ordering of human society, it is of vital concern to the kingdom of God.
>
> For after we have obeyed the Lord, and in His Spirit

nurtured on earth the values of human dignity, brotherhood and freedom, and indeed all the good fruits of our nature and enterprise, we will find them again, but freed of stain, burnished and transfigured. This will be so when Christ hands over to the Father a kingdom eternal and universal: "a kingdom of truth and life, of holiness and grace, of justice, love, and peace." On this earth that kingdom is already present in mystery. When the Lord returns, it will be brought into full flower. (GS, no. 34)

The Time of Christ's Return

When will the second coming of Christ, the general judgment, the resurrection of the body, and the transformation of the universe in Jesus Christ take place? Both the New Testament and the Catholic church concur in one answer: we don't know. The synoptic Gospels do describe proximate and immediate signs of the second coming of Christ that all should be able to recognize, but it is not revealed when this will occur. To the contrary, Jesus' parables and direct statements on the subject, indicate that his second coming will be sudden and unexpected "like a thief in the night" (1 Thes 5:2; 2 Pt 3:10; Mt 24:43). If the householder, bridesmaids, and servants in Jesus' parables knew when the master or the groom was returning, they would have been prepared. As it is, Jesus says, concerning the day of his return:

> "But of that day or that hour no one knows, not even the angels in heaven, nor the Son, but only the Father. Take heed, watch;... for you do not know when the master of the house will come, in the evening, or at midnight, or at cockcrow, or in the morning—lest he come suddenly and find you asleep. And what I say to you I say to all: Watch." (Mk 13:32, 33, 35-37)

Some Christians are convinced that we are living in the last days and that the end of the world is imminent. Catholics agree that the final age of the world has already come upon us (see 1 Cor 10:11; LG, no. 48), but view the entire period of time between the first coming of the Lord Jesus and his second coming as the end-times, the last days, or the final age. As the Letter to the Hebrews says, "in these last days he [God] has spoken to us by a Son" (Heb 1:2), we "upon whom the end of the ages has come" (1 Cor 10:11). We sometimes forget that God's timetable is not the same as ours:

> ... do not ignore this one fact, beloved, that with the Lord one day is as a thousand years, and a thousand years as one day. The Lord is not slow about his promise [of his return] as some count slowness, but is forbearing toward you, not wishing that any should perish, but that all should reach repentance. (2 Pt 3:8, 9)

The many warnings of Jesus and the other New Testament authors about the coming of the Son of man and the day of judgment are meant to convict us, and even disturb us, if we have fallen into complacency, unbelief, or sin. Even if the final coming of the Lord does not come suddenly during our lifetime, none of us know the day or the hour of our own death, our personal day of judgment.

The Catholic Response to the Last Things

In times past, some holy Catholic women and men would keep a skull on their desk to remind them of the shortness of life and their final end. Today, when most of us try to hide reminders of death, such a practice appears morbid. However, reflecting on the shortness of life and the possibility of Jesus' imminent return has a positive purpose: to lead us to turn to God, to repent of our sins, to live the new life that God offers to us in Jesus Christ. As Peter says in his Letter, God does not desire that anyone die eternally through sin, but that all should reach repentance.

A priest friend of mine, Father Augustine Donegan, T.O.R.,

put the human situation today in a nutshell. The problem, at least in Western society, is that people have lost their understanding of sin and the need for repentance. In losing their sense of sin and its horror, they cannot understand the cross of Jesus Christ, because the reason that Christ died on the cross was to take away the sin of mankind. And in losing their understanding of the cross of Christ, they lose the true understanding of Jesus himself. The sacrificial death of Jesus on the cross to take away the sin of the world becomes merely a symbol or an inspiring story, instead of the most important event in the history of humanity. Jesus, without the cross, becomes just a good man or a great teacher, instead of the one who alone gave up his life, his body and blood, in a way that definitively shattered the power of evil and sin in the world and reconciled the whole human race to God.

The basic message of the gospel is to call us to acknowledge our need for forgiveness and cleansing from the bondage of sin and to accept God's only remedy for sin—Jesus Christ and his death on the cross. To believe in and to follow Jesus as the one who saves humanity from sin is not just a one-time decision, although it must begin there. It is a decision that each person must make every day, "If any man would come after me, let him deny himself and take up his cross daily, and follow me" (Lk 9:23). That is the way that leads to eternal life and gives Christians hope for the day of judgment.

We may look at the lives of Christians who are following this way of daily discipleship, and often it seems their joy and desire for God grows greater as they approach closer to their goal of full union with Christ. St. Paul, for instance, spoke of having run the good race, fought the good fight. All that was left was to receive the crown of eternal life that was awaiting him (2 Tm 4:6-8).

Salvation and eternal life are gifts freely given by God. We cannot presume that we possess them before we finish the "race" of earthly life and receive our reward from God. Catholics, realizing this, are encouraged to pray for the grace of "final perseverance," the grace of God enabling them to remain faithful to God and his commandment to the very end of life, so that they may receive the crown of eternal life. The lives of Catholics who are always ready for the Lord's return by following him daily (daily discipleship) are marked by joy, peace, and a confident hope in their own salvation. They look forward expectantly to the day when they hear the Father say, "Well done, good and faithful servant; . . enter into the joy of your master" (Mt 25:21, 23). They remember even during the difficult times, the promises and words of encouragement that the Bible gives them, such as these words from the Letter to the Hebrews:

> For God is not so unjust as to overlook your work and the love which you showed for his sake in serving the saints, as you still do. And we desire each one of you to show the same earnestness in realizing the full assurance of hope until the end, so that you may not be sluggish, but imitators of those who through faith and patience inherit the promises. (Heb 6:10-12)

Those who turn from their sins through ongoing repentance, who believe in Jesus Christ, and who obey his commandments through a life of daily discipleship, have nothing to fear on the day when Jesus Christ comes again to judge all. The belief of the Catholic church about the final coming of Christ is best summarized by this section of the Dogmatic Constitution of the Church, no. 48:

> Since we know not the day nor the hour, on our Lord's advice we must consistently stand guard. Thus when we have finished the one and only course of our earthly life (cf. Heb 9:27) we may merit to enter into the marriage feast with Him and to be numbered among the blessed (cf. Mt 25:31-46). Thus we may not be commanded to go into eternal fire (cf. Mt 25:41) like the wicked and slothful servant (cf. Mt 25:26), into the exterior darkness where "there will be the weeping and the gnashing of teeth" (Mt 22:13; 25:30). For

> before we reign with the glorious Christ, all of us will be made manifest "before the tribunal of Christ, so that each one may receive what he has won through the body, according to his works, whether good or evil" (2 Cor 5:10). At the end of the world, "they who have done good shall come forth unto resurrection of life; but who have done evil unto resurrection of judgment" (Jn 5:29; cf. Mt 25:46).
>
> We reckon therefore that "the sufferings of the present time are not worthy to be compared with the glory to come that will be revealed in us" (Rom 8:18; cf. 2 Tm 2:11-12). Strong in faith we look for "the blessed hope and glorious coming of our great God and Savior, Jesus Christ" (Ti 2:13) "Who will refashion the body of our lowliness, conforming it to the body of His glory" (Phil 3:21) and who will come "to be glorified in His saints, and to be marveled at in all those who have believed" (2 Thes 1:10).

Thus Christians, rather than facing the end of the world or the final judgment with misgivings or fear, look forward to it with expectation and hope. ". . . we wait for new heavens and a new earth in which righteousness dwells" (2 Pt 3:13; also Rv 21:1 ff). Today Catholics must again learn to echo one of the oldest Christian prayers, that has resounded through the ages in the midst of our troubled and weary world. The prayer is *Maranatha!*—literally "Lord, come!"

> Come, Lord, to establish your kingdom in full glory and power!
> Come, Lord, to overthrow Satan's dominion and all the evil in the world!
> Come, Lord, to free us each from the bondage of our sin, and to share with us the gift of Your eternal life!
> Come, Lord, to reveal to all Your rightful place as King, Lord, and Master over the entire universe!
> Maranatha! Come, Lord Jesus!

Notes

Chapter One

1. See also Dogmatic Constitution *Dei Filius* (On the Catholic Faith), First Vatican Council, April 24, 1870, and Fr. Stanley Jaki, O.S.B., *Cosmos and Creator* (Edinburgh: Scottish Academic Press, 1980).
2. *Ibid.* See also Dogmatic Constitution on Divine Revelation (*Dei Verbum*) of The Second Vatican Council, no. 6.
3. Council of Trent, 4th Session, decree concerning the Canonical Scriptures (April 8, 1546), quoted in *The Sources of Catholic Dogma,* trans. by Roy J. Deferrari from Henry Denzinger's *Enchiridion Symbolorum* (St. Louis, Mo.: B. Herder Book Co., 1957), p. 244.
4. J. B. Phillips, *The Ring of Truth: A Translator's Testimony* (Wheaton, Ill.: Harold Shaw Publishers, 1977).
5. The statement of the *Shema* concerning God's oneness has various implications: (a) Yahweh is one, in contrast to many Baals; (b) Yahweh is the only god *for Israel,* the only god with whom they are to be in relationship; (c) Yahweh is one in the sense of simple being; this has implications for Christians who also believe in the Tri-Unity of the one Godhead.
6. Francis Thompson, *Selected Poems of Francis Thompson* (London: Burns and Oates Ltd., 1908), p. 51.
7. St. Augustine, *Confessions,* trans. by F. J. Sheed (New York: Sheed and Ward, 1943), Book I, p. 3.
8. John Paul II, address to general audience, September 11, 1986, in *L'Osservatore Romano* (English edition), September 16, 1986, p. 1.
9. Edmund J. Fortman, S.J., ed., *The Theology of God: Commentary* (New York: Bruce Publishing Company, 1968), p. 60.
10. Because God is Spirit, the personal name, "Father," does not specifically refer to God's gender. God is the author, or "father," of human masculinity and femininity, so they both must flow from God. But God, being spirit, transcends the simple sexual labelling applicable to his creatures. It is notable, however, that when God does reveal himself in human language, it is usually as "father," or in masculine terms. Though the Bible does compare God's care and tenderness toward humanity to motherly concern (Is 66:13; Ps 131:2; Lk 13:34), it nowhere explicitly

calls God "the Mother" or "Our Mother." This fact should not be interpreted merely as a prejudice of a patriarchal society, since Christians believe that the Holy Spirit of God inspired the biblical text, including the choice of specific language and images employed. God could have inspired the authors of Scripture to name God as "the Mother" as well as "the Father" (*no pater* in several New Testament passages), but he did not. See also, Louis Bouyer, *Woman in the Church* (San Francisco: Ignatius Press, 1979), pp. 29-39.

11. *L'Osservatore Romano* (English edition), December 2, 1985, p. 5.
12. *Ibid.*
13. "The reply which our reason stammers is based on the concept of 'relation.' The three divine persons are distinguished among themselves solely by the *relations* which they have with one another: and precisely by the relation of the Father to the Son, of the Son to the Father; of the Father and Son to the Spirit, of the Spirit to the Father and the Son. In God, therefore, the Father is pure Paternity; the Son pure Sonship; the Holy Spirit pure 'Nexus of Love' of the two, so that the personal distinctions do not divide the same and unique divine Nature of the Three.

    "The Eleventh Council of Toledo (A.D. 675) made it clear with great exactitude: 'What the Father is, that he is not in reference to himself, but in relation to the Son; and what the Son is, that He is not in reference to himself, but in relation to the Father; in the same way the Holy Spirit, inasmuch as He is predicated Spirit of the Father and of the Son, that He is not in reference to himself, but relatively to the Father and to the Son.' (DS, 528)

    "The Council of Florence (A.D. 1442) could therefore state: 'These three Persons are one God . . . because the Three have one substance, one essence, one nature, one divinity, one immensity, one eternity; in God in fact everything is one and the same where there is no opposition of relation.'" (DS, 1330)

    Pope John Paul, general audience of December 4, 1985, in *L'Osservatore Romano* (English edition), December 9, 1985, p. 1.
14. John Paul II, *L'Osservatore Romano* (English edition), December 2, 1985, p. 5.
15. "Creation is the work of the Triune God. The world 'created' in the Word-Son, is 'restored' together with the Son to Father, through that *Uncreated Gift,* the Holy Spirit, consubstantial with both. In this way the world is *created in that Love,* which is the Spirit of the Father and of the Son. This universe embraced by eternal Love commences to exist in the instant chosen by the Trinity as the beginning of time.

    "In this way *the creation* of the world is *the work of Love:* the universe, a created gift, springs from the Uncreated Gift, from the reciprocal Love of the Father and Son, from the Most Holy Trinity."

    John Paul II, general audience of March 5, 1986, in *L'Osservatore Romano* (English edition), March 10, 1986, p. 1.

16. *Ibid.*, January 20, 1986. From a general audience January 15, 1986.
17. "The first human being the Bible calls 'man' (*adam*), but from the moment of creation of the first woman, it begins to call him 'man,' *is*, in relation to *issa*, 'woman'—because she was taken from the man, *is*." Pope John Paul II, general audience, September 19, 1979, in *Original Unity of Man and Woman*, (Boston; Daughters of St. Paul, 1981), p. 24. Hence, the conventional usage of "man" as designating either a male person or the human race, or "mankind," will be employed in this book. The context should make clear which usage is intended.
18. John Paul II, *L'Osservatore Romano*, April 28, 1986, p. 1, from general audience of April 23, 1986.
19. *Confessions*, Book I, art. VI.
20. The only exceptions to birth into original sin are Jesus and his mother, Mary.
21. *Paradise Lost*, Book I, 1.263.
22. *L'Osservatore Romano*, from a general audience on January 8, 1986 (English edition), January 13, 1986, p. 2.
23. "Satan and Catholic Tradition," *New Covenant*, April 1974, p. 8.
24. "In modern times the theory of evolution has raised a special difficulty against the revealed doctrine about the creation of man as a being composed of soul and body. Many natural scientists who, with their own methods, study the problem of the origin of human life on earth, maintain—contrary to other colleagues of theirs—not only the existence of a link between man and the ensemble of nature, but also his derivation from the higher animal species. This problem, which has occupied scientists since the last century, involves vast layers of public opinion.

    "The reply of the Magisterium was offered in the encyclical *Humani Generis* of Pius XII in 1950. In it we read: 'The Magisterium of the Church is not opposed to the theory of evolution being the object of investigation and discussion among experts. Here the theory of evolution is understood as an investigation of the origin of the human body from pre-existing living matter, for the Catholic faith obliges us to hold firmly that souls are created immediately by God. . . .' (DS, 3896)

    "It can therefore be said that, from the viewpoint of the doctrine of the faith, there are no difficulties in explaining the origin of man, in regard to the body, by means of the theory of evolution. It must, however, be added that this hypothesis proposes only a probability, not a scientific certainty. The doctrine of faith, however, invariably affirms that man's spiritual soul is created directly by God. According to the hypothesis mentioned, it is possible that the human body, following the order impressed by the Creator on the energies of life, could have been gradually prepared in the forms of antecedent living beings. The human soul, however, on which man's humanity definitively depends, cannot emerge from matter, since it is of a spiritual nature." *L'Osservatore Romano*, April 21, 1986, pp. 1, 2. General audience, April 16, 1986.

Chapter Two

1. *L'Osservatore Romano,* (English edition), April 28, 1986, p. 5.
2. Biblical scholars debate exactly what body of water was crossed by the Hebrews, whether the Red Sea or the "Sea of Reeds." The crucial point for Jews and Christians is that the plagues, the crossing through a sea, and the entire Passover event was a miracle, a mighty intervention of God in human history that is not reducible to any purely naturalistic explanation.
3. The term "Messiah," or "anointed one," refers to the special blessing of God on this person. Anointing with oil was a way of setting apart kings for their ministry.
4. *L'Osservatore Romano,* (English edition), April 28, 1986, p. 5.

Chapter Three

1. Of course, there is no such thing as purely objective history or reporting. Every account, whether historical, factual, or scientific, is subjective to some extent since it represents the conclusions or interpretations of the person or persons presenting it. Therefore, to say that the New Testament accounts are not purely objective is not to impugn their truth or accuracy.
2. The Council of Chalcedon (A.D. 451), Christological Definition (author's translation).
3. Ralph J. Tapia, *The Theology of Christ: Commentary* (New York: Bruce, 1971), p. 262.
4. Cardinal Ratzinger, Prefect of the Sacred Congregation on the Doctrine of Faith of the Roman Catholic Church, was interviewed regarding his views of those theologians and biblical scholars who reject the reality of demonic powers as portrayed in the New Testament: "In this special case they admit—they have no choice—that Jesus, the apostles and evangelists were convinced of the existence of demonic powers. Then they go on to take it for granted that in this conviction of theirs they were 'victims' of current Jewish ways and thinking. But since they have already taken it to be absolutely certain that 'this idea can no longer be reconciled with our view of the world,' they have simply removed, by sleight of hand, whatever is regarded as unintelligible to today's average man."

   Consequently, the cardinal goes on, "in 'saying farewell to the devil' they are not basing themselves on Holy Scripture (which supports just the opposite view) but on our world view. Thus, they are saying farewell to every other aspect of faith which does not fit with current conformism; and they do so, not as exegetes, as interpreters of Holy Scriptures, but as contemporary men."

   For Ratzinger, these methods lead to serious consequences: "Ultimately the authority on which these biblical scholars base their judgement is not the Bible itself but the *weltanschauung* they hold to be contemporary. They are therefore speaking as philosophers or sociologists, and their philosophy consists merely in banal, uncritical assent to the convictions of the present time, which are always provisional." If I have understood him correctly, this would be to stand the traditional method of theological study on its head: Scripture no longer judges the world, but the world judges Scripture.

He further comments: "They are constantly trying to find a message that represents what we already know, or at any rate what the listener wants to hear. As far as the devil is concerned, faith today, as always, holds fast to the mysterious but objective and disconcerting reality. But the Christian knows that the person who fears God need fear nothing and no one. The fear of God is faith, something very different from a fear which enslaves, a fear of demons. But the fear of God is also very different from a pretentious daring which does not want to see the seriousness of reality. Genuine courage does not close its eyes to the dimensions of danger but considers danger realistically." Cardinal Joseph Ratzinger (with Vittorio Messori), *The Ratzinger Report* (Ignatius Press, 1985), pp. 143-144.

5. Catholic history... is replete with authenticated reports of extraordinary miracles worked through the saints, or in their lives in every age of the church. In fact, authenticated miracles through a person's intercession are required for that person to be canonized a saint by the Catholic church. It is ironic that some Catholic scholars will not attribute to Jesus what they must recognize in the lives of his followers: "No servant is greater than his Master..." (Jn 13:16; cf. Mt 10:24).
6. Michael Schmaus, *Dogma 3: God and His Christ* (Kansas City, Mo.: Sheed and Ward, 1971), p. 87.

Chapter Four

1. Expressions of Christian belief in the communion of saints are contained in the earliest creeds of the church, such as the Apostles' Creed. The doctrines of purgatory and the immediate union of the just with God upon death were first formally defined by the Catholic church at the First and Second Councils of Lyons (1245 and 1274), though they had long been believed by Christians. See Denzinger's *The Sources of Catholic Dogma*, trans. by Roy J. Deferrari, pp. 4-7, 180-181, 184.
2. It should be noted that not *all* councils of Catholic bishops are infallibly guided by the Holy Spirit in their doctrinal decisions. Only those worldwide or "ecumenical" councils of bishops that are recognized and defined as such by the Catholic church are considered by Catholics to be infallibly guided by the Holy Spirit and preserved from error in their formal definitions of doctrine and morals. As stated previously, the Catholic church recognizes twenty-one Councils in the church's history to be genuinely "ecumenical" in this sense.

3. The Catholic church distinguishes between Eastern churches not in union with the Pope (which usually call themselves Orthodox churches), and Eastern churches that are in union with the Pope (which we call Eastern Catholic churches) and whose rites are equal in dignity with the Roman rite of the Catholic church. This distinction, and the status of the Eastern Catholic churches, is explained more fully in the Decree on the Eastern Catholic Churches (*Orientalium Ecclesiarum*) of the Second Vatican Council.
4. St. Irenaeus of Lyons, *Against Heresies,* Book 3, Chapter 2, line 2, in *Early Christian Fathers,* ed. Cyril Richardson (New York: Macmillan, 1970), p. 371.
5. After the doctrine of papal infallibility was defined by the First Vatican Council in 1870, Pope Pius IX made it clear that he considered his definition of the doctrine of the Immaculate Conception, which he had defined in 1854, to be an infallible statement.
6. Religious who are not ordained are also considered part of the laity; this section, however, will focus on the role of the laity who have not committed themselves to the religious life through vows of poverty, chastity, and obedience.
7. This is why Pope John Paul II has been adamant that the clergy should not hold political office. Not only does this practice tend to identify the church with a particular political party or ideology, but it robs the laity of the role in the world and the church that is uniquely their own. It diverts the clergy holding office from their primary task of ministering to God's people.
8. Sacred Congregation for the Doctrine of Faith, *Mysterium Ecclesiae,* June 24, 1973, par. 1.
9. Fr. Feeney later clarified his views which were found to be in accordance with Catholic teaching, and he continued to minister as a priest in good standing in the Catholic church.

Chapter Five

1. Thus, the beliefs of the Unification church concerning Rev. Moon and religions that add to Christianity's basic revelation, such as Mormonism, are rejected by the Catholic church.
2. Fr. Avery Dulles, S.J., "The Bible in the Church: Some Debated Questions," in *Scripture and the Charismatic Renewal* (Ann Arbor, MI: Servant, 1979) p. 11.
3. "Canon" means an "official list," in this case, the official list recognized by the church of the inspired writings that make up the Old or the New Testament.
4. The 1964 instruction of the Pontifical Biblical Commission of the Catholic Church, entitled "On the Historical Truth of the Gospels," distinguished three stages of the tradition through which the life and teaching of Jesus have come down to us: (1) Our Lord's teaching—The New Testament originates in the teachings and works of Jesus himself. He is the source of the "tradition"—what is handed on—which is the

subject of the New Testament. (2) The apostles' teaching—The apostles "handed on" by preaching, proclamation, witnessing and other means of oral tradition, the good news of salvation through Jesus Christ. As the "Instruction" says, ". . . the apostles, in telling their listeners about our Lord's deeds and words, utilized the fuller understanding which they had acquired from the glorious events of Christ's life, and the guidance of the Spirit of Truth." (3) The four evangelists—Each of the writers of the four Gospels composed these written narratives based on the oral and written tradition which they had received. The "Instruction" emphasizes that each of the evangelists exercised a certain freedom, guided by the Holy Spirit, in composing his Gospel. It states, "Of the many elements at hand, they reported some, summarized others, and developed still others in accordance with the needs of various churches. From the material available to them, the Evangelists selected those items most suited to their specific purpose and their condition of a particular audience. And they narrated these events in the manner most suited to satisfy their purpose and their audience's condition." (Instruction of the Pontifical Biblical Commission, "The Historicity of the Gospels," II, April 21, 1964. In *The Pope Speaks,* Vol. 10, No. 1, 1964, Washington, D.C.

5. Bishops of the early church developed lists of writings, called "canons," that they considered to be inspired by the Holy Spirit. The canon developed by Bishop Irenaeus of Lyons around A.D. 185 is very similar to the present New Testament, but without mention of 3 John, James, or 2 Peter. Another canon similar to the present one is found written on the Muratorian Fragment, probably from the church of Rome, in about A.D. 200. Yet, even by the fourth century, the question of an official canon remained unsettled. In the early part of that century, Bishop Eusebius of Caesarea, refers to the letters of James, Jude, 2 Peter, and 2 and 3 John as "disputed, yet familiar to most." (See his *History of the Church.*) It took centuries for the bishops to come to an agreement on the complete New Testament canon. The bishops went through a similar process to recognize a canon for the Old Testament, though the dispute about the deuterocanonical, or apocryphal, books was more intense and confusing than the development of the New Testament canon. (See Henry Chadwick, *The Early Church,* [Baltimore, MD: Penguin Books, 1967], pp. 40-44, 81-82.)
6. A formal definition of the canons of the Old and New Testaments was made April 8, 1546, at the Council of Trent. There, the traditional Catholic canon generally agreed upon since the fifth century was challenged by the Protestant Reformation.
7. Bishop Irenaeus of Lyons looked to the church of Rome as preserving the apostolic tradition in a preeminent way. See St. Irenaeus of Lyons, "The Refutation and Overthrow of 'Knowledge' Falsely So-Called," Book III, Chapter 3, line 2, in Cyril Richardson, ed., *Early Christian Fathers,* p. 372.
8. Fr. Avery Dulles, S.J., "The Bible in The Church," pp. 7, 8.
9. Pius XII, *Divino Afflante Spiritu* no. 28, 29. "In the accomplishment of this task, the Catholic exegete will find invaluable help in an assiduous

study of those works, in which the Holy Fathers, the Doctors of the Church and the renowned interpreters of past ages have explained the Sacred Books. For, although sometimes less instructed in profane learning and in the knowledge of languages than the scripture scholars of our time, nevertheless by reason of the office assigned to them by God in the Church, they are distinguished by a certain subtle insight into heavenly things and by a marvellous keenness of intellect, which enables them to penetrate to the very innermost meaning of the divine word and bring to light all that can help to elucidate the teaching of Christ and promote holiness of life.

"It is indeed regrettable that such precious treasures of Christian antiquity are almost unknown to many writers of the present day, and that students of the history of exegesis have not yet accomplished all that seems necessary for the due investigation and appreciation of so momentous a subject. Would that many, by seeking out the authors of the Catholic interpretation of Scripture and diligently studying their works and drawing thence the almost inexhaustible riches therein stored up, might contribute largely to this end, so that it might be daily more apparent to what extent those authors understood and made known the divine teaching of the Sacred Books, and that the interpreters of today might thence take example and seek suitable arguments."

10. Final report of the Extraordinary Synod—1985, 11, 8, a), 1. Daughters of St. Paul Edition, p. 49.
11. Pius XII wrote in *Divino Afflante Spiritu*: "... the Angelic Doctor [St. Thomas Aquinas] already observed in these words: 'In Scripture divine things are presented to us in the manner which is in common use among men.' For as the substantial Word of God became like to men in all things 'except sin' (Heb 4:15), so the words of God, expressed in human language, are made like to human speech in every respect, except error" (no. 37).
12. Pontifical Biblical Commission, "The Historicity of the Gospel," April 21, 1964, explains that: "The evangelist felt duty-bound to narrate his particular account in the order which God suggested to his memory. At least this would seem to hold true for those items in which order of treatment would not affect the authority or truth of the Gospel. After all, the Holy Spirit distributes His gifts to each as he chooses. Since these books were to be so authoritative, he undoubtedly guided and directed the sacred writers as they thought about the things which they were going to write down; but he probably allowed each writer to arrange his narrative as he saw fit. Hence anyone who uses enough diligence, will be able to discover this order with the help of God."
13. See Pope Leo XIII, *Providentissimus Deus,* November 18, 1893; Pope Benedict XV, *Spiritus Paraclitus,* September 15, 1920; Pius XII, *Divino Afflante Spiritu,* September 30, 1943; *Humani Generis,* August 12, 1950, and many instructions of the Pontifical Biblical Commission, including those of May 13, 1950, and April 21, 1964.
14. Note by Fr. R.A.F. MacKenzie, Footnote 31 to Dogmatic Constitution on Divine Revelation in *The Documents of Vatican II,* Walter Abbot, S.J.,

ed. (New York: American Press, 1966), p. 119.
15. *Ibid.*
16. *Humani Generis,* Encyclical Letter of Pope Pius XII, August 12, 1950, N.C.W.C. translation (Boston, MA: Daughters of St. Paul), no. 22, p. 9.
17. Instruction of the Pontifical Biblical Commission, April 21, 1964, Section 1.
18. *Ibid.*, May 13, 1950, II, 2b.
19. *L'Osservatore Romano,* English edition, April 21, 1986, p. 3.
20. A good, concise history of biblical reading by laity in the Catholic church may be found in Nick Cavnar's article, "Did the Catholic Church Ever Ban the Bible?" *New Covenant,* November, 1983, pp. 10-11. "Plenary indulgence" will be explained in Chapter Seven.

Chapter Six

1. Certain sacraments, such as baptism, may be administered by any Christian (or in baptism, even by a non-Christian) in an emergency as long as the person has the intention to perform the sacrament as the church intends and the basic form of the sacrament is correct.
2. See Fr. Michael Scanlan, T.O.R., *The Power of Penance.*
3. Pouring or sprinkling water on the head was viewed as a sufficient alternative to immersion since the head is the most noble member of the body, which represents the whole. Notice, we often send people photos of our faces, but not our arms!
4. In an emergency, the Apostles' Creed should be recited before baptism, if time permits, to replace the normal baptismal rite of the church. Each baptismal candidate should have at least one godparent who would assume the responsibility of seeing the baptized person is taught the Catholic faith and raised in a Christian environment.
5. Cyril C. Richardson, ed., *Early Christian Fathers* (New York: Macmillan, 1970), p. 114.
6. *Ibid.*, p. 286.
7. *Ibid.*, p. 388.
8. See Walter Kasper, "Unity and Diversity in the Eucharist," *Theology Digest,* vol. 33, no. 2 (Summer, 1986), p. 221.
9. "The Call of the Whole Church to Holiness," in Dogmatic Constitution of the Church, chapter 5.
10. The Catholic church does grant annulments of marriages in cases where the church judges that the marriage covenant was not entered into properly or responsibly. In such cases, the church judges that a true Christian marriage never existed. Much serious preparation and prayer is necessary to enter into the Christian marriage covenant, as the Catholic church is increasingly emphasizing today. Divorce of couples properly married within the church has never been recognized as legitimate by the Catholic church.
11. The most recent doctrinal statement of the Catholic church on why only men are ordained to the ministerial priesthood is the "Declaration on the Question of the Admission of Women to the Ministerial Priesthood,"

issued by The Sacred Congregation for the Doctrine of the Faith on October 15, 1976.

Chapter Seven

1. The Jesus Prayer is "O Lord, Jesus Christ, Son of God, be merciful to me a sinner."
2. A modern example of this is the Catholic church's establishment of the feast of St. Joseph the Worker, May 1, to stress the real purpose and dignity of work in contrast with the communist "May Day," which anticipates the triumph of the working class through Marxist ideology, methods, and military might.
3. Pope Paul VI, *Marialis Cultus,* February 2, 1974 (Washington D.C.: USCC, 1974), p. 34.
4. "The Didache," 8:1 in Cyril C. Richardson, ed., *Early Christian Fathers* (Macmillan, 1979), p. 174. The Jews, it notes, fasted on Mondays and Thursdays.
5. The modern Catholic teaching on indulgences is contained in Pope Paul VI's *Apostolic Constitution on the Doctrine of Indulgences* (January 1, 1967), and further specified in the *Enchiridion of Indulgences* (Vatican Press, 1968). What must be done to obtain an indulgence? In general, Pope Paul's Apostolic Constitution explains that besides carrying out the particular prescribed prayer or work, the faithful must also have the "... necessary dispositions, that is to say, that they love God, detest sin, place their trust in the merits of Christ and believe firmly in the great assistance they derive from the Communion of Saints" (no. 10). The "Norms on Indulgences" issued from Rome on June 29, 1968, states that to obtain a plenary indulgence, one must participate in the sacrament of reconciliation, receive Holy Communion, and pray for the intention of the Pope, along with the prescribed prayer or work to which the indulgence is attached (no. 27). These three conditions may be fulfilled several days before or after the actual prayer or action of the plenary indulgence, although it is fitting that Holy Communion be received and prayer for the Pope's intention said on the same day (no. 17).

   Plenary indulgences may be received for such things as adoration of the Blessed Sacrament *or* devout reading of the Bible for at least one-half hour, "the pious exercise of the Way of the Cross," or recitation of the rosary any time in a church or family group, a religious community, or a pious association of persons.

   Partial indulgences are attached to many prayers and meditations. It is noteworthy that the Catholic church proclaims three "general grants" of indulgences that are "... intended to serve as a reminder to the faithful to infuse with a Christian spirit the actions that go to make their daily lives and to strive in the ordering of their lives toward the perfection of charity" (*Enchiridion on Indulgences,* 1968). The *Enchiridion on Indulgences* lists these indulgences as "(1) a partial indulgence is granted to the faithful who, in the performance of their duties and in bearing the trials of life, raise their mind with humble confidence to God, adding—even if only mentally—some pious invocation; (2) a partial indulgence is granted to the faithful, for a contribution of their goods to serve their brothers in need; (3) a partial indulgence is granted to the faithful, who in a spirit of penance voluntarily deprive themselves of what is licit and pleasing to them."

6. *Charisms and Charismatic Renewal: A Biblical and Theological Study* (Ann Arbor, MI: Servant Books, 1984) pp. 71-72.
7. *Ibid.*, p. 72.

Chapter Eight

1. *Basic Teachings for Catholic Religious Education,* National Conference of Catholic Bishops, January 11, 1973 (Washington, D.C.: USCC Publications Office, 1973), nos. 17 and 18.
2. *The Teaching of Christ,* Ronald Lawler, O.F.M.; Bishop Donald W. Wuerl; Thomas Comerford Lawler, editors, second edition (Huntington, IN: Our Sunday Visitor, 1983), p. 292 ff.
3. "What are the greatest needs of the Church today? Do not let our answer surprise you as being oversimple or even superstitious and unreal: one of the greatest needs is defense from that evil which is called the Devil. . . . we know that this dark and disturbing spirit really exists, and that he still acts with treacherous cunning; he is the secret enemy that sows errors and misfortunes in human history. . . . The question of the Devil and the influence he can exert on individual persons as well as on communities, whole societies, is a very important chapter of Catholic doctrine which is given little attention today, though it should be studied again. . . ." (Pope Paul VI, General Audience on Nov. 15, 1973, *New Covenant,* April 1974, p. 8.)

   In response to the Pope's exhortation, the Sacred Congregation for the Doctrine of the Faith published a thorough study on the Catholic understanding of Satan on June 26, 1975, entitled, "Christian Faith and Demonology" (in *Vatican II: More Post-Conciliar Documents, Vol. II,* Austin Flannery, O.P., ed., Grand Rapids, MI: Eerdmans, 1982, pp. 456-485). This study, which was based on sacred Scripture, the teaching of the ecumenical councils, and Catholic tradition from the patristic period to the present, concluded that existence of Satan and demons (evil spirits) is an essential matter of Catholic and Christian faith. While warning against certain extremes, such as denying the existence of Satan (rationalism), placing Satan on the level of God instead of a creature (manichaean dualism), avoiding personal responsibility for evil doing (blaming sins on the devil), or gullibility regarding diabolic intervention, the study concludes: All these considerations notwithstanding, the church is simply being faithful to the example of Christ when it asserts that the warning of St. Peter to be "sober and alert" is always relevant.

4. C.S. Lewis, *The Screwtape Letters,* Letter VII (Old Tappan, N.J.: Fleming H. Revell, 1976), pp. 45, 46.
5. Fr. Daniel Sinisi, *Christian Moral Living* (Steubenville, OH: Franciscan University Press, 1983), p. 63.
6. *Ibid.*, p. 69.
7. See John XXIII, Litt. Encyclical, *Ad Petri Cathedram,* 29 June, 1959: AAS 55 (1959), p. 513, quoted in the Pastoral Constitution on the Church in the Modern World, no. 92.
8. *To Live in Christ Jesus: A Pastoral Reflection on the Moral Life,* National Conference of Catholic Bishops, November 11, 1976 (Washington, D.C.: USCC Publications Office, 1976), pp. 8, 9.
9. C.S. Lewis, *Mere Christianity* (New York: Macmillan Paperbacks, 1960), pp. 17-39. Also see C.S. Lewis, *The Abolition of Man* (Toronto, Canada: Macmillan Paperback Edition, 1965), Appendix "Illustrations of the *Tao,*" pp. 95-121.
10. *The Teaching of Christ,* p. 315.
11. Fr. Daniel Sinisi, T.O.R., *Christian Moral Living,* p. 14.
12. *Ibid.*, p. 19.
13. *Ibid.*, p. 37.
14. *Basic Teachings for Catholic Religious Education,* pp. 20, 21.

Chapter Nine

1. John Paul II, "*Urbi et Orbi* Message, Christmas, 1985," in *L'Osservatore Romano,* English edition, January 6, 1986, pp. 1, 2.
2. *The Weight of Glory and Other Addresses* (Grand Rapids, MI: Eerdmans, 1965) pp. 14, 15.
3. T.S. Eliot, "Choruses from 'The Rock,'" in *T.S. Eliot: Collected Poems 1909-1962* (New York: Harcourt Brace, and World, 1963), p. 154.
4. John Paul II, "Apostolic Exhortation on Catechesis in Our Time" (*Catechesi Tradendae*) October 16, 1979 (Boston, MA: Daughters of St. Paul, 1981) pp. 18, 21, 22.
5. Sacred Congregation for the Doctrine of Faith, *Instruction on Certain Aspects of the "Theology of Liberation,"* August 6, 1984, and *Instruction on Christian Freedom and Liberation*, March 22, 1986. (Both published in English by the office of Publishing and Promotion Services, USCC, Washington, D.C.)
6. *Familiaris Consortio*, no. 6 (Boston, MA: Daughters of St. Paul, 1981), p. 17.

Chapter Ten

1. Raymond Brown, Karl Donfried, Joseph Fitzmeyer, John Reumann, eds., *Mary in the New Testament* (New York: Paulist, 1978).
2. St. John Chrysostom, in his *Homily V* on the Gospel of Matthew, notes that the word "until" was used similarly in other parts of Scripture. For

example, in the story of Noah's ark, the Bible says, "The raven returned not until the earth was dried up" (Gen 8:7). Yet, St. John notes, the raven did not return *after* that time either. This is a particular usage of the Greek word "until," to stress the action prior to a certain time—not afterward.

3. *Mary in the New Testament,* pp. 65-67, 291.
4. Pope Pius IX, *"Ineffablilis Deus,"* December 8, 1854, quoted in *The Sources of Catholic Dogma,* p. 413.
5. Irenaeus of Lyons, "On the Refutation and Overthrow of Knowledge Falsely So-Called," or "Against Heresies," book III, 22, 4, in *The Faith of the Early Fathers,* vol. 1, W.A. Jurgens, ed., p. 93.
6. Frances Parkinson Keyes, "Bernadette and the Beautiful Lady," in *A Woman Clothed with the Sun,* John Delaney, ed. (Garden City, NY: Doubleday, 1960), p. 137.
7. Pope Pius XII, *"Munificentissimus Deus,"* quoted in *Theotokos: A Theological Encyclopedia of the Blessed Virgin Mary,* p. 55.
8. The Catholic church has always made a clear distinction between the adoration given only to God (*latria* in Latin) and the special honor given to Mary the Mother of God (*hyperdulia* in Latin). St. Augustine, for example, warned against giving to any martyr, angel, or saint (including Mary) the worship and adoration due to God alone, when he wrote:

   > . . . the veneration strictly called "worship," or *latria,* that is, the special homage belonging only to the divinity, is something we give and teach others to give to God alone. The offering of a sacrifice belongs to worship in this sense (that is why those who sacrifice to idols are called idol-worshippers), and we neither make nor tell others to make any such offering to any martyr, any holy soul, or any angel . . .

   Augustine of Hippo, "Against Faustus the Manichaean," (c. A.D. 400), 20, 21, in *The Faith of the Early Fathers,* vol. 3, W.A. Jurgens, trs., p. 59.
9. Juniper B. Carol, O.F.M., in *Mariology,* Vol. 1 (Milwaukee: Bruce, 1954) pp. 32-33, states:

   > There is no Catholic theologian who denies to Our Lady the title: Mediatrix of all graces. But since the term "mediation" has many shades of meaning, the sense in which the Mother of God is called Mediatrix must first be explained.
   >
   > A mediator is a person who stands in the middle and unites individuals or groups which are opposed. Our blessed Lord, the God-Man, was uniquely fitted to be the Mediator between God and man. St. Paul says, "For there is one God, and one Mediator between God and man, himself man, Christ Jesus, who gave Himself a ransom for all . . ." (1 Tm 2:5-6).

   He continues, "If there is only 'one Mediator,' as St. Paul writes, then any other Mediator can only be such in strict dependence and in a secondary sense." He ends by quoting Pope Leo XIII as he referred to St. Thomas Aquinas in his teaching on the possibility of other mediators: "... As the Angelic Doctor teaches, 'there is no reason why certain others should not be called in a certain way mediators between God and man, that is to say, insofar as they co-operate by predisposing and ministering in the union of man with God.' Such are the angels and saints, the prophets and priests of both Testaments; but especially has the Blessed Virgin a claim to the glory of this title. For no single individual can even be imagined who has ever contributed or ever will contribute so much toward reconciling man with God. She offered a Savior to mankind, hastening to eternal ruin, at that moment when she received the announcement of the mystery of peace brought to this earth by the angel, with that admirable act of consent—and this, 'in the name of the whole human race.' She it is from whom Jesus is born; she is therefore truly His mother, and for this reason a worthy and acceptable 'Mediatrix to the Mediator.'" [*Fidentem piumque,* Tondini, pp. 248-250; Lawler, pp. 150-151; D.B., 1940 a. Quotes from Juniper B. Carol, O.F.M., *Mariology,* vol. 1 (Milwaukee: Bruce, 1954), pp. 32-33.]

10. Pope John Paul II, homily at Fatima, Portugal, May 13, 1982.
11. William C. McGrath, "Our Lady of the Rosary," in *A Woman Clothed with the Sun,* pp. 175-212.
12. *Ibid,* pp. 202-203.

Chapter Eleven

1. "The Reality of Life after Death," *Recentiores episcoporum synodi,* Sacred Congregation for the Doctrine of the Faith, May 11, 1979. "The Church affirms that a spiritual element survives and subsists after death, an element endowed with consciousness and will, so that the 'human self' subsists. To designate this element, the Church uses the word, 'soul,' the accepted term in the usage of Scripture and Tradition. Although not unaware that this term has various meanings in the Bible, the Church thinks that there is no valid reason for rejecting it; moreover, she considers that the use of some word as a vehicle is absolutely indispensable in order to support the faith of Christians."
2. Sacred Congregation for the Doctrine of the Faith, "The Reality of Life after Death," (*Recentiores episcoporum synodi*) 11 May 1979, in *Vatican II: More Postconciliar Documents,* Vol. II, ed., Austin Flannery, O.P., pp. 502-503.
3. The doctrine of purgatory must be understood in terms of the full meaning of salvation. For Catholics, salvation includes both "justification" (restoration to a right relationship with God through Jesus Christ) and "sanctification" (being cleansed from personal sin and made holy, that is, remade into the image of God, freed from the corruption of sin). Purgatory completes the process of sanctification, by which we are cleansed from sin and restored to the image of God as fully as our nature allows.

4. Catholic doctrine traditionally speaks of this as remission of the "temporal punishment due to sin," meaning the punishment that comes upon each person as a result of the bondage and other ill effects of sin (e.g. bad habits, character weaknesses, inability to overcome a sin) that still linger in a person's life, even after the sin has been forgiven. See Chapter Seven for a further explanation of indulgences.
5. *Confessions,* Book I.

Index